WITHDRAWN

EDUCATION IN BRITAIN
SINCE 1900

EDUCATION IN BRITAIN
SINCE 1900

by

S. J. CURTIS, M.A., Ph.D.
Senior Lecturer in Education, The University of Leeds

GREENWOOD PRESS, PUBLISHERS
WESTPORT, CONNECTICUT

LA
631.8
C87
1970

Originally published in 1952
by Andrew Dakers Ltd., London

First Greenwood Reprinting 1970

Library of Congress Catalogue Card Number 71-104264

SBN 8371-3913-9

Printed in the United States of America

CONTENTS

Chapter		Page
I	THE STATE OF EDUCATION IN ENGLAND AND WALES AT THE CLOSE OF THE NINETEENTH CENTURY	7
II	FROM STATE ASSISTANCE TO STATE SUPERVISION	23
III	THE REIGN OF SIR ROBERT MORANT	45
IV	TOWARDS A WIDER CONCEPTION OF EDUCATION	68
V	FROM STATE SUPERVISION TO STATE CONTROL	113
VI	THE PUBLIC SCHOOLS	158
VII	UNIVERSITY EDUCATION, 1900-50	181
VIII	ADULT AND TECHNICAL EDUCATION, 1900-50	208
IX	EDUCATION IN SCOTLAND, 1900-50	236
X	EDUCATION IN H.M. FORCES, 1900-50	270
	SUGGESTIONS FOR FURTHER READING	303
	APPENDIX	311
	INDEX OF NAMES	313
	INDEX OF SUBJECTS	315

CHAPTER I

THE STATE OF EDUCATION IN ENGLAND AND WALES AT THE CLOSE OF THE NINETEENTH CENTURY

ONE of the best known scenes in *Uncle Tom's Cabin* is that in which Miss Ophelia asks the small negro girl, Topsy, who made her and receives the somewhat disconcerting answer, 'I spect I grow'd'. That reply characterizes the development of English education prior to the commencement of the present century. It had developed from a number of widely different beginnings and some aspects of its growth were indeed spectacular. At the commencement of the century, education had been entirely in the hands of voluntary agencies. Secondary education was represented by the public schools and the endowed grammar schools. Elementary education was provided by the Sunday schools and by philanthropic institutions of which the National Society and the British and Foreign School Society were the most influential. It soon became apparent, however, that voluntary effort was quite unequal to the task of providing schools for the nation's children and the State, reluctantly at first, was obliged to intervene. The first act of Government intervention was in 1833 when a half-empty House of Commons approved a grant of £20,000 to be divided between the National and the British and Foreign School Societies as an aid to the building of schools.

For several years the continuance of the grant was uncertain. Thus in 1839, when Parliament approved the establishment of the Select Committee of the Privy Council for Education, the annual grant was passed by the slender majority of two. From this year, however, the principle of assisting voluntary effort through the expenditure of public money became well established and because of the work of the Secretary of the Committee of Council, Dr. Kay (afterwards Sir James Kay-Shuttleworth, the scope of Government aid became greatly extended. The grant came to include assistance for the provision of books and apparatus and the payment of teachers and pupil-teachers. In spite of Government help, the voluntary bodies failed to provide the number of school places required and the State was obliged to take a further step. The Elementary Education Act of 1870 was designed, as Mr. Forster expressed it, 'to fill the gaps', that is to establish schools in those areas which were inadequately served by the voluntary agencies. The latter were allowed a period of grace in which to remedy the deficiencies, but where they failed to do so the School Boards stepped in to supply the need.

The development of secondary education had proceeded at a slower pace. Two Royal Commissions on secondary education, the Clarendon Commission, 1861-4 (Public Schools) and the Taunton Commission, 1864-7 (Endowed Schools) had suggested lines of reform and although the Government was not willing to enforce most of the recommendations of the Commissioners, the Public Schools Act of 1868 and the Endowed Schools Act of 1869 went part of the way and left the remainder to the good sense of the schools concerned. The latter Act established the Endowed Schools Commission which was given authority to construct schemes for the better government and management of the endowed grammar schools. In 1874 the powers of this body were merged in those of the Charity Commission but the work of framing new schemes for schools went steadily ahead. By 1895, schemes had been approved for 902 schools out of a total of 1448 and although on the surface it might seem that improvements in the constitution of governing bodies were of minor importance, yet in fact, the character and educational work of the schools were materially raised.

At the beginning of the century higher education was provided by the two ancient universities of Oxford and Cambridge, whilst technical education was practically non-existent. The next ninety years saw the rise of the University of London, the foundation of the University of Durham, and the creation of two federal universities: the Victoria University which included Owens College at Manchester, University College, Liverpool, and the Yorkshire College at Leeds, and the University of Wales which consisted of the university colleges of Cardiff, Aberystwith and Bangor. In addition, university colleges had been established at Sheffield, Birmingham, Nottingham, Bristol, Exeter, Southampton, and Reading. These colleges prepared their students for the external degrees of the University of London but some of them were already aspiring to full university status. Technical education had developed through the aid given by the

Science and Art Department, and in the latter part of the century, progress had been stimulated by the competition of foreign countries in the field of industry and commerce. Government technical institutes had been established in London and the examples of the Polytechnic and the City and Guilds of London Institute had encouraged the growth of provincial technical colleges. Adult education, at first carried on in the Mechanics' Institutes and Adult Colleges, had acquired a new lease of life through the activities of University Extension.

Altogether substantial progress had been made in the fields of education enumerated above, but another side of the picture revealed a number of serious defects. Two Royal Commissions had been appointed with a view of taking stock of the educational situation. The Cross Commission of 1888 had surveyed the field of elementary education and the problems discussed showed such wide divergences of opinion that agreement was impossible and it was necessary to issue a majority and a minority report. These differences were specially acute in regard to the problems of the higher grade schools, the pupil-teacher system, and the training of teachers. The Bryce Commission of 1895 was concerned with secondary education but it was unable to survey the field adequately without, on the one side, taking account of elementary education, and on the other, of technical and higher education. The Bryce Commission was rendered inevitable by the increasing confusion, and muddle in the sphere of educational administration, both central and local.

By 1895 the country had arrived at what Adamson termed 'administrative muddle' in regard to education. The first part of the Commission's report describes the chaos and overlapping which was the result of the piecemeal development of English education. In view of subsequent developments it will be necessary to describe in some detail the situation as regards educational administration as it appeared to the Bryce Commission. The Commissioners realized quite clearly what was at fault and why the muddle had arisen. The Report stated, 'There is one feature in this growing concern of the State with education which must not be here overlooked. The growth has not been either continuous or coherent; i.e., it does not represent a series of logical or even connected sequences. Each one of the agencies ... was called into being, not merely independently of the others, but with little or no regard to their existence. Each has remained in its working isolated and unconnected with the rest. The problems which Secondary Education presents have been approached from different sides, at different times and with different views and aims'.[1]

Elementary education was supervised by the Education Department of the Privy Council and one might at least expect that this sphere would present a clear-cut situation. This, however, was not the case. For some years there had been an increasing tendency for a considerable number of children to remain at school after they had passed the sixth standard. This development had resulted in the creation of a seventh standard and even ex-standard classes. Foreign competition was forcing this country to adopt more scientific methods of manufacture, and mass production processes were being introduced. The differences between skilled and unskilled work were being accentuated and parents were discovering the advantages which education could confer. Those who were able to afford it were only too willing to allow their children to remain at school for a year or two longer. The upward movement had continued and had resulted in the establishment of higher grade elementary schools in London and the larger cities. Although classed as elementary, these schools provided what amounted to a secondary education and really corresponded to the third grade secondary schools proposed by the Taunton Commission. They gave instruction in more advanced mathematics, modern languages and natural science. On the financial side, the higher grade schools were supported by Parliamentary grants for elementary education and by the rates which the local School Boards were empowered to levy. The Science and Art Department, however, had a finger in the pie. Higher grade schools were eligible for the grants paid by that Department and in order to qualify as organized schools of science, they developed a decided bias towards the teaching of scientific subjects. The Education Department because of its interest in the training of teachers was concerned with higher education. Following the recommendation of the Cross Commission, it had recognized day training colleges attached to universities and university colleges and issued regulations fixing the amount of grant payable to such institutions.

The Charity Commissioners, whose province it was to frame schemes for the government of endowed schools, did

[1] *Bryce Commission Report*, Vol. I, p. 17.

not confine themselves to secondary education. Elementary endowed schools which possessed an income from endowments exceeding £100 a year came under their jurisdiction. At the other end of the scale, the Charity Commissioners were not concerned with the seven public schools considered by the Clarendon Commission; Eton, Winchester, Charterhouse, Harrow, Rugby, Shrewsbury, and Westminster. The Endowed Schools Acts did not apply to endowed schools maintained by voluntary contributions, choristers' schools, and endowments founded less than fifty years before the Act of 1869, though all these foundations came under the operation of the Charitable Trusts Acts.

The Science and Art Department paid grants on the results of a yearly examination to organized science classes which included endowed grammar schools, evening classes, and higher grade elementary schools. In addition, it gave aid to teachers training at the Royal College of Science and the National Art Training School and paid subsidies to local museums of science and art.

The Board of Agriculture had jurisdiction over institutes (excluding elementary schools) in which instruction was given in any subject related to agriculture. It inspected endowed grammar schools, evening classes, and adult classes in which the education provided was connected with agriculture. Moreover it paid grants to university colleges which provided agricultural instruction and also to one county council. Each of the above central authorities issued its own codes and grant regulations which were framed as often as not without reference to the other central bodies.

A similar overlapping could be found in local administration. Apart from the voluntary schools which received grant from the Education Department and were administered by their own managers, the School Boards were responsible for elementary education in their own areas. We have already seen that the higher grade schools came under their jurisdiction. There were 2568 School Boards and in country areas many of them were responsible for small districts containing not more than two or three schools. In some parts of England, School Boards had not been established and some of their functions were carried out by School Attendance Committees. It should be realized that these Boards, together with the 14,238 bodies of voluntary school managers, had direct access to the Education Department. Small wonder then that one board of managers complained that it had to wait ten months for an answer to a letter it had sent to Whitehall. The public schools and the endowed grammar schools had their own governing bodies.

The situation was complicated by the newly acquired powers of the county and county borough councils. The Technical Instruction Act of 1889 had empowered these councils to levy a rate not exceeding 1d. in the pound for aiding or supplying technical instruction. In 1890 the Local Taxation (Customs and Excise Act) made further sums of money available. The licences of certain publicans had been withdrawn and in order to compensate them the Chancellor of the Exchequer proposed a tax on whisky and other spirits. Some members of the Commons had strong objections to this use of public money and the Chancellor found himself with a substantial surplus. He decided to hand over the money to the county borough and county councils and one of the purposes for which it might be employed was the encouragement of technical education. The 'Whisky Money' could be used for maintenance and capital expenditure in building and equipment. Much of the amount, which in 1893-4 came to £423,080, was devoted to secondary education and in this way many endowed grammar schools were rescued from their financial difficulties. The experience gained by the councils in administering the 'Whisky Money' was to prove useful to them in later years.

The Bryce Commission gave priority to the administrative problem. 'A general survey of Secondary Education, as it now exists in England, appears to show that the first problems to be solved are those of organization. Large powers are already distributed among the various separate agencies which deal with particular parts of Secondary Education. It is not so much the extension of those powers, as the harmonizing of the agencies which exercise them, that is urgently required. The first need is for greater unity of control. Local authorities are required, which shall be responsible for all Secondary (including Technical) Education within their respective areas. There should be also one central authority, which, while leaving due freedom of action to the local bodies, could supervise the general interests of Secondary Education in England as a whole'.[1]

Most of the witnesses examined by the Commission were in complete agreement about the necessity of constituting a central authority for education but there was considerable

[1] Vol. I, pp. 78-9.

divergence of opinion about the form it should take. It was generally agreed that a Minister of Education, assisted by a Council or Board of Education, should be appointed but a variety of views as to the powers of the Council and its relation to the Minister and to Parliament was expressed. It was felt that the Minister should be responsible for both secondary and elementary education since considerable benefits would follow if the whole field of education and not its component parts could be surveyed. Some witnesses expressed their fears about what State control might involve. They were influenced by their experience of the Education Department and its policy of 'Payment by Results'.

Others were afraid of the consequences that would follow the appointment of a Minister of Education. They were most anxious that education should be free from the influence of party politics. Thus the Bishop of London in reply to the question whether some substantial advantage might be obtained from having such a Minister, said, 'There are some advantages, no doubt. The disadvantage is obvious enough, namely, that you let in upon education, which ought to be a steady thing, all the fluctuations of political parties . . . The advantage of not having education under Parliament is, of course, that it ought to be independent of all those fluctuations of opinion, and ought to go upon higher lines than the party politics of the day'.[1] That these fears were not groundless has since been illustrated by the attitude of the Liberals towards the Education Act of 1902 and the spirit in which some of the sections of the Act of 1944 have been interpreted. Few of the numerous Presidents of the Board of Education have left a permanent mark upon the educational system of the country and that office has usually been regarded as a stepping stone to higher cabinet appointment.

The general view was that the Minister should be assisted by an Education Council composed of representatives of the Crown, the universities, and the teachers. Amongst its functions would be that of making and keeping a register of teachers and also that of regulating examinations. In the question of the relations between the Council and the Minister, there was again divergence of opinion. Was the control of education to rest with the Council which would be largely a professional body, or was the Minister to be supreme and the Council to be constituted as a consultative or advisory body?

[1] *Minutes of Evidence*, 4921-2.

All witnesses agreed on the necessity of local authorities for secondary education but there were many differences of opinion in regard to their powers and functions, their constitution and the size of the area which they should control. Many were in favour of authorities responsible for both elementary and secondary education. The answers given by some witnesses revealed the central problem of local educational administration which has not been satisfactorily solved at the present time. On the one hand, the area administered by a local authority should be large enough to constitute a satisfactory unit, i.e. its child population should be sufficient to make possible the supply of primary and secondary schools. On the other hand, it should not be so extensive as to swamp local interest and initiative. In many rural districts, great disatisfaction has been expressed with regard to the School Boards. The areas they controlled were too small: in some cases their population was less than 5,000.

The following extracts from the evidence presented to the Commission show that some witnesses fully appreciated the problem.

(a) Can you give us any opinion on the suggestion that has been made that the counties are in many cases much too small, and that it would be better to divide England into 12 educational districts independently altogether of the county councils. Would that suggestion meet your acceptance?—No, you would destroy the essence of the whole thing, which is the county feeling of pride in its schools and the feeling of the unity of the whole of local self-government.[1]

(b) ... we want to secure two things. As to the educational area, we want an area sufficiently large to secure an educational body that would be broad in their sympathies, and also we want to have a sufficiently large area to make the burden of expense fairly easy. On the other hand—I lay very great stress upon this—that those who are admitted upon the educational board, whatever it may be, should, to some extent at all events, be drawn from the districts where the school work will be carried on.

(Sir Henry Roscoe). You would like to have local interest properly developed?—Yes. We want to get the local interest distinctly in our governing body.[2]

(c) Have you thought of any county in England which

[1] *Minutes of Evidence*, 4641.
[2] *Ibid.* 7394–5.

would be too big when you take out of it all the county boroughs in it?—Yes, Lancashire, my own county.

Even taking Lancashire, supposing that all the county boroughs which are towns of 50,000 inhabitants and upwards were eliminated, do you think that what would remain of the population would be too big an area?—It would be too much scattered. I should say the same of the West Riding. We are 50 or 60 miles from one end of the county to the other. There can be no local knowledge on the part of a body that represents such a district. You might just as well have it administered by Parliament, as it appears to me.[1]

The recommendations of the Bryce Commissioners reflected the views of the majority of the witnesses. They offered the following solution of the administrative problem. They approved the establishment of a Government department presided over by a Minister of Education who would be responsible to Parliament. He would supervise both elementary and secondary education. His chief executive officer should be a permanent secretary but since much of the work of the department would be purely professional in character, the Minister should be assisted by an Education Council. This should be an executive body and one of its functions ought to be the compilation of a register of teachers.

It was considered that the Council should consist of twelve members—one-third appointed by the Crown, one-third by the Universities of Oxford, Cambridge, London, and Victoria, and the remainder chosen by the rest of the Council from educationists well known because of their expert knowledge and long experience. The Council should hold office for six years and should have power to co-opt additional members when necessary. The Education Department, the Science and Art Department, and the Charity Commission as regards its educational functions, should be merged in the new central authority.

Although many of the professional witnesses had been suspicious of local control, there was, on the part of the others, a strong feeling in favour of the establishment of local authorities. As a compromise, it was recommended that the county councils, the county boroughs, and other boroughs which had a population of over 50,000 should become responsible for local administration. The experience these bodies had gained in administering the grants for technical education and the manner in which the Welsh Intermediate Education

[1] *Ibid.* 13,431–2.

Act had worked suggested that this would be the most suitable plan. Amongst their functions would be those of providing adequate secondary education in their areas, of initiating schemes for schools and conducting the inspection of schools. They should also be given the power to recognize private and preparatory schools which attained a satisfactory standard as regards their buildings and their instruction. It was felt that the local authorities were the right and proper bodies for awarding scholarships and exhibitions, including scholarships for pupils of merit in the elementary and higher grade schools of the district.

The problem of the higher grade schools thrust itself upon the Commissioners. Some witnesses had drawn attention to them by alleging that they trespassed upon the secondary school domain. This did not seriously disturb the Commissioners. They regarded the higher grade schools as equivalent to the third grade of secondary school recommended by the Taunton Commission in 1868, and seemed to show no objection to the fact that they were managed by the School Boards. They stated their belief that the 'higher grade elementary school largely corresponds with a demand for secondary education from the lower social strata, and the region of its special activity is the space left practically vacant between elementary education and the second grade secondary school.'[1]

The Bryce Commission took a wide and generous view of the nature of secondary education. Technical instruction was fast coming into its own and it was important for both types of education that they should not be regarded as mutually exclusive. One of the most striking passages in the report is that which asserted the essential relationship between these two forms of education. It should be remembered that one of the Commissioners was Mr. (later) Sir Michael E. Sadler, and there is no doubt that his was the inspiration which resulted in this paragraph.

'Secondary education is the education of the boy and girl not simply as a human being who needs to be instructed in certain rudiments of knowledge, but it is a process of intellectual training and personal discipline conducted with special regard to the profession or trade to be followed. . . . All secondary schools . . . in so far as they qualify men for doing something in life, partake more or less in the character of institutes that educate craftsmen. Every profession, even

[1] Vol. I, p. 67.

that of winning scholarships, is a craft, and all crafts are arts. . . . No definition of technical instruction is possible that does not bring it under the head of secondary education, nor can secondary education be so defined as absolutely to exclude from it the idea of technical instruction. Technical instruction is secondary, i.e. it comes after the education which has awakened the mind by teaching the child the rudiments, or, as it were, the alphabet, of all knowledge, and the better the whole of this alphabet has been mastered, the better and the easier will later learning be. And secondary education is technical, i.e. it teaches the boy so to apply the principles he is learning, and so to learn the principles by applying them, or so to use the instruments he is being made to know, as to perform or produce something, interpret a literature or a science, make a picture or a book, practise a plastic or manual art, convince a jury or persuade a senate, translate or annotate an author, dye wool, weave cloth, design or construct a machine, navigate a ship, or command an army. Secondary education, therefore, as inclusive of technical, may be described as education conducted in view of the special life that has to be lived with the express purpose of forming a person fit to live it'.[1]

The Bryce Commission acknowledged that the position as regards secondary education had greatly improved since the Taunton Report of 1868. In the majority of the schools the standard of the work had become higher and as a consequence the number of pupils attending the schools had increased. When Fitch had investigated the provision of secondary education in the West Riding of Yorkshire on behalf of the Taunton Commission, he reported that only three first grade schools existed, the grammar schools at Leeds, Doncaster and York. The number had now risen to eight. As the grammar schools became more popular, the number of private secondary schools tended to diminish. Nevertheless much needed to be accomplished before the situation could be considered as satisfactory. The Commission selected certain districts as being better served by endowed schools than the rest of the country but even in these areas there was room for much improvement. Thus, although the Manchester Grammar School had increased the number of its pupils from 360 to 806, it had to serve as a first grade school for pupils living as far away as Fleetwood and Huddersfield. About two-thirds of its pupils came from

[1] *Ibid.* pp. 135–6.

Manchester and Salford and the remainder from neighbouring towns. The only other endowed school in the city was the Hulme Grammar School, which ranked as a second grade secondary school. As a witness told the Commissioners, only about 1200 boys out of a population of more than five millions were receiving an efficient secondary education.

In some of the country districts and the smaller towns the plight of the grammar schools was indeed desperate. Their work was crippled by lack of endowments and they were obliged to make do with buildings which had been out of date for more than a generation. There were certain cases in which the school governors had been forced to adopt the practice of 'farming' the school to any headmaster who was willing to accept responsibility for running the school with the help of such fees as he could obtain. Examples of 'farming' were to be found in South Lancashire and at Knaresborough in the West Riding of Yorkshire. In London and in the industrial North and Midlands, there was an increasing demand for secondary education but this was offset by the apathy prevalent in some of the country districts. Mr. H. T. Gerrans reported to the Commission the speech made by a Devonshire farmer at a meeting of an agricultural society.

'A man consists of three parts—back, belly, and brains— and what we have to do is to fill the belly. Now this technical education may work the brains, but it won't fill the belly, and so I say it is of no practical use; but if you work the back then you can fill the belly, and so get on. My boys want to go in for bicycling and athletics and these 'ologies, but I say to them: "They won't fill your belly, and how are you to get on if your belly is not filled?" And so I say you must always recollect that a man consists of three parts—back, belly, and brains'.[1]

In spite of the progress made since 1868, the number of pupils receiving efficient secondary education in 1895 was deplorably small. It is impossible to obtain the exact figures. The Bryce Commission had only time to investigate conditions in six counties since it had been asked to make its report as quickly as possible. Mr. G. A. N. Lowndes carefully studied the available figures and came to the conclusion that about 75,000 attended the endowed secondary schools and about 34,000 the proprietary schools. The distribution

---

[1] *Bryce Commission—Report on the System of Secondary Education in the County of Devon*, p. 71.

of endowed schools throughout the country was very irregular. Thus Huddersfield, which had a population of over 95,000, had no endowed school. Apart from private schools and the higher grade schools, the nearest endowed grammar school was Almondsbury, which was some distance beyond the borough boundary. In many cases the existence of an endowed school depended upon purely accidental circumstances.

'Let us glance at the history of a typical endowment. One day towards the end of the sixteenth century, as Mistress Alice Wilkes was walking abroad in the fields at Islington, she observed a woman milking, and had a mind to try whether she could milk. "At her withdrawing from the cow," so the story continues, "an arrow was shot through the crown of her hat, which so startled her that she then declared if she lived she would erect something on that spot of ground to commemorate the great mercy shown by the Almighty in that astonishing deliverance." Accordingly, in 1609, after completing the romance by marrying the archer (who turned out to be Sir Thomas Owen), she granted certain lands, called the Ermitage fields in Islington and Clerkenwell to the Brewers' Company, for the support of ten poor widows. Four years later she expanded the charity by providing for a "free" school as well as almshouses, and set apart a farm of forty-one acres in Essex for the endowment of the school, to provide instruction for thirty children, twenty-four from Islington and six from Clerkenwell, in "grammar, fair writing, cyphering, and casting of accounts".

'To this incident in the life of Lady Owen the districts of Islington and Clerkenwell are indebted for the possession of one of the most efficient secondary schools in London. Had the narrow escape occurred on any other spot, Islington might now be as ill-provided as regards secondary schools as the most neglected regions in the North-West of London, while some other district would be enjoying the educational advantages of "Dame Alice Owen's Schools".[1]

Standards of instruction varied considerably but on the whole the teaching was bad. In many schools the masters relied entirely upon homework. The pupil learnt his lesson at home and then was tested at school the next day, a method which is not entirely absent from some present day grammar schools. The science teaching in some schools was especially

[1] *Studies in Secondary Education*, edited by Arthur Acland and Llewellyn Smith, Percival, 1892, pp. 152–3.

weak. We hear of cases of pupils being prepared for the examinations of the Science and Art Department who had never performed or witnessed an experiment in the whole of their school career. In one Yorkshire school a number of pupils passed the London Matriculation in chemistry on the strength of memorizing the contents of their textbook. Practically all the schools paid considerable attention to Latin and it was a common custom for those who were unable to make much progress in their Latin to be sent to learn shorthand. The main reason for the poor teaching in the schools was the scarcity of trained teachers. If a person had graduated it was assumed that he would be able to teach. In fact some headmasters regarded training as a mark of inferiority. Training smacked too much of the elementary school. The writer remembers a headmaster of those days who afterwards boasted that during the whole of his term of office he had refused to appoint a trained teacher on his staff.

Considerable progress had been made in elementary education. Thanks to the activities of both the voluntary bodies and the School Boards, by 1895 it might be said that elementary school places had been provided for every child and that in spite of the large birthrate in the latter quarter of the nineteenth century. It was, however, one thing to provide school places and another to fill them. As regards the towns, by 1895, the worst cases of non-attendance had been eliminated though here and there we read of parents who were repeatedly fined because of their neglect to send their children to school. One may feel a certain amount of sympathy for many of them. Wages were extremely low; many factory workers only received about a pound a week and agricultural workers much less than that. Hence the extra money which a child could bring home might make all the difference to the family. There was a special temptation for parents living in country districts. Children could earn an appreciable amount at hay or harvest time, or by hoeing turnips, lifting potatoes, picking hops or beans or peas. Small wonder then that many children were kept away from school at these busy and profitable times. In addition, the half-time system which dated from Sir James Graham's Factory Act of 1844 was still in force. Most of the half-timers were to be found in the industrial areas of the North and Midlands. The Elementary Education (School Attendance) Act of 1893 had raised the age of exemption from ten to eleven. Since this also applied to part-timers, there was a marked falling off in their numbers. The half-time system continued until it was finally abolished in 1918. The voluntary schools still outnumbered the Board Schools but because the religious bodies were finding, it difficult to meet the rising cost of education the School Boards were fast overtaking voluntary effort. Many of the voluntary school buildings had been erected earlier in the century and compared most unfavourably with the newer and more up to date Board Schools. It is sad to think that many of these old buildings are still doing duty as schools more than half-a-century after this date. Some of the earlier Board Schools were almost as unsatisfactory. Cheapness was often the order of the day and schools were often erected upon most unsuitable sites, e.g. at the junction of busy thoroughfares or in close proximity to the gas works. The cost of sites in large cities was largely responsible for the huge barrack-like buildings of two or three stories in which the younger children had sometimes to climb narrow staircases to reach the second or third floor. The more recent schools were of the central hall type. Classes were often large and many teachers had to cope with numbers as large as sixty or even more.

Payment by Results was still in force but much of its severity had disappeared with the issue of the Codes of 1891 and 1895. More subjects had been recognized as specific or class subjects on which grant could be earned and the last vestiges of the system disappeared in 1897. There had been a considerable increase in the proportion of college-trained certificated teachers, and graduates from the new day training colleges were beginning to find their way into the higher grade and even into the elementary schools. The salaries of teachers varied from district to district but already the large towns by expressing their willingness to adopt better rates of pay were attracting the best teachers. The method of 'chalk and talk' was supreme in most schools but here and there, practical activities such as woodwork and metal-work, cookery and domestic science were beginning to appear. The object lesson still held its own in many places although the Heuristic approach advocated by Professor Armstrong was already influencing the teaching of elementary science. Some School Boards such as those at London and Bradford were experimenting with school medical inspection and had made a start with the provision of special schools for handicapped children but as yet such services were not obligatory. Physical training was generally represented by military drill or exercises with dumb-bells or clubs but some schools had introduced musical drill and Swedish exercises. Kindergarten methods had been introduced into infant schools but with no very clear understanding of Froebel's principles. During the half-century which followed, changes were to take place which completely revolutionized both the elementary and the secondary schools and it is these developments which it is the object of this book to consider.

CHAPTER II

FROM STATE ASSISTANCE TO STATE SUPERVISION

FOR more than a half-century previous to the Bryce Commission the relations between the State and education had been undergoing continuous change and the original view that State intervention should be limited to making grants to supplement voluntary effort had gradually disappeared. By means of the grant system, the State had step by step taken over the supervision of elementary education but so far its action had been spasmodic, piecemeal, and in some ways ineffective because of the absence of co-ordination between the Government departments concerned. In recommending the establishment of a central authority for education, and local authorities responsible for all types of education within their areas, the Bryce Commission was taking a decisive step towards the substitution of State assistance by State supervision. Few were sufficiently bold at this time to suggest replacing State supervision by State control but there was a strong feeling that the State should be more actively concerned with education than it had been so far. Consequently there was a large domain consisting of the public, proprietary, and private schools into which State intervention had scarcely entered. We have already noted the wide differences of opinion in regard to the machinery through which State supervision ought to be exercised.

The voluntary schools presented an additional problem. They did not concern the Bryce Commission but nevertheless they constituted a factor which had to be considered. In many respects the position of the voluntary schools had deteriorated. It should be realized that at this time more than half of the elementary school population of the country was contained in the voluntary schools, the majority of which were Church of England schools supervised by the National Society. Between 1870 and 1895, the cost per child had been steadily rising. When Mr. Forster introduced the Elementary Education Act in 1870, he estimated that the cost per head was not likely to rise beyond thirty shillings. By 1880, however, the cost per head in the National schools was £1 14s. 10½d. Although subscriptions from Church people had more than doubled, the voluntary schools were finding it impossible to compete on equal terms with the Board Schools which could call upon the rates for assistance. Lord Sandon's Act of 1876 had indeed helped managers of voluntary schools by increasing the grant from 15s. to 17s. 6d. per child but this was only a temporary relief. Hence the Government had to consider the problem presented by the voluntary schools. Another difficulty was that religious differences were still so acute that any suggestion of rate aid for Church schools was bound to arouse fierce opposition from the Nonconformists.

The Liberal Government of Lord Rosebery was defeated in the General Election of 1895 and its successor was a Conservative administration headed by the Marquis of Salisbury. The new Government was as anxious as its predecessor to carry out the recommendations of the Bryce Commission and it also wished to do something to relieve the situation of the voluntary schools. The Liberals were not unanimous in their views on education but on the whole one can say that the party favoured the retention of the School Boards and even wished to increase their powers. The Bill of 1896 which was framed by the Vice-President of the Education Department, Sir John Gorst, with the assistance of the Secretary, Sir George Kekewich, and Mr. Michael Sadler, failed to meet the approval of the House and to avoid a possible defeat was abandoned by the Government. In one respect, the Bill went a step further than the proposals of the Bryce Commission. It suggested that the county and county borough councils should be constituted as the local authorities for elementary, secondary, and technical education, whereas the Bryce Commission had assumed that elementary education might be left in the hands of the School Boards. The Liberal opposition, supported by the School Boards and the Nonconformists, threatened to bring down the Government. It is said that the Lord President of the Council, the Duke of Devonshire, was requested by the Prime Minister to break the news of the failure of the Bill to Sir John Gorst as gently and as diplomatically as possible. He carried out his mission by bursting into Sir John's office with the remark, 'Gorst, your damned Bill's dead'.

In spite of this reverse, the Government was determined to help the voluntary schools. In the following year it passed a Voluntary Schools Act which freed the schools from the payment of rates, abolished the 17s. 6d. limit for grant and made available an aid grant of 5s. per head to be paid through the Association of Voluntary Schools. To placate the opposition, similar relief was given to necessitous School Boards. It was freely recognized that these were merely temporary expedients which would last until an opportunity arose for surveying the whole situation more comprehensively.

The Government considered that it was now time to deal with the recommendations of the Bryce Commission. They selected the problem of the central authority as a start, knowing that it had not only a logical priority but that it was also free from the highly controversial issues connected with the establishment of new local authorities and the relief of the voluntary schools. The new central authority was created by the Board of Education Act of 1899 which came into operation at the beginning of the financial year, April 1st, 1900. The Government had in mind certain fears expressed by the witnesses called by the Bryce Commission and therefore refrained from giving the Board the control of education. It was content to emphasize the Board's function as that of 'the superintendence of matters relating to education in England and Wales'. In introducing the Bill, the Duke of Devonshire quite frankly admitted that nobody supposed that an actual Board would be constituted. It nominally consisted of the President of the Board, the Lord President of the Council (unless he was appointed President of the Board), the Principal Secretaries of State, (i.e. the Secretaries of State for the Home Department, Foreign Affairs, Colonial Affairs, War, and India), the First Lord of the Treasury, and the Chancellor of the Exchequer. As the Duke intimated, the Board only existed on paper. During its long history, it never once met and for practical purposes it consisted of the President, the Parliamentary Secretary, the Permanent Secretary, and the senior administrative officials. This is one of the standing puzzles to overseas students of the British Constitution.

The Education Department, the Science and Art Department, and the Charity Commission, in so far as it was concerned with education, were merged in the Board. The President was to be responsible to Parliament. One important section of the Act gave powers to the Board to 'inspect any school supplying secondary education and desiring to be so inspected'. It was under this provision that in later years certain public and preparatory schools opened their doors to Government inspection and were placed on the Board's list of recognized secondary schools.

The Bryce Commission's proposal for the establishment of an educational council was considerably modified. The Act provided for a Consultative Committee which could be summoned by the President of the Board to advise him on any matter which he referred to it. The Committee was in the position of not being able to speak until it was spoken to but in spite of this handicap, considerable use was made of it and the Committee was able to perform valuable service in the issue of such reports as the Hadow Reports on the Adolescent, the Primary School, etc. The Committee consisted of eighteen members of both sexes who held office for six years. It also had the duty of compiling a register of teachers. One of the reasons for weakening the recommendations of the Bryce Commissioners was the attitude of the public schools, who, through the Headmasters' Conference, were opposed to any step that might interfere with their independence.

It must be admitted that the Board of Education Act was a sorry attempt to interpret the real opinions of the Bryce Commission. The substitution for a Minister of Education by a President of a Board that never really existed and the whittling away of the powers of the Educational Council had results that could have been foreseen. There was another factor that may have swayed the Government in favour of a Board instead of a Ministry. It was expense. As the salary of the President was a mere £2,000 a year, a Board was a cheaper proposition than a Ministry. The first President was the Duke of Devonshire, but what was to be done about Sir John Gorst, the Vice-President of the Education Department? Although neither office nor Department now existed, he still continued to draw the salary belonging to his former appointment. The Presidency of the Board was therefore a comparatively junior appointment and was often to fall to members of the Government whose eyes were fixed on the attainment of more important and more lucrative offices. Small wonder, then, that of all the many occupants of that office, only four have held it sufficiently long and have possessed the experience, personality, and initiative to make a permanent mark upon the educational system of this country. These were: Mr. Fisher, Sir Charles Trevelyan, Lord Eustace Percy, and Mr. Butler. This does not mean that the long reign of the Board was a period of inefficiency. Far from it. The Board often meant in practice the permanent officials, and all who have had experience of the work of the senior members of the British Civil Service know that it has been distinguished by sound judgment and administrative competence. In 1899 the Board of Education was a new venture and it had to win its spurs, especially in the opinion of the many who mistrusted any move towards the centralization of policy.

The second cardinal part of the Bryce Commission's recommendations had to wait seven years before it was fulfilled by the establishment of local education authorities by the Education Act of 1902. A still longer delay might have occurred had it not been for the astonishing action of Robert Morant, who at this time was a rather junior member of the Civil Service. The Act of 1902 was not only the outcome of a struggle between opposing ideas, but it was also a contest between rival personalities who embodied those ideas and through whom the final compromise that resulted in the Act may best be understood. Let us then attempt a brief review of the individuals who controlled the destiny of education in the year 1899.

In order of seniority, the Duke of Devonshire comes first. Originally Lord President of the Council, he had been appointed the first President of the Board of Education. One is tempted to ask why. Probably the prestige won by his forebears in the political arena had much to do with the appointment. A man of his influence and importance could not be left out of office and although his age precluded him from a higher appointment, it was to be said in his favour that he had held numerous other positions, if not with distinction, yet without causing any acute embarrassment.[1] According to Sir George Kekewich, he was 'dull, silent, and impassive', but such comments should be accepted with a certain amount of reserve if one considers the circumstances under which they were made. It is true that the Duke's personal appearance suggested impassivity and this feature was seized upon in the numerous cartoons depicting members of the Government which appeared in *Punch* at this period. There are evidences that the Duke was far more shrewd than his op-

---

[1] Spencer Compton, 8th Duke of Devonshire, entered Parliament as Marquis of Hartington in 1857. He held successively the posts of First Lord of the Admiralty, Secretary of State for War, Postmaster General, and Secretary for Ireland. For a period, whilst Mr. Gladstone was out of office, he was leader of the Liberal Opposition. In 1880, he was offered the Premiership but declined it in favour of Gladstone. The Home Rule policy of Gladstone caused his break-away from the Liberals and as a Unionist, he accepted the office of Lord President of the Council in Lord Salisbury's administration of 1891.

ponents gave credit. Nevertheless it must be admitted that the Board of Education had not achieved a startling 'take-off' under his rule. If he had but little knowledge of educational matters, he was a good judge of the political situation of the time and he had some realization of the difficulties involved in transferring the powers of the School Boards to the local education authorities.

Kekewich describes him as follows: 'He was a living wet blanket, and he seemed to consider that his principal duty was to pour cold water upon every proposition that was made to him, and to show a chronic lack of appreciation of the merits of any reform suggested to him'.[1] Sadler was not misled by the Duke of Devonshire's impassive appearance. Although he spoke of the 'abysmal sleep of the Duke', he also recorded that he 'certainly was not continuously active in official business, but who, more than any chief I have served under, jerked out the essential question which lay under fluffy generalizations'.[2]

The Vice-President, Sir John Gorst, was a man of very different character and temperament. He was undoubtedly clever and able and if he had not possessed such a flair for irritating friends and foes alike by his sarcastic remarks, he might have become a really eminent statesman. When the Education Bill of 1896 was abandoned, Gorst, who could never condone a failure, blamed those who had assisted in drafting it and from that time his relations with Kekewich and Sadler seem to have changed. Gorst stirred even the impassive Duke to wrath and on one occasion the latter asked Kekewich 'whether any inducement worthy of his acceptance could be offered him to transfer his energies elsewhere. I suggested that a colonial governorship would be tempting, "not one of the two thousand pounds places, but a four thousand pounds one, such as Trinidad or Jamaica". Said the Duke, slowly and deliberately, not moving a muscle of his face, "I cannot imagine that the Government would offer Sir John Gorst the governorship of any colony that they desired to retain".' Sir John's spiteful temper and his penchant for fishing in troubled waters added a good deal of excitement to life in the Education Department during the last four years of its existence.[3]

---

[1] Sir G. W. Kekewich. *The Education Department and After*, p. 96. Constable, 1920.
[2] Michael Sadleir. *Michael Ernest Sadler*, p. 194, Constable, 1949.
[3] Sir G. W. Kekewich, *op. cit.*, pp. 94–5.

Sir George Kekewich was the Secretary of the Education Department. He was an experienced official who had the cause of education at heart but he had not a sufficiently robust personality to deal with men of the stamp of Sir John Gorst. Kekewich had been appointed Secretary in 1890 in succession to Mr. Cumin and within a few months of his acceptance of office he gained the confidence of the teachers. 'My creed was that the children came first, before everything and everybody', he wrote, and in support of this principle one of his first acts was the issue of the Code of 1890 which marked the beginning of the end of the system of Payment by Results which had been established by Robert Lowe's Revised Code of 1862. The teachers had experienced several attempts to woo them and at first they were inclined to mistrust the intentions of the new Secretary, but they quickly discovered that he was a man of his word. When he retired, the National Union of Teachers registered their appreciation of his work by conferring upon him the honorary membership of the Association. After the abortive Bill of 1896, Sir John Gorst took an active dislike to Kekewich and in 1901 *Truth* published an article which described the state of affairs in the Board of Education. 'The Duke of Devonshire is President of the Board of Education, and Sir John Gorst is his lieutenant. The Duke sometimes visits his Department; Sir John Gorst goes there a little more frequently. . . . The permanent Secretary for the past twelve years has been Sir George Kekewich, a pleasant, sensible man of business, and not at all a hide-bound official. Sir George Kekewich, however, and Sir John Gorst have practically ceased to be on speaking terms with each other. Sir John, in fact, is hardly on speaking terms with anybody—even with himself. The Duke of Devonshire well knows the unhappy condition of his department, but he is too lazy to interfere. He yawns and lets things slide'.[1]

In 1894, Mr. A. Acland, Vice-President of the Education Department in the Liberal Government, applied to the Treasury to obtain sanction for the appointment 'of an officer charged with the special duty of keeping, so far as may be found practicable or expedient, a systematic record of educational work and experiments, both in this country and abroad, and also with the further duty of obtaining and supplying information upon any special educational question

---

[1] Sir G. W. Kekewich, *op. cit.*, p. 335.

which may be referred to him for a report'.[1] This was the
first move towards the establishment of the Office of Special
Inquiries and Reports. The Treasury approved the application and gave authority for the appointment of a Director
with the appropriate staff. The result was that at the beginning of the year 1895, Michael Ernest Sadler was appointed
Director of Special Inquiries and Reports. At the time of his
appointment, Sadler was Secretary of the University Extension Delegacy, Oxford, and Steward of Christ Church. He
was already a recognized authority on educational matters
and he had served as a member of the Bryce Commission.
For some time, Sadler had been intimately acquainted with
Mr. Acland and it was the latter who proposed him as the
Director of the new sub-department.

One of Sadler's first tasks was to sort out the valuable
collection of books and reports which had lain untouched for
years in the cellar of the Education Department. These
formed the nucleus of the Reference Library of the Board of
Education. Sadler was quite aware of the possibilities and
value of the new department. His immediate chief, Sir
George Kekewich, also realized the importance of Sadler's
work. In later years, he wrote: 'The reports of this subdepartment, which were largely concerned with education
in foreign countries, were, and are still, of quite inestimable
value. Mr. Sadler brought to bear on the questions and
inquiries submitted to him, a knowledge of education, both
generally and in detail, which was then, and is still, second
to that of no man in this or perhaps in any other country.
When, years afterwards, he found it necessary to resign his
position, I could not help feeling that his resignation was a
real loss to the State, and that it would be exceedingly difficult, if not impossible, to find a man who could adequately
fill his place. Such cases are exceedingly rare. But that
place was not one in which a man could make up for any lack
of knowledge by picking the brains of his subordinates. Mr.
Sadler had to depend exclusively on his own knowledge and
his own ability, and the excellence of the work that he
accomplished stands as a testimony to the greatness of both'.[2]

The truth of this appreciation will be recognized by anyone who studies the first three volumes of *Special Reports*,
published in 1897 and 1898. These contain a large number of

---

[1] *Papers relating to the Resignation of the Director of Special Inquiries and Reports*, p. 3-4 (Cmd. 1602), H.M.S.O., 1903.
[2] Sir G. W. Kekewich, *op. cit.*, pp. 90-91.

exceedingly able studies prepared by the Director, his staff, and other experts in education and it is no exaggeration to say that Sadler's work prepared the way for that liberal conception of post-primary education which first received official mention in the Education Act of 1918, was elaborated in the Hadow Reports, and finally achieved full legal recognition in the Education Act of 1944.

In addition to collecting information and drafting reports on educational progress and experiments in Great Britain, the Dominions and Empire, and in foreign countries, and building up the Board of Education Library, Sadler's department had many other kinds of work to do. Visitors from the Empire or from foreign countries who wished to study English education were given into the charge of the Office of Special Inquiries and Reports. Ministers and senior officials who required at short notice authoritative information on educational matters, sent their requests to Sadler. When a very important person had to make a speech for a special occasion, Mr. Sadler was in demand. Thus, on the occasion of the Paris Exhibition, the sub-committee in charge thought it would be desirable to collect a number of exhibits to illustrate different aspects of English education and that before despatching the collection it might be useful to invite teachers and the general public to see it. The Prince of Wales agreed to open the exhibition and his speech was to be followed by one given by the Duke of Devonshire. The Prince's speech was written for him by Sir George Kekewich, who relates: 'Next the Duke of Devonshire followed suit and asked that he also might be supplied with a type-written speech, and as I really did not feel equal to concocting two speeches on the same exhibition, I asked Mr. Sadler if he would undertake the preparation of the Duke's speech. He kindly agreed to do so, and certainly compiled a speech worthy of the occasion, for which the Duke obtained much vicarious credit. That speech was also type-written, and was handed to the Duke on the platform. Neither the Prince nor the Duke had ever seen the speeches they had to deliver, but each of them read out his oration without turning a hair. Happily the speeches did not get mixed. They were both successes, and it was exceedingly interesting and somewhat amusing to the real authors to read the comments upon them in the newspapers the next day'.[1]

As the scope of the work of the Office of Special Inquiries

[1] Sir George Kekewich, *op. cit.*, p. 134.

and Reports extended, it became necessary for Mr. Sadler to visit other countries and he felt that he needed an Assistant-Director to take charge when he was away from England. His request was granted and Robert L. Morant was appointed in August, 1895. Morant (1863–1920) had been educated at Winchester and New College, Oxford. His original intention was to take Holy Orders but events changed his mind and in 1888 he became tutor to the family of the Siamese ambassador and later to the Crown Prince of Siam. He remained in that country until 1893, when on account of popular resentment at French attempts at annexation, he, in company with other Europeans, had been forced to leave. During his residence in Siam, Morant gained a reputation for educational organization and was often referred to as 'the uncrowned King of Siam'. It would seem, also, that he gained an intimate knowledge of the methods of Eastern intrigue. When he applied for the post of Assistant-Director, he made a profound impression on Sadler, who wrote to Mrs. Sadler: 'I hope they'll appoint Morant. He's the best man—very keen and active and has refused a good Indian appointment in the hope of coming into the new office'.[1]

When Morant took up his work in Sadler's department, he quickly discovered that during his absence from England much had happened with which he was unfamiliar. Hence his first task was to make himself acquainted with the educational situation at this time. Mr. Lowndes in *The Silent Social Revolution* gives a vivid picture of Morant's 'midnight reading' which resulted in his acquiring an expert knowledge of the details of evidence submitted to the Cross and Bryce Commissioners. His study soon revealed to him the muddle and chaos which had overtaken educational administration and his quick logical mind saw that there was only one practicable solution of the problem. The local administration of education must be delegated to the county and county borough councils. In his view, the School Boards had long outlived their period of usefulness but he realized that they would not willingly consent to their liquidation. The problem had been complicated by the development of the higher grade elementary schools. Sir George Kekewich, who was his chief as well as Sadler's, had great faith in the future of these schools. He had recently toured the country explaining to School Boards that the higher grade schools were no longer a 'mere luxury but an absolute necessity'.

[1] Michael Sadleir, *op. cit.*, p. 142.

Morant would also know Sadler's views on the matter. The latter regarded these institutions as containing in themselves the germs of a wider and more liberal conception of secondary education than this country had yet recognized. Hence the problem of Morant was how to discredit the School Boards and the answer seemed to him to be tied up with the question of the legality of the higher grade schools. Had not witnesses before the Cross Commission suggested that the use of money voted for elementary education but spent on what in fact was secondary education was a matter of doubtful legality?

Moreover Morant had not to be long in the Education Department to realize the internal dissension that was rife—in particular, the antagonism against Sir George Kekewich that was displayed by Sir John Gorst. Anything that was detrimental to the policy of the Secretary would find willing support from the Vice-President. A junior civil servant, however, would have to play his hand with supreme care and it would not be expedient to come out into the open prematurely. Morant laid his plans with great skill. His experience in the Far East had taught him the type of tactics likely to succeed.

Robert Morant's character is difficult to assess. The main sources of information are avowedly partisan. Dr. Allen, by the title he adopts for his work, *Life of Sir Robert Morant, a great Public Servant*, suggests that he is both an admirer and an apologist but even he seems at times to experience a difficulty in explaining away Morant's actions at this period. Mr. Michael Sadleir naturally ranges himself on his father's side and the extracts from private papers which he publishes are intended to testify to Morant's ruthlessness and overpowering ambition. Mr. Lowndes has obviously great admiration for Morant but he freely admits, 'Mr. Morant's strategy had been learnt in Siam, and looked at from the point of view of strategy alone this ruthless and apparently premeditated indiscretion was a master stroke, purchased at a price which it has taken educational opinion thirty-five years to appreciate, and regret. Looked at from the point of view of modern civil service ethics, it is better to admit frankly that it seems to have been an astonishing step for a comparatively junior official to have taken'.[1]

Morant has been described as unscrupulous but much depends upon the precise meaning to be attached to this

[1] G. A. N. Lowndes, *The Silent Social Revolution*, p. 78. O.U.P., 1937.

term. If it is used to suggest that he was a mere self-seeker with no high and far-reaching ideals, then nothing could be more false. Morant had his ideals just as Sadler had, but the misfortune of it all was that their aims were completely disparate. Morant in the pursuit of his ends let nothing stand in the way—not even personal loyalty or old friendships. On the other hand there is nothing to show that his ambition was merely a personal one. It is charitable to suppose that he sought high office as the means of carrying out the ideals in which he believed and which were so vital to him that he could brook no opposition, nor could he appreciate that others might have views about which they felt just as strongly, and that he might be mistaken and they right. He was in the front rank of administrators but we shall see that his autocratic and dictatorial manner made him less efficient than he might have been. Few loved him but many feared him and when an indiscretion of a subordinate brought about his fall from power, his many enemies rejoiced. This same autocrat, however, was, if not the creator of the pre-war elementary school, the stimulus which accounted for its development. He had a deep interest in adult education for working men and women and it was his support and sympathy which sustained the McMillan sisters in their pioneer work for nursery school education. Truly he was a man of many parts.

The strategy to which Mr. Lowndes refers may be briefly summarized. In the course of his work for the Department of Special Inquiries and Reports, Morant visited Switzerland to make a study of the educational system of that country. His article on Swiss education appeared in *Special Reports on Educational Subjects*, vol. 3, 1898, and he slipped into it a paragraph drawing attention to the illegality of spending public money ear-marked for elementary education on the upkeep of higher grade schools. He hoped, as actually happened, that it would pass unnoticed by both Kekewich and Sadler. Very soon the opportunity to make use of it presented itself. A dispute was in progress between the London School Board and the London Technical Education Board in which the latter claimed responsibility for secondary education, and was supported by the County Council. Morant felt that he was in a position to intervene. It seems that Sir John Gorst had asked Sir George Kekewich to release Morant temporarily from his duties in the Office of Special Inquiries and Reports so that he might act as his private secretary. Why Gorst should single out Morant for this duty is a matter for conjecture. When Gorst's private secretary resigned in November 1899, Morant was appointed in his place. It should be realized that technically he was still an assistant to Sadler and Kekewich. The result was that Morant was able to act in independence of Sadler.

Dr. Garnett, the Secretary of the London Technical Education Board, was preparing the case for the County Council. Morant contrived that his reference in the Swiss report should be placed in a position where Garnett could not avoid seeing it. No doubt Sir John was privy to the affair and would be delighted at the chance of striking a blow at Kekewich. He decided in favour of the County Council and suggested to Dr. Garnett that at the next meeting with the Government Auditor, Mr. T. B. Cockerton, the legality of the London School Board's action in maintaining higher grade schools ought to be challenged. This was done. The auditor was satisfied with the evidence and surcharged the School Board with the amount which had been spent on higher grade schools. The School Board contested this decision in the Queen's Bench Division of the High Court. The court decided in favour of Mr. Cockerton but the School Board resolved to appeal. The Court of Appeal not only upheld the previous decision, but also declared that the School Board had acted illegally in conducting evening continuation schools for persons who were not children and using the elementary grant to finance the instruction. The Cockerton Judgment created an extremely difficult situation and in 1901 the Government had to pass a special Act to legalize the position of the School Boards for one year until a comprehensive measure could be prepared.

Morant's promotion was now rapid. He assisted Sir John in drafting the Act of 1901 and his connection with Sadler's department was severed by his appointment as Senior Examiner in the new secondary school branch of the Board of Education. As a comprehensive education Act was inevitable, Mr. Balfour requested Morant to draw up a memorandum on the problems that had to be faced and he was so impressed with Morant's ability that he invited him to prepare the draft of the new Bill which was to be introduced in the following session. The Cockerton Judgment must have been a severe blow to Sadler's hopes of a more liberal spirit in secondary education, but whatever may have been his misgivings, he immersed himself in the work of his department.

When Mr. A. J. Balfour succeeded Lord Salisbury as Prime Minister in 1902, several important changes were made in the Cabinet. Lord Londonderry became President of the Board of Education and Sir William Anson, Parliamentary Secretary. The latter appointment involved the retirement of Sir John Gorst. Sir George Kekewich was not due to retire until April, 1903, but Morant doubted whether he was the type of man who could carry out the Government's policy successfully. Rumour had it that Kekewich had not favoured the Board of Education Act. When he published his book, some eighteen years later, Kekewich showed himself an ardent Liberal who believed that the Government's intentions about education were mistaken. Although he declared that during his term of office nobody at Whitehall knew his political creed. Morant was convinced that Kekewich was not heart and soul in support of the new Bill. Hence he persuaded Lord Londonderry to write to the Prime Minister asking for the appointment of a really good man, thoroughly acquainted with the educational situation, to take the place of Kekewich. It was obvious that Lord Londonderry would recommend Morant because of his work in the preliminary drafting of the Bill. The President sent for Kekewich and suggested that he should retire at the end of October but might nominally hold the office of Secretary in order to qualify for full pension. Morant was installed as Acting-Secretary and received the official title of Permanent Secretary of the Board of Education in April 1903.

Meanwhile the new Bill had been presented to the House of Commons. The situation was bristling with difficulties but both Balfour and Morant were determined to face them boldly. In accordance with the recommendations of the Bryce Commission, the Bill proposed the abolition of the School Boards and their substitution by the County Councils and the County Borough Councils as the new local education authorities. The way for the acceptance of this had been prepared by the publication by the Webbs of the Fabian Pamphlet, No. 106, entitled *The Education Muddle and the Way Out*. Few mourned the decease of the School Boards save the School Boards themselves, and Mr. Joseph Chamberlain, who fortunately for the success of the Bill had been incapacitated by a street accident at the time the measure was being discussed in Parliament. The blow to the School Boards, possibly on the advice of Morant, was softened.

Although the new local authorities under Part II of the Act took over the control of elementary education in their areas, they were also empowered to supply or aid education 'other than elementary'. The latter phrase included secondary and technical education and the provision of training colleges for teachers. In order to carry this out, they were allowed, in addition to 'Whisky Money', to levy a rate not exceeding twopence in the pound. At the same time they were charged with the general co-ordination of all types of education in their areas. Part III of the Act permitted borough councils with a population exceeding 10,000 and urban districts with a population of over 20,000 to become local education authorities with control over elementary education only.

It was argued that this would lead to the fostering of local initiative and lead to the development of local interest. In fact it was an attempt to conciliate the out-going School Boards. In later years, no section of the Act received such severe criticism and caused so much administrative difficulty as this, but at the time attention was diverted by the intense denominational antagonism aroused by the Act. Both Part II and Part III authorities normally delegated their powers, except those of levying a rate or raising a loan, to education committees. London presented a special case and an Act of 1903 replaced the London School Board by the County Council.

The religious issue was raised by the proposal to place voluntary schools as regards secular instruction under the L.E.A.s and to secure rate aid for them. The board schools now became council schools and since the school buildings were provided by the local authority, they were also known as provided schools. The school buildings of the voluntary schools remained the property of the religious denominations, who were responsible for the upkeep of the fabric except for repairs due to fair wear and tear. These non-provided schools were to be controlled by four foundation managers to whom were added two managers appointed by the local authority. Some critics were anxious that the appointment of a new incumbent should not involve the teaching of Anglo-Catholic doctrines in the school. Again, on the advice of Morant, consent was given to the Kenyon-Slaney Clause which provided that the religious instruction given should be in accordance with the trust deed of the school.

The L.E.A. was to be responsible for the secular instruction whilst the managers controlled the kind of religious teaching provided. Under this Dual System, the head and assistant-teachers were appointed by the managers but the L.E.A. could veto the appointment of any candidate who was deemed unsuitable as regards his professional qualifications. On the other hand, the managers retained the power to dismiss a teacher on religious grounds. There were cases in which this power was exercised. Thus in a village school in the south of England, a head teacher, who had been warned about the low standard of the religious instruction in the school and who did not take steps to improve it, was dismissed by the managers. Their action was upheld by the Court and the individual was eventually given an appointment as an assistant-teacher in a neighbouring council school. The maintenance of non-provided schools, the provision of books and apparatus, and the salaries of the staff were charges on the local authority.

It is perhaps difficult for us in these days of religious tolerance and friendliness to understand the fierce resentment which these proposals aroused. To appreciate it, one must cast one's mind back to the earlier days of the nineteenth century, when the claim of the Church of England to control education was bitterly resisted by the Nonconformists. The idea that the rates they paid should be used to support religious teaching in schools from which they dissented was abhorrent to them. On previous occasions, the suggestion of applying rate aid to voluntary schools had caused the abandonment of educational legislation. Religious disputes had almost wrecked the prospects of the Elementary Education Act of 1870 and it was only the introduction of a Conscience clause, and the well known Cowper-Temple Clause which enabled the measure to be approved by the Commons.[1] In the first draft of the Bill of 1902, Balfour and Morant actually contemplated the abolition of the Cowper-Temple Clause but further reflection convinced them that the attempt would not be successful.

As soon as the proposal to place the voluntary schools on the rates became known, the fighting spirit of the Nonconformists was aroused and following the example of Dr. Clifford many of them announced their intention of refusing to pay their rates. A considerable number carried out this threat and for some years after the passage of the Act,

---

[1] The Clause applied to schools which received aid from the rates and stated 'no religious catechism or religious formulary which is distinctive of any particular denomination shall be taught in the school'.

Passive Resisters submitted to fines and distraint upon their belongings.[1] The Liberal party adopted the Nonconformist cause and Mr. Lloyd George concentrated the attack upon the Government. He realized that the Government had presented the Liberals with a heaven-sent opportunity of healing their differences and forming a united party. As the debate continued, Mr. Lloyd George's opposition came to have less and less to do with education and became a strenuous attempt to bring down the Government. The Bill formed a rallying point for all the Liberal factions and the Government's education policy was one of the most influential factors which contributed towards the great landslide at the General Election of 1906.

Not all Liberals, however, adopted Mr. Lloyd George's point of view. Some of them put ideas of party triumph aside because they saw quite clearly the necessity for a comprehensive policy in education. Mr. Haldane was one of these and his speech from the Opposition bench in support of the Bill was one of the most constructive of the whole debate. Mr. Sidney Webb had been a supporter of the Bill from the beginning and he wrote in the *Daily Mail*, October 17th, 1902, this oft quoted paragraph.' For the first time the Bill definitely includes as a public function education as education, not primary education only, or technical education only, but anything and everything that is education from the kindergarten to the university. This renders the Bill of 1902 epoch-making in the history of English education.'

The Liberals and the Nonconformists were not prepared to give up the struggle. In addition to the campaign of passive resistance, certain local authorities in Wales threatened open disobedience. Morant advised the Government to take firm action. The consequence was the passage of the Education (Local Authorities Default) Act of 1904 which stated that in cases where the local authority refused to make adequate grants to the voluntary schools in its area, the Board of Education would deduct an equivalent amount from its grant to the authority and pay it direct to the managers of the voluntary schools. Mr. Lloyd George challenged the Government to put the Act into operation. He declared that the Welsh authorities would reply by refusing to carry on elementary education and would close the council schools. Mr. Balfour was not to be intimidated and

[1] According to Mr. G. A. N. Lowndes there were about 70,000 prosecutions for non-payment of rates.

immediately took action against two defaulting authorities. Lloyd George's threat was not carried out. The Liberals realized that the general public would resent any movement which made school children pawns in the political game.

After the election of 1906 which returned the Liberal party to power with the largest majority of modern times, three different attempts were made to reverse the Act of 1902. The first was a Bill introduced by the Liberal President of the Board of Education, Mr. Birrell. It sought to transfer the voluntary schools to the local authorities. The Bill was drastically amended by the Lords and as neither House was willing to compromise, the Government decided to abandon it. Dr. Clifford was intensely disappointed with this decision and tried to work up the constitutional issue of the Lords versus the Commons. As the Act of 1902, thanks to Morant, was working so well, the Government was not prepared to support Dr. Clifford. The second attempt was made by Mr. McKenna in 1908. He proposed that rate aid should be limited to schools which provided undenominational teaching. The trustees of non-provided schools were to be invited to transfer their schools to the local authority. If they did not wish to do so, they would cease to receive rate aid, and would be given, if the school was approved by the Board of Education as efficient, an Exchequer grant not exceeding 47s. per head per annum. They would also be permitted to charge fees up to 9d. a week. This option was not to apply to single school areas, i.e. parishes where the non-provided school was the only one. The Roman Catholics joined the Anglicans in opposition to the Government's proposals. Both had learnt from the tactics of the Nonconformists and they threatened passive resistance on a nation-wide scale. The Government withdrew the Bill but it made one concession to Welsh national feeling. A special Welsh Department of the Board of Education was created to supervise educational matters in the Principality. The last attempt to reverse the 1902 Act was made in the same year by Mr. Runciman, who had succeeded Mr. McKenna at the Board. This time the Anglicans and Roman Catholics were supported by the teachers who resented the fact that education was becoming the sport of party politics. Moreover, they felt that it was now time that the teaching profession had a say in affairs. Once more the Government was forced to yield.

After the lapse of half a century, one is now in the position to review the Education Act of 1902 in a spirit which is free from partisan prejudice and which enables one to appreciate those qualities of foresight and statesmanship which produced it. That is not to say that the measure was free from blemishes. In order to make certain of its acceptance by the House of Commons certain complications had to be introduced and various compromises were made, but on the whole one can say that it made a number of contributions of the greatest value. Although it would be an exaggeration to claim that the Act created a national system of education, yet one can justifiably assert that it laid the foundation on which such a system could be built. Taken in conjunction with the Board of Education Act of 1899, it represents the half-way house between State assistance and State control, namely, the stage of State supervision. One of its most important achievements was the recognition that the service of public education is a function belonging to local government and although not expressly stated in the Act, there was implicit in it what has been termed the tri-partite partnership between the central authority, the local authorities, and the various bodies of governors and managers responsible for individual schools. The exact relations between the partners were not defined and it was left to subsequent events to clarify them.

Although some powers of the Board of Education with regard to special provisions of the Act were named, yet many of its clauses were permissive rather than mandatory. Thus it was left to the initiative of the local authority to make provision for higher education; it was no part of its duty. Most local authorities freely accepted the implied responsibility but there was left the opportunity for a niggardly authority to adopt a passive resistance policy. In the last resort, as the power of the purse was in the hands of the Board of Education, recalcitrant authorities could always be brought to heel by the intimation that grants would be withheld or reduced. The Board was always reluctant to take such a step and it relied on the indirect means of suggestion, exhortation and encouragement. If few authorities were sufficiently bold to defy the Board, a considerable number procrastinated and delayed schemes for improvement until the last possible moment.

The Act produced a considerable simplification in administration. The Board of Education now had to deal with 318 local education authorities in place of 2,568 School

Boards and School Attendance Committees and 14,238 boards of voluntary school managers. The system of 'Payment by Results' had disappeared and the state grant was reorganized as an Aid grant which however took insufficient note of the fact that the expenditure per head of some local authorities, through no fault of their own, was excessively high, whilst the amount derived from the rates was correspondingly low. This placed an unfair burden on some authorities and when in 1906 the L.E.A. for East Ham found it impossible to carry out the Act, the Government found it necessary to make additional grants to necessitous areas.

One of the most significant features of the Act was the power given to L.E.A.s to provide secondary and higher education. The idea of secondary education for all was only present in the minds of a few advanced thinkers but the Act prepared the way for the eventual acceptance of this view. In the eighteenth century, secondary education was the privilege of the wealthier sections of the community who were able to afford the fees of the public schools and the endowed grammar schools. Foundation statutes did indeed provide for the free education of a number of poor scholars but the financial condition of many of the schools was rapidly making such provision a farce. The Taunton Commission considered that the name 'Free School' had completely lost any meaning by the middle of the nineteenth century. Primary education for the poorer classes was regarded as a gift bestowed through the generosity of philanthropic individuals and societies. As the Industrial Revolution progressed, it became evident that something would have to be done in respect of the education of 'the lower orders'. Such provision was conceived as being very different from the kind of education considered suitable for the children of country gentlemen or of well-to-do merchants and manufacturers. The tendency to broaden the basis of primary education received a setback through the introduction of the Revised Code and Lowe had openly acknowledged that it was right that the training given to poorer children should differ essentially from that enjoyed by the upper and middle classes. Gradually other subjects had been added to the three Rs but at the beginning of this century the line of division between primary and secondary education was still the ability or inability to pay fees.

When the Act of 1902 gave power to local authorities to

provide for education other than elementary and directed them to co-ordinate all forms of education within their areas, this very fact forced them to consider the relations between the secondary and the elementary school. The time was not ripe for any considerable development of the idea of secondary education for all but it was becoming generally recognized that a certain number of elementary school scholars had the ability to profit from a secondary course of instruction. We shall see that this idea was strongly supported by the Liberals and resulted in the adoption of the Free Place system. Thus in a very real way we may consider the 1902 Act as containing in germ the idea of the scholarship ladder from the elementary school to the university.

Unlike previous education acts, that of 1902 took the whole of education under university level in its survey. The local authorities were given power to build training colleges for teachers. Hitherto entrants to the teaching profession had received their training in colleges supported by voluntary bodies or in the day training departments attached to institutions of university rank. The Board of Education expressed willingness to defray three-fourths of the building costs of the municipal training colleges. The result of this expansion was that between 1900 and 1913 the output of trained teachers was practically doubled. Many of the old higher grade schools became secondary schools and new county and municipal secondary schools were erected. At first the building programme went ahead very slowly but once the Free Place system became general, there was considerable speeding up.

The distinction between the Part II and Part III authorities proved a source of much contention. It is true to say that some Part III authorities were very progressive, indeed more so than some of their Part II neighbours, but at the same time they were restricted and handicapped. They had the power of levying a penny rate for assisting higher education but the provision of this instruction was the concern of the county authority. The Part III authority was generally responsible for a small area the rateable value of which was not adequate to the provision of amenities in the form of scholarships, playing fields, and swimming baths on the same scale as was possible for the more wealthy authorities. Thus, in theory, a child in a Part III area had more restricted opportunities than his more fortunate neighbour. In practice, British common sense tended to iron out many of the discrepancies. It became the general custom for the Director of the Part III authority to be the secretary to the governors of the local grammar school for which the county authority was responsible. Thus, to give an illustration, the Director of Education for Morley in the West Riding was the Secretary to the Governors of Morley Grammar School and thus established a link between the two authorities.

CHAPTER III

THE REIGN OF SIR ROBERT MORANT

MORANT was now firmly established as the Permanent Secretary of the Board of Education but he was quite aware that as soon as the Liberal party came to power, strenuous efforts would be made to reverse the situation created by the Act of 1902. The most effective means of preventing this was to ensure that the Act was working smoothly and efficiently so that there would be little chance of a return to the School Boards. One of Morant's first tasks was the re-organization of the central authority. Although the Board of Education had been entrusted with the superintendence of all forms of education, there was still a possibility that the separate branches which were formerly represented by the Science and Art Department, the Charity Commission, and the Education Department might go their own ways. This possibility was the more real since Morant had to use the staffs of these departments. Hence his problem was to devise means of bringing the different sections into harmony and to prevent overlapping. The solution he adopted was to re-organize the work of the Board into three main branches—Elementary, Secondary, and Technical, each in charge of a Principal Assistant Secretary. The country was divided into seven geographical districts each in charge of a Principal[1] who was responsible for the work of the three branches in the area. Means for co-operation between the branches were arranged and also for consultation with the local authorities.

At the same time the Inspectorate was re-organized. The Board's Inspectorate was divided geographically into nine districts with Wales as a tenth and the distribution of inspectors was arranged to correspond with the three main branches so that each branch had its own staff of inspectors. Additional inspectors were appointed for the training of teachers and the work of schools of art. Women inspectors were also appointed 'to undertake inspection and inquiry

[1] Principals and Assistant Principals were at one time called Examiners on account of their duties connected with examining the papers worked by pupil teachers and students in training.

into all matters especially needing the scrutiny and advice of a woman'.[1]

Morant took special care in the selection of his inspectors and endeavoured to choose them with regard to their particular kind of experience. He exercised a personal supervision of their work and set a very high standard of efficiency for them to follow. No longer was it possible for an inspector to drop into a school for a short time at the beginning of a morning and then lunch with the squire and perhaps spend the remainder of the day in shooting or fishing. Morant was concerned to see that the inspectors carried out their jobs in an efficient and conscientious manner. There is a story which has been vouched for, of an inspector who was a good batsman. He was asked by the local squire to play for the village team. The inspector hurriedly paid a visit to the parish school and by the middle of the morning had changed and was ready for the cricket match. Unfortunately for him, his photograph was reproduced in one of the popular illustrated journals and Morant happened to see it. The result was a short interview with the offending inspector and that was the finish of his career.

Morant was concerned to enunciate a definite policy with regard to elementary and secondary education. He had very clear ideas about what he desired and he was not prepared to allow anything or any person to stand in the way of accomplishing his purpose. Lester Smith remarks that there was 'nothing normal about Morant, for he was as autocratic, ruthless and ambitious as any self-made industrial magnate'.[2] As Sir Maurice Holmes declared, 'he was incapable of thinking in terms of partnership,' and he realized that there was only one quarter from which effective opposition might be expected; his old chief Sadler. Hence he resolved that he would have to get rid of him. Sadler had become too independent for Morant's liking and his ideas about secondary education were very different from those in which Morant believed.

The opportunity presented itself to Morant early in 1903. Sadler had suggested a report on Italian education but Morant wrote to the Parliamentary Secretary, Sir William Anson, giving his opinion that the need for economy made it imperative that this particular inquiry should be postponed.

---

[1] Women inspectors had previously been appointed in 1883 and again in 1890 to supervise needlework and domestic subjects.
[2] *Education in Great Britain*, p. 117. O.U.P. (Home University Library), 1949.

Sadler protested to both Anson and Morant but he received the following reply: 'Pray understand that neither Sir W. Anson nor I have the least desire to undervalue the interest and importance of these reports, or to hinder the progress of any which can properly be described as urgent. But we cannot admit that the Italian report is urgent: and this being so, we cannot admit that your Division is entitled to exemption from the demand of the Treasury for economy in all branches of our work, in view of the heavy expenditure arising in connection with the Education Act.'[1]

On Morant's suggestion, Sadler asked for an interview with the President of the Board, who eventually sanctioned the preparation of a report on Italian education. Sadler had by this time realized that he would have to work in the face of constant opposition from Morant and he felt that the only course left to him was to tender his resignation. He accompanied this with a memorandum which set forth his views about the function of the Office of Special Inquiries and Reports.

Sadler's memorandum showed that he had a thorough grasp of the issues involved. He stated that 'the office of Special Inquiries and Reports is the Intelligence Department of the Board of Education. The need for an Intelligence Department at the Board of Education is as great as at the War Office or Admiralty. Industrial and commercial rivalry under modern conditions is largely governed by comparative educational efficiency. It is, therefore, necessary that Great Britain shall know, accurately and quickly, what educational advances are being made by her commercial and industrial competitors in Europe and America. The Intelligence Department at the Board of Education has the duty (1) of giving information to the Board on educational matters referred to it by the Board for inquiry and report, and (2) of publishing accurate information on educational methods and developments at home and abroad, for the guidance of public opinion, and for the help of local educational authorities, teachers, governing bodies of schools, etc.'[2] Towards the end of the memorandum he added, 'The Office has been seriously overworked for many years. The Director's request for more help has been three times refused since January 1900. It has now become impossible

---

[1] *Papers relating to the Resignation of the Director of Special Inquiries and Reports*, p. 38. H.M.S.O., 1903.
[2] *Ibid.*, p. 39.

for him to maintain the Intelligence Department at its necessary level of efficiency for the supply of important and well-digested information, without further aid.'[1] Sadler requested certain very modest additions to the establishment, and asked that if the Treasury wished for further satisfaction, he hoped it would institute a special inquiry into the organization and work of the office.

A second memorandum from Sadler gave a detailed account of the work which his office had already accomplished. Evidently Morant was not getting the best of the argument and he replied as follows: 'The President is fully sensible of the value not only of the Reports, but of the inquiries made, the information supplied, and the library work done by you and your staff; but it cannot be too clearly impressed upon you that the work of the Office of Special Inquiries and Reports is done, and must be done, for the benefit of the Board, at the instance of the Board, and under the direction of the Board.'[2]

Sadler believed that the conditions prescribed were intolerable. He was being asked to publish what the Government desired and to refrain from giving any information, however true it might be, which might run counter to the purposes of the administration. In other words, he was being asked to sell his soul for the sake of administrative expediency. Such a course, he was firmly convinced, was in the highest degree dishonest and dishonourable. His reply was unequivocal: 'In order that the scientific work of educational inquiry may be searching and fruitful, it must be intellectually independent. Those engaged in it must be free to state what they believe to be true, apart from pre-considerations as to what may at the time be thought administratively convenient. But the Secretary's minute lays down a principle of administrative control which would, if pressed, be fatal to the freedom of scientific inquiry, and therefore to the independence of the Reports.'[3] As a consequence, he reaffirmed his intention of resigning. Some further interviews between Sadler, the President and the Parliamentary Secretary took place but it was found impossible to reach an agreement. The following official notice appeared in the newspapers of May 11th-12th, 1903. 'Mr. M. E. Sadler has placed in the hands of the President of the Board of Education his resignation of

[1] *Ibid.*, p. 40.
[2] *Ibid.*, p. 57.
[3] *Ibid.*, p. 58.

the Office of Director of Special Inquiries and Reports to the Board, the point at issue being proposals, which, in his judgment, would impair the scientific value and thoroughness as well as the practical efficiency of the work of his Office. The Office of Special Inquiries and Reports is the Intelligence Division of the Board of Education. Mr. Sadler has been Director of the Office from its establishment in 1895.'

Sadler's resignation caused considerable discussion in the press. Mr. Emmott, M.P. for Oldham, put a question in the House of Commons which was answered by Sir William Anson. The latter suggested that the Board of Education had made no proposals affecting the Office of Special Inquiries and Reports but had rigidly adhered to the conditions stated in Mr. Acland's Minute of 1895 when the appointment was made. It was Mr. Sadler who had asked for a new departure and the Board had considered that his proposals were inconsistent with the terms of the original appointment. Mr. Acland denied this and wrote to the *Times* warmly supporting the action of Sadler. The result was the issue of the Blue Book—*Papers relating to the Resignation of the Director of Special Inquiries and Reports.* Morant, however, had achieved his purpose, and with Sadler out of the way, he was now ready to press forward his own policy without fear of opposition. For the next eight years his reign at the Board of Education was supreme and the policy of the Board was really that of Morant.

One of Morant's chief problems was concerned with the expansion and re-organization of secondary education. As a result of the 1902 Act, many of the higher grade schools and pupil teacher centres were taken over by the local education authorities and became secondary schools. The Board had issued a Minute recognizing higher elementary schools which were to provide a four year course for pupils of 10 to 15 years of age but there was a noticeable lack of encouragement for this scheme. Having got rid of the higher grade schools, Morant did not wish to find himself saddled with a substitute for them. According to Graves, 'The number of schools recognized between 1905 and 1917 never exceeded 45, and at no time were as many as 10,000 pupils being educated in them.'[1] Morant's interest was in what are now termed secondary grammar schools.

The distinction between elementary and secondary educa-

[1] J. Graves. *Policy and Progress in Secondary Education*, p. 75. Nelson, 1943.

tion had never been clearly defined. The Bryce Commission had given a good deal of thought to the essential characteristics of both secondary and technical education and, guided by Sadler, had shown that there was no real opposition between the two types. This, we have seen, was not Morant's view. The difficulty was accentuated by the fact that the only definition of an elementary school was given in the Education Act of 1870. An elementary school was described as a school in which elementary education is the principal part of the education given and in which the fees did not exceed 9d. per week. It was assumed that everybody knew what was meant by elementary education. No further assistance was given by the Act of 1902, which referred to both secondary and technical education as 'education other than elementary'. In the *Regulations for Secondary Schools*, 1904, the Board defined a secondary school as 'a day or boarding school which offers to each of its scholars up to and beyond the age of 16 a general education, physical, mental, and moral, given through a complete graded course of instruction, of wider scope and more advanced degree than that given in elementary schools.' It should be noted that the definition was framed in terms of the kind of instruction given. The age of the pupils concerned was a supplementary item. The idea that every pupil should pass through a stage of secondary education had not yet developed. Bearing this restriction in mind, at first sight the definition seems an admirable one but when the Regulations are examined more closely, it is seen that the interpretation reveals a certain school of thought, of which Morant was representative and which was in essence opposed to the view expressed by the Bryce Commission.

This school of thought derived its ideas of a liberal education from von Humboldt and Matthew Arnold. It considered that the normal grammar school course would last until 18 or 19 years of age and for many pupils would lead to university studies. Morant's own experience of secondary education had been gained at Winchester and even when he had resigned his office at the Board of Education, so many of his colleagues had been appointed from the same school, that this influence, in a modified form, still lived on. This idea of secondary education did not fit the facts. The majority of secondary school boys and girls left at 16 or even earlier, but it was thought that even so the school should be modelled with a view to university requirements. Hence the

Regulations demanded a four-year course in certain groups of subjects. These were: (1) English language and literature, history and geography for at least 4½ hours a week; (2) at least one language other than English studied for a minimum of 3½ hours a week (six hours if two languages were taught); (3) mathematics and science, both theoretical and practical for 7½ hours a week; and (4) drawing. Morant's views were clearly shown in the following paragraph. 'Where two languages other than English are taken, and Latin is not one of them, the Board will require to be satisfied that the omission of Latin is for the advantage of the school.' It seemed as though nothing had been learnt from the work carried on so successfully by the higher grade schools. Even as late as 1910–11, the Board of Education Report considered that practical housewifery ought not to be included in the curriculum of girls' secondary schools 'because the educational value of the proposed arrangements and its connection with the ordinary work of the school were not clearly made out.' In justice to Morant, one should realize that conditions had changed from the days when the Taunton Commission had investigated the curriculum of the endowed grammar school. Then the claims of physical science for inclusion in the curriculum were only beginning to be heard. Now it was the other way about. The demand for scientific and technical instruction had grown to such an extent that there was a very real danger that the literary subjects might be rated as being of secondary importance. The Bryce Commission had commented on the undue bias placed on scientific instruction in the higher grade schools. No doubt Morant had this in mind.

Dr. R. F. Young in his historical sketch at the beginning of the Spens Report, indicates the errors in Morant's views. He says, 'The most salient defect in the new regulations for secondary schools issued in 1904 is that they failed to take note of the comparatively rich experience of secondary curricula of a practical and quasi-vocational type which had been evolved in the higher grade schools, the organized science schools, and the technical day schools. The new regulations were based wholly on the tradition of the grammar schools and the public schools.[1] He then continues by pointing out that an unreal and unnecessary distinction was introduced between secondary and technical education, in opposition to the view expressed by the Bryce Commission

[1] *Spens Report*, pp. 66–7. H.M.S.O. 1938.

and that the meaning of the term 'general education' was confused. The result of the new regulations was that secondary education was regarded from the standpoint of subjects rather than from that of the pupil, his needs, outlook, interests and abilities at different stages of his development. Moreover, Morant was a believer in the faculty psychology even though it was being rejected by some of his younger contemporaries. This inclined him to attach special value to subjects as a means of training different faculties of the mind.[1]

Morant's approach to the problems of elementary education was far different. In this case, he had no pre-conceived notions to govern his outlook and his *Code for Public Elementary Schools*, 1904, marks an entirely new departure. Morant wrote the introduction himself and the opening paragraphs, which seem like a breath of fresh air after the stifling atmosphere of the earlier codes, are well worth quoting in full.

'The purpose of the public elementary school is to form and strengthen the character and to develop the intelligence of the children entrusted to it, and to make the best use of the school years available, in assisting both girls and boys, according to their different needs, to fit themselves, practically as well as intellectually, for the work of life.

'With this purpose in view it will be the aim of the school to train the children carefully in habits of observation and clear reasoning, so that they may gain an intelligent acquaintance with some of the facts and laws of nature; to arouse in them a lively interest in the ideals and achievements of mankind, and to bring them to some familiarity with the literature and history of their own country; to give them some power over language as an instrument of thought and expression, and, while making them conscious of the limitations of their knowledge, to develop in them such a taste for good reading and thoughtful study as will enable them to increase that knowledge in after years by their own efforts.

'The school must at the same time encourage to the utmost the children's natural activities of hand and eye by suitable forms of practical work, and manual instruction; and to afford them every opportunity for the healthy development of their bodies, not only by training them in appropriate physical exercises and encouraging them in organized

---

[1] For examples of phrases which illustrate Morant's adherence to the faculty psychology see S. J. Curtis, *History of Education in Great Britain*, note, p. 328. U.T.P., 2nd edition, 1950.

games, but also by instructing them in the working of some of the simpler laws of health.' Morant here stated an ideal which it took many years for the schools to attain, hampered as they were by memories of Payment by Results and the era of chalk and talk. Nevertheless it was a noble ideal and one can say that even now it has not been reached by quite a number of schools.

The new Code was followed in 1905 by the publication of the *Suggestions for the Use of Teachers and Others concerned in the work of Elementary Schools*. This volume represented such a change from the rigid dictation of the days of the Revised Code that Dr. Leese very rightly refers to it as 'the teachers' new charter of liberty'.[1] The Preface struck an entirely new note. 'The only uniformity of practice that the Board of Education desire to see in the teaching of public elementary schools is that each teacher shall think for himself, and work out for himself such methods of teaching as may use his powers to the best advantage and be best suited to the particular needs and conditions of the school. Uniformity in details of practice . . . is not desirable even if it were attainable. But freedom implies a corresponding responsibility in its use.

'Teachers who use the book should therefore treat it as an aid to reviewing their aims and practice, and as a challenge to independent thought on such matters.'

Although the book was not free from the faculty psychology yet its issue marked the beginning of a new era for the teacher because it encouraged him to think out the details of his job in his own way. Later editions in 1908 and 1918 were published and the advice given was enriched by the experience of teachers and inspectors. A new edition in 1926 was entitled the *Handbook of Suggestions for Teachers* and this was again revised in 1937. Since the last war the book has been reprinted.

Another of Morant's reforms was in regard to the training of teachers. The pupil-teacher system originated by Sir James Kay-Shuttleworth in 1846, and modified in subsequent years, was, at the beginning of the century, the chief means of securing recruits for the teaching profession. The would-be entrant offered himself as a candidate and after six months, if it was decided that he showed promise of teaching ability, he was promoted to be a pupil-teacher. Part of his time

[1] J. Leese. *Personalities and Power in English Education*, p. 240. E. J. Arnold, 1950.

was spent as a kind of supernumerary member of the staff of an elementary school, and the remainder as a student at a pupil-teacher centre, where he studied for the King's Scholarship examination. A few of the more able students received preparation for London Matriculation, by which, if they were successful, they became qualified to enter a university or university college to read for a degree. Whilst in school, the pupil-teacher was supposed to be trained by the head teacher, who gave him all kinds of hints and tips, the value of which depended upon the interest, experience and ability of the head teacher. If he gained the King's Scholarship, the pupil-teacher had the option of entering the profession as an uncertificated teacher or of entering a college for professional training. The training colleges offered a two-year course for the Board of Education Teachers' Certificate. Many pupil-teachers were debarred through financial reasons from entering college. When they became uncertificated teachers, they hoped eventually by means of special classes or correspondence courses to qualify for certification.

The weakness of this system was apparent to Morant. In the majority of cases, the academic background of the pupil-teacher was slender. Moreover, there was a decided disadvantage in early segregation. The would-be teacher's experience was gained within the narrow circle of the elementary school, followed by the pupil-teacher centre and training college and then the elementary school again. There was much to be said for leaving the candidate in a secondary school until at least 16 years of age. The chief drawback was that in many districts secondary school accommodation was not yet adequate. Morant was able, through the *Regulations for the Instruction and Training of Pupil Teachers*, to make 16 the normal age of entry. In many areas, the centre was still a necessity, but where there was accommodation, Morant encouraged local authorities to send young aspirants to the secondary school.

In 1906, the Board adopted the bursary system as alternative to the pupil-teacher system. Bursars remained at the secondary school until 17 or 18, and after passing a qualifying examination, either the Preliminary Examination for the Certificate or one of its many equivalents, they either entered a training college direct or passed a preliminary year as a student teacher. The new scheme marked the beginning of the end of the pupil-teacher system, although in rural districts pupil-teachers were still to be found as late as the year before the outbreak of the second World War.

In the eyes of Morant, technical education was a poor relation. Most of the organized science schools, after 1902, became units in the secondary system. A few lingered on as higher elementary schools but they received little encouragement. Sadler had seen in them a means of enriching and extending the conception of secondary education, but not so Morant. Under the plea of attending to one thing at a time, he expended his energies upon the secondary grammar school. The *Regulations for Evening Schools, Technical Institutions, and Schools of Art and Art Classes*, 1903–4, concentrated upon evening classes. There was little provision for day classes for pupils between 14 and 16 years of age. Technical institutions were for students over 16 and one of the conditions of entry was that the student should have spent at least three years in a secondary school. In 1905, the Board tentatively offered grants to day technical classes for ex-elementary school pupils, but it was not until the Board of Education Report of 1908–9 that these classes were recognized as junior day technical classes. The further development of the junior technical school was delayed until after Morant had left the Board. It is significant that when in 1944, Mr. Chuter Ede, then Parliamentary Secretary to the Board of Education, replied to criticisms about the backwardness of our system of technical education, he replied, 'Then we had the misfortune that, when the Act of 1902 was passed, its administration was left to one of the greatest autocrats who ever dwelt in the Civil Service—the late Sir Robert Morant, of whom it is said, "He was not unprincipled but he was unscrupulous".'

While this re-organization was proceeding, the new local education authorities had been surveying their areas and making plans for the extension and co-ordination of different types of education within them. Their work was ably assisted by Mr. Sadler. He had been appointed to the Chair in the History and Administration of Education at the University of Manchester. His previous work was well known and he was an acknowledged expert in educational matters. It was to him that a number of local authorities turned for assistance and he wrote a series of reports upon areas which included about one-ninth of the population of England. His first report was prepared for the Sheffield Education Committee and was so well received that other authorities, both borough and county, approached Sadler to do a similar thing for them. There is no doubt that these reports played a material part in stimulating public interest in education as well as providing local authorities with the reliable information they needed. Their value received recognition from Morant in the *Report of the Board of Education*, 1904–5 (p. 49). 'More than fifty reports of varying scope, length and elaboration, dealing with higher education, and prepared or published since the beginning of 1903, have come under the notice of the Board. Amongst the most valuable of those published are the series of reports on secondary and other higher education in Sheffield, Birkenhead, Huddersfield, Liverpool, Newcastle-on-Tyne, and Exeter, and in the administrative counties of Derbyshire and Southampton, by Professor Michael Sadler'.

The report on *Secondary Education in Liverpool* is typical of the series. It began by summarizing the state of secondary education in that city in the year 1904. Sadler realized that 'the educational problem in Liverpool is the education of commercial England in epitome' and this led him to make a number of extremely valuable observations concerning the secondary education of boys in a great commercial city. Nowhere does his grasp of the situation appear more clearly than in the following paragraphs: 'It would be a great misfortune for a commercial city to make commercial knowledge the dominant aim of its secondary education. The more likely that a boy's future life-work is to absorb him in questions which necessarily have some sordid sides, the more need is there to insist that throughout his education there shall be a strong vein of idealism which will stand him in good stead, and keep his aims fresh and high, throughout his after-life. And, at bottom, the business relations of a great commercial city with the outside world are human relations. In no education, therefore, is it more necessary than in the education of a commercial community to give large place to the vivid and real teaching of the humanities. ... What a school can do is not create business ability or show short cuts to commercial success, but quicken the imagination, train the faculties of the mind and lay the foundations of a manly character. It cannot do these things quickly. It needs time for its work. It cannot be hurried.' (p. 12).

'The fundamental aim of a secondary education is the human aim. The school should humanize. It should give to each of its scholars the chance of that development most congenial to his native powers. Its business is to help him to a wide outlook and to sincerity of judgment, to sympathy but also to self-control. And by thus humanizing its pupils, it can best serve the community which supports it. It will train up citizens who will be alert for work, and who will uphold the honour of the city's name. It will inspire them with a sense of civic duty. It will make them feel that they do not live for themselves alone.' (p. 18).

These quotations are typical of the whole chapter and one may regard Sadler's reports as manifesting similar ideals with regard to secondary education as Morant's *Code for Elementary Schools* did for elementary education. It was a misfortune for England that differences of temperament and outlook prevented both men from working in partnership at the Board of Education.

The Liverpool Report presented a detailed description of the public boys' and girls' secondary schools in that city and even included a brief survey of the work which was being carried out in the private schools. The whole was supported by detailed statistical tables. The education committee was told the causes of the weakness in secondary education and practical suggestions for eliminating them were added. The whole problem of the supply and training of elementary school teachers was investigated and separate chapters were given to the consideration of the functions of the School of Art, the School of Commerce, the teaching of domestic science, and the position of evening continuation schools and technical classes in the city. The Report concluded with what was perhaps the most valuable feature: a series of suggestions and recommendations for the improvement of secondary education in Liverpool. Sadler was perfectly frank in his appreciation of the situation. He told the education committee in his preface: 'I cannot disguise from the Committee the grave concern with which at the close of my inquiry I regard the present state of much of the secondary education of Liverpool. Its defects are very serious. They seem to me to threaten some of the vital interests of the city. They allow a large part of its intellectual resources to run to waste. They put, each year, numbers of promising boys and girls at a growing disadvantage in the struggle of life. They impair the efficiency of every other part of the educational organization. In regard to much of the secondary education which it provides for those destined to take an active part in the work of a great commercial community, Liverpool has allowed itself to remain, as compared with its rivals, in the state in which its port would now have been, had little been done to deepen the channels of the Mersey and the entrance to the docks. Is it too much to hope that, when the consequences of the present weakness and anæmia of many of the secondary schools have been taken into account, an effort may be made to place Liverpool, in respect of this vital part of its educational equipment, in the front rank of the great commercial cities of the world?' Those who know what has been accomplished in the sphere of secondary and technical education in Liverpool since those days, will realize that Sadler's question has been answered in the affirmative and no small part of the credit belongs to him.[1]

By 1906, the preliminary work of laying the foundations for state supervision had been completed and the Act of 1902 was working successfully. So thoroughly had the work been accomplished, that the attempts of the Liberal government, as we have seen, failed to reverse the situation. Morant was now free to develop some of the latent possibilities of the Act. This was a policy which was enthusiastically supported by the President, Mr. McKenna. By placing the responsibility for the provision of education upon the local authorities, the Act had brought it into relation with the other functions of local government and it was soon realized that education was one of the most essential of the social services. In many areas, it had long been a matter of common knowledge that considerable numbers of children, because of lack of food, were unable to take full advantage of the educational facilities provided. One has only to read the log books of schools situated in the poorer districts of London to appreciate this. Many instances are recorded of food and hot drinks being supplied at their own expense by members of the school staff. In some cities, voluntary associations gave considerable assistance by providing dinners for necessitous children at the price of one penny per head. In the new Parliament, a Labour member (for the first time the Labour Party was represented by 40 members) proposed a

[1] In 1911, Sadler received an invitation from the Council of the University of Leeds to follow Sir Nathan Bodington as Vice-Chancellor. He held this office until 1923, when he was elected Master of University College, Oxford. He died in 1943. In 1917, he was appointed Chairman of a Royal Commission on Calcutta University and the excellent work which he did in India was rewarded by a knighthood.

private member's bill which received the support of the Government. The Education (Provision of Meals) Act, 1906, became law and gave authority to L.E.A.s to provide premises and facilities so that voluntary associations could serve meals to necessitous children. In cases where the funds of voluntary associations were insufficient, the L.E.A., with the approval of the Board of Education, could provide the meal and levy a rate not exceeding one halfpenny in the pound to defray the expense.

In the following year, the Government passed the Education (Administrative Provisions) Act which introduced a number of changes of such importance that they merit more detailed consideration. The Act marks the beginning of compulsory medical inspection in elementary schools. Medical inspection goes back to the last years of the nineteenth century. In 1890, the London School Board appointed a medical officer to examine mentally defective children. In 1902, the appointment was made full-time and the medical officer was given three part-time assistants. The following year, a number of oculists were added to test the eyesight of school children. A staff of six trained nurses was also appointed to inspect children notified by head teachers. In some cases they inspected whole classes, discussed problems of cleanliness and hygiene with the teachers and visited the homes of children who had been absent or excluded from school because of illness or supposed infection. Bradford had taken a further step when in 1893 it undertook the medical inspection of its children. For many years, this city was a pioneer in the provision of school medical services. The Defective and Epileptic Children Act of 1899 gave power to School Boards to provide suitable instruction for such children in special schools. Similar powers for blind and deaf children had already been granted by an act of 1893. These powers were permissive and not mandatory.

The reports of medical officers who had examined recruits for the South African War caused considerable disquiet. Many men had been rejected for medical reasons and this had raised the question whether the physique of the nation was as satisfactory as it should have been. The consequence was the appointment in 1904 of the Committee on Physical Deterioration. In the following year, a report was received from certain women inspectors who had investigated children under five in the London elementary schools. They drew attention to the valuable work being carried out by trained school nurses in London.

Morant had always been convinced of the importance of the good health and physique of school children. In the Code of 1906, he had added organized games to the table of physical exercises. All this was preparatory to the introduction of compulsory medical inspection by the Act of 1907. A complete school medical service was not provided by the Act. For example, it did not apply to secondary schools nor did it place an obligation on parents to carry out the recommendations of the school doctor. Many of the larger secondary schools had their own medical officers, and in any case, since the majority of the pupils were fee payers, it was considered that their parents could afford the expense of medical examination and treatment for their children. This section of the Act was very welcome to Morant. A Medical Department of the Board of Education was established with the duty of supervising the work of local authorities under the Act. Morant's choice of Dr. (later Sir) George Newman as Chief Medical Officer of the Board was a most fortunate one. The Board announced its intention of publishing annual reports on the work of the School Medical Service and those who have read Sir George Newman's annual reports until he was appointed Chief Medical Officer of the Ministry of Health in 1919, realize the immense value of his work. Lowndes claims that Sir George was responsible for saving more lives than had ever been lost in our great wars.[1]

The inception of the School Medical Service brought Morant into contact with Miss Margaret McMillan, who had already accomplished splendid work in this field under the Bradford L.E.A. Miss McMillan paid tribute to the value of Sir George Newman's reports as follows: 'The new Medical Reports from Whitehall show plainly to any unprejudiced mind the new and strong desire to grapple with a momentous question, to meet, at least, with open mind and strenuous endeavour a situation big with bewildering possibilities for the whole race'.[2] Morant knew a great deal about her work in Bradford and shortly before the Act became

---

[1] That the measure was not premature can be ascertained by reading the *Reports of the Chief Medical Officer to the Board of Education* for the years 1908 and 1909. These reports should be compared with those for 1917 and 1931. Alternatively, the summary given by G. A. N. Lowndes in *The Silent Social Revolution*, pp. 221-5, O.U.P., 1941, can be consulted with profit.

[2] Quoted by A. Mansbridge. *Margaret McMillan, Prophet and Pioneer*, p. 69. Dent, 1932.

operative he wrote to her giving his own views. 'For myself, I have for some time past come to feel that for the good of the children and the people, what subjects are taught *do not matter anything like so much* nowadays as attention (a) to the *physical* condition of the scholars and of the teachers, and (b) to the physiological aspect of school'.[1] When the service had been launched, he wrote to Miss McMillan and asked her to let him have her views on medical inspection as a basis for a Circular on that subject and added that he was very anxious to keep the zealous interest of 'those who care for this new development, so that we may get it started right and that it shall neither hang fire nor get started on wrong or futile lines'. Morant was fully alive to the defects of the Act of 1907 and he pressed for medical treatment to follow medical inspection. This was not accorded until after he had left the Board of Education. In 1912, the Board made grants for treatment as well as inspection, and the Regulations of the following year brought both aspects of the work of the School Medical Service under State assistance. When the Education Act of 1918 made medical treatment compulsory, most L.E.A.s had for some years been carrying this out.

The second major consequence of the Act of 1907 was the institution of the Free Place system. *The Regulations for Secondary Schools*, 1907, authorized a grant of £5 per head on each pupil between the ages of 12 and 18. Certain conditions were to be observed in order to qualify for the grant. The school could no longer insist upon restricting entry to pupils belonging to a particular religious denomination, and its governing body had to include a number of representative members, among whom should be individuals appointed by the local education authority. The third condition was the most significant one. Secondary education was to be accessible to all classes of the community. It marked the break-down of the idea that secondary schools were only for those who could afford to pay fees. On the other hand, the idea of secondary education for all had not yet gained general acceptance. The principle involved was later stated as the conviction that no child should be deprived of the opportunity of secondary education because of the parent's inability to pay fees. One had, however, to wait until the Education Act of 1918 before this principle was explicitly stated. It is important to bear in mind that secondary education meant education in the secondary grammar

[1] *Ibid.*, p. 64.

school. The idea of secondary education for all could not make much headway until it became recognized that there might be more than one type of secondary school.

The principle was applied through the following regulation: 'In all fee-charging schools, a proportion of free places must be open in each year to pupils entering from public elementary schools. This proportion will ordinarily be 25 per cent of the total number of pupils admitted to the school during the previous year, but may be reduced or varied by the Board on sufficient grounds in the case of any particular school or any particular year'.

For many years, secondary schools had been receiving an increasing number of pupils from the elementary schools.[1] Some of them were fee-payers, others had gained exhibitions paid for from the endowments of their schools. Some local authorities had offered a limited number of free or half-fee places to pupils who passed a qualifying test. Obviously the numbers admitted varied from district to district. The effect of the regulation was that every area now offered these facilities. The reception accorded to the new requirements was mixed. Some schools viewed with horror the idea of opening their doors to 'barbarians' from the elementary school and saw in the regulation a threat to their independence. They preferred to forego the grant rather than submit to the new requirements. At the other extreme, there were schools which hailed the new conditions as a means of deliverance from their financial difficulties and it is no exaggeration to say that the institution of the Free Place system saved many grammar schools from having to close down. Others, again, were glad of the extra grant but adopted a suspicious, a supercilious or patronizing attitude towards scholarship pupils. The writer well remembers the attitude of the staff of an old foundation school to which, in 1904, he with five others was fortunate enough to proceed by means of a scholarship examination. They were constantly reminded by the masters that they were scholarship pupils, were looked upon in the light of poor relations, and any little mistake on their part was magnified. This attitude passed over from the staff to the boys, who showed that in every way they regarded scholarship pupils as belonging to an inferior category. When, after three years at the school,

---

[1] At the end of the 19th century, it is estimated that about 5,000 elementary school children were holding scholarships of one kind or another in secondary schools.

increased numbers of scholarship pupils were arriving, the tone changed and the new-comers were regarded as quite normal. In this particular school, as in many others, most of the scholarship holders obtained an extension of their scholarship so that the sixth form contained a majority of them and they won the major number of successes in public examinations and university entrance tests. This was a common experience and as a result the demand for free place holders grew. Headmasters asked for them in greater numbers and more parents sought the opportunity of providing in this way a secondary education for their children. In seven years the number of free places awarded had risen from 47,200 to 65,799.

Two further results followed from this expansion. The original qualifying examination became severely competitive and the age of admission for elementary scholars to the secondary school gradually became standardized at between 11 and 12. As most pupils left school at or about 16, this enabled them to complete a three or four year course and rendered their introduction to new studies such as classics, mathematics, modern languages and science less burdensome. There is no doubt that the Hadow Report in 1926 was influenced by this fact when it suggested 11 plus as marking the transition from primary to secondary education.

The Act also gave L.E.A.s compulsory powers to acquire land for building secondary schools, and this, taken in conjunction with the new rate of grant, stimulated the opening of new secondary schools. The long-delayed establishment of a Teachers' Registration Council was taken in hand. This had been urged by the Bryce Commission and in 1902 the Board had attempted to form a register. Very unwisely, the register was divided into two columns, one for elementary teachers and the other for secondary. The National Union of Teachers raised strong objections to this procedure and as a result the register was withdrawn. The Teachers' Registration Council of 1907 issued a list containing the names of teachers in alphabetical order and included all types of service from the elementary school to the university. Registration was voluntary and teachers who were accepted for inclusion in the register were entitled to use the letters, M.R.S.T. (Member of the Royal Society of Teachers) after their names. It was hoped that registrations would do much to raise the status and dignity of the profession. Unfortunately, neither the central nor the local authorities used the register in selecting candidates for appointments and the consequence was that many teachers were unwilling to pay the small fee demanded for registration. The register has recently been abolished but teachers who are already registered preserve their right to the title of M.R.S.T.

Morant had reigned supreme at the Board of Education for eight years when the circumstance arose which caused his resignation. Although the era of Payment by Results had come to an end in 1897, the outlook upon education for which it was responsible was slow in disappearing. Local education authorities tended to appoint as local inspectors men from the older and more experienced elementary school teachers. This practice was followed in some instances by the Board so that a few successful elementary teachers were appointed to junior ranks of the inspectorate. The majority of the new recruits had grown up under the system of Payment by Results and their earlier experiences tended to restrict and narrow their outlook. It was not an easy matter for them to discard the habits of years. When Mr. Edmond Holmes was appointed H.M.I. in the north of England, he found, to his distress, that progress was being hampered by the formal and rigid views of these officials. Later, when in 1905 he became Chief Inspector of elementary schools, he discovered that similar traditions existed in other parts of England. Holmes was so concerned that he drafted a confidential report intended for the personal attention of Morant. By some curious means, which has never been satisfactorily explained, the report found its way to the bottom of a pile of memoranda on Morant's desk, with the result that he signed it and thereby authorized its publication. In the report, Holmes had expressed his views quite frankly. He wrote, 'Apart from the fact that elementary school teachers are, as a rule, uncultured and imperfecly educated, and that many—if not most—of them are creatures of tradition and routine, there are special reasons why the bulk of the local inspectors in this country should be unequal to the discharge of their responsible duties.'

The storm burst immediately the contents of the report became known. Sir Samuel Hoare saw in it a heaven-sent opportunity for launching an attack on the Liberal Government. The N.U.T. had long resented Morant's attitude towards the association. Kekewich had carefully cultivated friendly relations with the N.U.T. and had taken its officials into his confidence. Morant had consistently ignored the

THE REIGN OF SIR ROBERT MORANT

association. The N.U.T. read the report as an unmerited attack upon the integrity of the teaching profession. Dr. Clifford had never forgiven Morant for his part in securing the passage of the Education Act of 1902. Moreover, Morant's autocratic rule had produced many personal enemies. Even Dr. Allen, who regards Morant in a most favourable light, has to admit that 'there were some, both among his colleagues in the office and in the larger world outside, who regarded him with awe and even with dislike'.[1] The N.U.T. made no secret of its intention of taking up the gage of battle, which would never be laid down until the last remnants of a bureaucratic despotism had been removed. In the face of opposition in Parliament, in the press and in public meetings, the Government saw that only one course was open. Morant had to go. With him went Holmes,[2] who was regarded as the originator of the trouble, and Mr. Runciman, the President of the Board, who was held responsible for the actions of his subordinates. Although Morant resigned in 1911, it was felt that he was too able an administrator to be lost to the country. Mr. Lloyd George offered him the Chairmanship of the National Health Insurance Commission. Morant's enemies asserted that he had long foreseen the possibility of resignation and for this reason he had cultivated the friendship of Lloyd George. There is, however, little evidence to substantiate this.

Whatever were Morant's faults, and they were in some ways serious ones, to him belongs the credit for the creation of the English elementary school which endured successfully until in 1944 the adoption of a more liberal conception of education completely changed the scene. Morant well and truly laid the foundations of the system and many writers have emphasized that the soundness of his conception was vindicated by the thousands of ex-elementary school pupils

---

[1] B. M. Allen. *Sir Robert Morant, a great Public Servant*, p. 245. Macmillan, 1934.

[2] After his retirement, Holmes wrote *What Is and What Might Be* (Constable, 1911). This book is most valuable evidence in regard to the new ideas in education which were developing at this period. In the first part, '*What is, or the Path of Mechanical Obedience*,' a picture is presented of the actual conditions under which teachers worked in the Edwardian elementary schools. The description of the large classes, the narrow outlook, and the mechanical methods employed in the classroom is based on Holmes's own experience as an inspector. The second part expresses Holmes's vision of what school might be in the hands of enlightened teachers freed from the task of imposing quietness and obedience in impossibly large classes taught under most unsatisfactory conditions. In the ideal school, 'Egeria', conditions would be such that the children would lead the happiest of existences with freedom and opportunities for self-realization.

who gave of their best in the war of 1914–18 and saved England from subjugation by Germany. As an administrator, Morant was in the first rank. He was responsible for that high standard of administrative efficiency and integrity of which the Board of Education was justly proud. The standards he set were maintained and enhanced by the spirit of friendliness and co-operation which the Board, under his successors, Sir Selby-Bigge and Sir Maurice Holmes, displayed towards the local authorities and the teachers.

Both his strength and his weakness were admirably summarized in an article in *The Daily Mail*, April 28th, 1911, entitled, *A Master-Man, Sir Robert Morant, by One who knows him.* 'Sir Robert Morant is a tall man of commanding appearance, who would never pass unnoticed in any crowd of celebrities. His powerful face would at any time cause those who saw him for the first time to turn round and ask, "Who is that?" He can wreathe that commanding face in the most winning of smiles or cloud it with the most forbidding of frowns. He is a man of great strength of character, of high ideals, and of enormous powers of work.... He is masterful; he despises shams, and goes striding to his ends swerving never to right or left. He is certain of what he wishes to do, does not particularly want advice, and is lacking in fear. On the other hand, he is unselfish in so far as he works not for himself but for a cause. His mind and heart are always aflame with educational ideals, with schemes for the uplifting of his fellow-man. There is probably not a more sincere or earnest man in all Whitehall. Some officials he offends by his autocratic methods; others are angry because he insists on an earnestness in work which is perhaps foreign to the spirit of some Civil Servants; not a few are jealous; many are cross because of the ruthless way in which he despises their stupid labour-saving conventions.

'He owes a certain number of his enemies to his method of working. When, let us say, he wants to build a house, he erects a scaffolding like any other builder. In order to get the scaffolding to stand steadily to its duty he will impress upon it that without its aid the house can never be built. The scaffolding, of course, gets an exalted idea of its own importance. When the walls are up and the roof is on he kicks the scaffolding away and leaves it lying in the dust ready to be returned ignominiously to the builder's backyard. Naturally the scaffolding grumbles.

'The National Union of Teachers is probably wrong in

assuming that the Permanent Secretary is animated by any antagonism to the order of teachers, who may be well assured that whatever his methods may be he has but a single ideal—the elevation of our present chaotic educational system to a higher level. This ideal he will pursue to the end with passionate enthusiasm.'

Morant's work with the National Health Insurance Commission was marked by the same high degree of efficiency that he had displayed when at the Board of Education. When the war-time Ministry of Health was formed, he was appointed Chief Permanent Secretary. He died from a sudden attack of pneumonia in March 1920.

CHAPTER IV

TOWARDS A WIDER CONCEPTION OF EDUCATION

EDUCATIONAL progress during the first decade of the present century may not have been spectacular; nevertheless, those years showed slow, steady, but solid achievement. The system inaugurated in 1902 had proved its worth to the extent that it was not likely to be drastically affected by political changes. The partnership between the central authority, the local authorities, and the managers and governors of schools had become cemented. The partners had got to know and understand one another and were becoming accustomed to working together. There was a growing realization that education as one of the most important social services was linked with the other social services. The period was essentially one of consolidation following the changes of the beginning of the century and the time had come when it was possible to take stock of the situation. The outstanding defect, as it appeared to progressive thinkers, was the narrowness of the system. For the majority of English children, the school course was little longer than eight years. Pupils entered school at five and could leave at thirteen years of age, though some local authorities had used their powers to ensure that except in special cases schooling was prolonged to fourteen. Those who entered secondary schools, in spite of the expansion of the Free Place system, represented, even as late as 1910, but a small proportion of the nation's children. Of these, a considerable number left school before sixteen.

The schools themselves were restricted in their outlook. The rigidity of the days of Payment by Results had not entirely disappeared. New ideas were infiltrating very slowly. In the infant school, the principles of Froebel, for long misunderstood in England, were beginning to be intelligently applied. 'Chalk and talk' still predominated in the schools and owing to Morant's policy the secondary school was confined to a narrow academic path, though from 1907 onwards the Board of Education had in a very modest way shown itself ready to encourage experiment, with the proviso that a full report should be submitted and should be published if it was thought fit to do so. Thus the experiment of Dr. Rouse and his colleagues in applying the direct method of teaching languages to the study of the classics at the Perse School, Cambridge, was the subject of a full report in 1910.

The standards of school buildings were improving, though many schools, both council and voluntary, were being carried on in premises which were a legacy of the worst days of the nineteenth century. Before further progress on a large scale could become effective, education required to be re-vitalized through the medium of fresh ideas and a new outlook. Strange to say, the new ideas sprang from the lower end of the educational scale and worked upwards. It was in 1911 that the sisters Rachel and Margaret McMillan opened their nursery school at Deptford. The earlier policy of the Board of Education had been to deprecate the attendance at school of children under five and L.E.A.s were at liberty to refuse them admittance. In 1907, the Board asked the Consultative Committee to consider the problem of the education of children under five. In the course of the inquiry, developments in France, Germany, and Switzerland were considered, and although it was thought that nursery schools in certain industrial areas might be advisable, on the whole, the Committee recommended that it was not opportune to lower the age of admittance.

The work of Margaret McMillan with the school medical service at Bradford and the encouragement she received from Morant have been mentioned in the previous chapter. On account of ill-health, Miss McMillan had left Bradford in 1902 for London. Here she continued her fight to secure medical inspection and treatment of school children and she was fortunate enough to be able to co-operate again with Dr. Kerr, the Medical Officer of the L.C.C., who had previously been the first school doctor to be appointed at Bradford.

Margaret McMillan's work in London started with the opening of a clinic at Bow in 1908. Later, this was transferred to Deptford, where through her instrumentality the first L.C.C. dental clinic was founded and officially opened by Sir John Gorst in 1910. Many of the patients came from overcrowded and unsatisfactory homes. The next step was the formation of a night camp for girls in the garden of Evelyn House and this was followed by a day and night camp for boys in St. Nicholas churchyard. The idea of a churchyard being used in this way shocked many of the residents in the district and Miss McMillan had to find another site. She rented a piece of waste land in the neighbourhood and there she transferred the open air camp and opened her nursery school. At that time it was not possible to obtain assistance from public funds, so that the venture depended for its continued existence upon the generosity of supporters and sympathizers. Both the Board of Education and the L.C.C. watched the experiment carefully and did all that was in their power to encourage it. No assistance from public funds was available until after the outbreak of war, when the Ministry of Munitions allowed sevenpence a day for minding each child belonging to munition workers. The full significance of the experiment was only recognized by a few and the realization that a completely new development in education was taking place did not come until the end of the war period.

Corresponding to this extension of education at the lower end of the age scale, a movement concerned with the older pupils was developing. It was felt that the elementary school curriculum and methods of teaching were not entirely suitable for the older boys and girls who would be leaving in the space of a few years to take their place in industry and commerce. The higher elementary school had not been a success. A new type of school was needed and this sprang from the initiative of certain local authorities, particularly in London and Manchester. London was the first in the field and adopted in 1911 the central school system into which its higher elementary schools were absorbed. In 1912, Manchester followed the example of London.

Each central school was fed by older pupils from the neighbouring elementary schools. The curriculum had a definitely practical bias, either industrial or commercial, or both, but it was not narrowly vocational. The central school provided a four year course, 11 plus to 15 plus, and a limited number of bursaries was available for children whose parents could not afford to keep them at school beyond the age of fourteen. Classes were smaller than those common in elementary schools and the pupils had the benefit of tuition from specialist teachers. At first the Board of Education regarded the experiment somewhat suspiciously and it was not until the Education Act of 1918 that central schools and central classes received official recognition. Just as contemporary opinion failed to see in the experiment of

Margaret McMillan a revolutionary conception as regards infant education, so the advent of the central school produced little comment. The fact that a new type of secondary school alternative to the grammar school had been born escaped notice.

Most central schools were selective, that is, pupils were admitted on the result of an entrance examination. The free place examination was made to serve a dual purpose. Those pupils whose performance was moderately good but not sufficient to justify a place in a grammar school, were given the opportunity of attending a central school. One unfortunate consequence was that certain central schools tended to ape the grammar school. The writer had some teaching experience in a central school where the curriculum was barely distinguishable from that of a grammar school. Candidates were freely entered for the senior Local examinations of Oxford and Cambridge, and as the school was staffed by trained specialist teachers, the examination results were immeasurably superior to those obtained by the two local old foundation schools, in which the majority of the staff were untrained graduates. Such a school, in spite of its examination successes, had departed from the original aim of the central school, which was that of preparing pupils for entering industry or commerce immediately after leaving school without the need for a further course of training.

Another innovation was the issue in 1913 of the Board's *Regulations for Junior Technical Schools* which raised the status of the day technical classes. This, however, though long overdue, was but a half-way measure. The recommendations of the Bryce Commission still fell on deaf ears, for it was specifically stated that the junior technical school was not to be regarded as a secondary school. The Regulations emphasized: 'These schools are definitely not intended to provide courses furnishing a preparation for the professions, the universities, or higher full-time technical work, or again for commercial life: they are intended to prepare their pupils either for artisan or other industrial employment or for domestic employment.' The normal age of entry was 13 and a grant of £5 per head was authorized. A limited number of pupils could be admitted before 13 but in this case the grant payable was £3. Pupils were selected from elementary school children and it should be noted that the junior technical school was a fee-paying institution. As in secondary and central schools, free places were offered dependent on an entrance examination. The junior technical school gave both a general and a vocational training up to the age of 16. Some local authorities preferred to emphasize vocational training and developed day trade instead of junior technical schools. The Regulations for art schools in the same year authorized what were to be known later as Junior Art Departments.

The Government outlined proposals for the development of a comprehensive system of education which would include all types of secondary school, central schools, technical and trade schools and evening and day continuation schools. Mr. J. B. Pease (afterwards Lord Gainford), the President of the Board of Education, also announced his intention of giving Part III authorities control over higher as well as elementary education in their areas. The Government proposed to make it obligatory for local authorities to prepare schemes for 'the development of a progressive system of education in their areas, and to afford children during the latter years of their elementary school life opportunities of obtaining more advanced instruction than was possible in the ordinary elementary school'. These intentions were to be postponed for five years because of the outbreak of war in 1914.

As regards education, the war of 1914–18 was not altogether a calamity. It certainly faced the authorities and the schools with a large number of problems but at the same time, while actual progress was halted for a period, an opportunity was given for serious thought about the lines on which re-construction ought to proceed once peace was secured. Public interest in education was raised to a level which it had never reached before. Thus, when after the war the work of educational re-construction began, it sprang from plans which had matured during the period of hostilities and which had been most carefully debated. The historian will no doubt point out as one of the peculiarities of the British race that towards the end of a war its thoughts seem naturally to turn to education. It was so in 1902 and it was repeated in 1918 and 1944. The Elementary Education Act of 1870 was the product of peace, yet even that measure became law at a time when this country was occupied with the 'cold war' of commercial and industrial competition.

When war came, the total unpreparedness of the country was reflected in the educational situation. It was obvious that problems of staffing would arise and that many schools would be requisitioned as centres for military training or as hospitals. It was to the credit of all concerned that the improvisations adopted worked with such smoothness and that the damage inflicted on the children's education was much less than might have been expected. Up to 1916, nearly 20,000 teachers had volunteered for military service and when in the following year conscription was introduced, all men in medical categories A1 and B1 who were under 31 years of age were called up for service. At the same time, men of a lower medical category who were being employed on home defence, were released to take their places in school once more. In addition to men, quite a number of women joined the nursing and the women's auxiliary services. Naturally the staffing of schools became a most serious problem. Classes became larger and in boys' schools the majority of the teachers were women. Grammar schools, in which specialization was more extensive than in elementary schools, were hit the hardest. Nevertheless, immense efforts were made to maintain the work of the schools and these had to be re-doubled when the heavy casualty lists towards the later period of the war necessitated the call-up of all A1 men under 45 and B1 under 36. Harassed local authorities and school governors were only too glad to accept as temporary teachers any whose knowledge and experience enabled them to fill the gaps. Retired and married women teachers were requested to come back to the service. Clergy, lawyers, professional men who had sufficient qualifications—all did their bit and although the schools suffered as regards efficiency, the main problem, that of keeping them open, was solved.

The military authorities requisitioned 743 schools for training purposes and over 80 schools and training colleges were used as military hospitals or for the accommodation of refugees from the Continent. In such areas use had to be made of Sunday schools, places of worship, and public halls to accommodate the pupils. In other districts, a two-shift system was the only possible expedient and this led to what seemed a surprising discovery. The Board of Education Report of 1914–15 recorded: 'By curtailing instruction it concentrates the efforts of teachers and scholars on essential matters. Further, the half-day out of school has sometimes been used to excellent purpose for games and physical exercises, swimming, open-air work, excursions, visits to museums and galleries, needle-work parties and the like. In a large town where both open-air expeditions and visits to galleries have been particularly well organized, the Inspector mentions that one headmaster in a school favourably situated is so convinced of the advantage of open-air work that he would not object to continuing the half-time plan when the war is over. The effect on the health of the children has also been good.'

Teachers and pupils contributed nobly to national needs. Many schools by knitting socks and helmets, or making splints and crutches, or collecting wild fruits for jam, or constructing emergency gas masks. performed invaluable service. Oundle School, which had been equipped in pre-war days with a forge and up-to-date machine shops, was able to turn the older pupils on to the task of producing munitions. Older pupils from the secondary and central schools were able to perform important services for the community. Members of the Scouts and Guides rendered considerable assistance to over-worked local officials. When the submarine campaign began to prove a serious menace to our food supply, the Government intensified the effort to secure as much home-grown produce as possible. Through school gardens and allotments, children added to the supply of vegetables and soft fruits. The Board appealed to local authorities to do all in their power to step up the supply. Even town schools cultivated gardens and in the rural districts the growth in the number of allotments was striking. Thus, after the Board's Circular of July 1917, the West Riding of Yorkshire added 349 new school gardens and allotments to those already under cultivation.

Towards the end of the war farmers were handicapped by the increasing demands made upon them to grow more food at a time when larger numbers of farm labourers were being drafted into the Forces. The Board of Education, in order to ease the situation, encouraged older pupils to work on farms during vacations and even in term time, permitted them to be excused attendance for a limited period so that they could assist in agricultural work. Inspectors and school attendance officers kept a very close watch to see that children of school age were not being exploited.

The War Savings campaign was materially assisted by contributions received from elementary schools. Most schools had for a number of years possessed a penny bank. Its object was to encourage habits of thrift and large numbers of children on bank morning (usually Monday), brought their contributions to the school bank. Parents also made use of the school bank by sending their savings through their children. In this way, pupils accumulated useful deposits on which they could draw for holidays and emergencies. In 1916 the Board requested teachers to give special lessons on the War Savings movement and a leaflet was printed to show in detail the different ways in which the money lent to the Government was being used for the war effort. War Savings Associations were formed and since they continued to function after hostilities had finished, when the second World War broke out the machinery for a renewal of the savings effort was at hand. Altogether there were about 35,000 War Savings Associations in the country and of these, those connected with the schools formed approximately one third. To quote one instance: 'In Leeds in 1890, there were 9915 school accounts and the sum deposited from 1890 to 1926 amounted to £1,747,143 8s. 10d. In 1916, War Savings Certificates were introduced and could be purchased through the school bank. During the war Leeds children bought Savings Certificates to the value of £52,233 9s.'[1]

As a consequence of the absence on war service of many fathers and the employment of many mothers in munition factories, parental control became relaxed and children lacked adequate home supervision. This led to an increase in juvenile delinquency and hooliganism. In 1917 the Government attempted to deal with this problem. The Board of Education encouraged education authorities and voluntary associations to open evening play centres for children and offered to pay up to half the cost of maintaining such institutions. It was hoped that this step would keep children off the streets and provide them with an opportunity for organized games and healthy recreation and amusement. The health of the children was a constant care of the authorities but in spite of the absence of large numbers of doctors on war service, medical inspection and treatment were maintained. Special attention was given to school meals. With, in many cases, both parents absent, it was essential to extend the school meals service. The Education (Provision of Meals) Act of 1914 empowered local authorities to supply school meals during holidays and abolished the restriction that the cost of provision should not exceed a half-penny rate. Thanks to these measures, the health and physical well-being of the

[1] S. J. Curtis. *History of Education in Great Britain*, p. 340. U.T.P., 2nd Edition, 1950.

children, far from deteriorating, was more satisfactory than it had been in pre-war days. This encouraged the Board to continue these measures after the war and the wisdom of this policy was proved during the difficult period of strikes and wide-spread unemployment that shortly followed the peace.

The war produced one very striking effect upon secondary education. There was an unprecedented demand for entrance to secondary schools with the result that the existing schools had to accommodate nearly twice the number of pupils for which they had been built. The problem of additional accommodation was met by the erection of temporary classrooms and huts. Unfortunately these improvised additions, intended to serve for a few years only, are still being used in some of our schools.

The demand for more secondary school places may be considered from two aspects. On the one hand, the high wages paid to munition workers and employees in key industries had raised the general standard of living. One can still remember stories of munition workers who got rid of their extra earnings by purchasing fur coats and grand pianos. Such instances were the exception rather than the rule. Most parents found themselves with more money to spend than they had possessed before in their lives and the more sensible of them were desirous of giving their children a better start in life than they had had. That meant to them a secondary education for their children and many were both able and willing to pay the moderate fees demanded. From another point of view, it was essential to keep the secondary schools full; even to overcrowd them if necessary. Thousands of our best trained young men had perished as the result of enemy action or of disease contracted in the war area. Any doubt on this point can be dispelled by studying the Rolls of Honour displayed in our secondary schools and colleges. Their places had to be filled if Britain was to meet the requirements of the post-war period. As G. A. N. Lowndes succinctly remarks: 'William of Wykeham, contemplating the dearth of "a due supply of men fitted to serve their country in Church and State" caused by the ravages of the Black Death, founded his College at Winchester. His successors in a modern age, the local education authorities, contemplating the ravages of the Great War, set about modernizing and adding to the number of their grammar and county schools'.[1]

[1] *Op. cit.*, pp. 114-5.

Apart from this wastage which had to be made good, there was the further problem of what to do about those adolescents who left the elementary school at 14, of whom only a small percentage received any adequate kind of education after that age. The Prime Minister, Mr. Lloyd George, amongst all his other worries, was seriously perturbed about the future of education. There was only one thing to be done. The policy of the Board of Education would have to be guided by the best brains and the most experienced educationists that could be found. It was in this situation that he offered the Presidency of the Board of Education to Mr. H. A. L. Fisher, one of our most distinguished historians who at that time was Vice-Chancellor of the University of Sheffield. Mr. Fisher possessed both vision and high ideals and it was most unfortunate for the nation that circumstances combined to nullify the fulfilment of so many of his plans. He saw quite clearly that a start must be made at each end of the scale—with both the nursery school and the young adolescent. But from whence should come the initiative to commence these reforms and the power to ensure their continuous development? Mr. Fisher had no doubt about the answer. They must come from the Board of Education working through efficient local authorities. Hence, when he presented his Education Bill to Parliament he proposed two administrative changes. The Board of Education must be given sufficient power to coerce reluctant and laggard authorities. On the other hand, the local authorities must be so constituted that they would be able to carry out the policy of the Board effectively.

Many of the smaller Part III authorities were incapable of carrying out his programme. He proposed, therefore, that certain of them should be merged in the County Councils. Events have since shown that Mr. Fisher's proposals were sound. They awakened, however, so much opposition that the administrative clauses had to be deleted if the Bill was to be accepted. Hence the powers of the Board were left as they were while those of the local authorities were augmented. Mr. Fisher hoped and believed that the partnership of the local and central authorities would be sufficiently strong to ensure the accomplishment of his main ideas. As a result, two vital features of the Act, those concerned with the nursery schools and the part-time education of the adolescent, were not made mandatory but left as permissive. There is no suggestion that the majority of L.E.A.s were unwilling to work the Act in the spirit in which it was framed. It simply happened that when attacks came from outside, they were not powerful enough to withstand them and so took refuge in the permissive character of the clauses.

As a paper manifesto, the Education Act of 1918 promised much. Its keynote was the clause which stated that 'children and young persons shall not be debarred from receiving the benefits of any form of education by which they are capable of profiting through inability to pay fees' (section 4 iv.). Perhaps the best way of considering the Act is to concentrate first on those features which were permanent. The school leaving age was definitely fixed at 14. No pupil could leave school until the last day of the term in which his fourteenth birthday occurred. Local authorities had the power to advance the leaving age to 15 but very few of them did so. Another permanent provision was the complete abolition of the half-time system from July, 1922. Sir James Graham's Factory Act of 1844 had permitted children between the ages of eight and thirteen to spend the equivalent of three days in school and the remainder of the week in industrial employment. Subsequent legislation had raised the lower age limit to twelve but the half-time system still lingered on. The number of half-timers had dwindled but they still amounted to about 70,000, most of whom were employed in agricultural work. The Act also abolished the payment of fees in elementary schools.

A most important section of the Act was that which restricted the employment of children of school age in and out of school hours. It was made illegal to employ any child under twelve and those over that age could only be employed for a maximum of two hours on Sundays. On school days, a child could not be employed during school hours nor on any day before six in the morning nor after eight in the evening. Local authorities by means of a byelaw could permit the employment of children over twelve on a school day for one hour before 9 a.m. if the same child was not employed for more than one hour in the afternoon. This enabled local tradesmen such as newsagents to use children to deliver the morning newspapers. No child of school age was to be employed in factories or mines or in street trading. This immediately ended the selling of newspapers by young boys. A local education authority could issue a licence allowing children to take part in entertainments. This was frequently given to enable children to dance or form a chorus in the pantomime. The school medical officers watched these children carefully to see if their employment in any way affected their health. As a result of an investigation carried out by the school medical officer at Bradford, it was discovered that child dancers, because of the constant exercise, actually improved in physique.

Medical inspection and treatment were extended to pupils in maintained secondary schools but remained optional as regards aided schools. The provisions of the Defective and Epileptic Children Act of 1899 had already become obligatory in 1914. Mr. Fisher's Act went a step further by imposing on local authorities the duty of ascertaining physically defective children and providing suitable instruction for them. The system of government grants to local authorities was also overhauled. We have seen that the grant system of 1902 placed a heavy burden upon areas of low rateable value, and that supplementary grants had been introduced to assist them. The Act of 1918 abolished all specific grants and substituted for them a single block grant paid to each education authority and which amounted to not less than half of the net approved expenditure of the authority. Mr. Fisher hoped that the change would encourage progressive authorities to go ahead with their schemes.

Mr. Fisher had been greatly impressed by the nursery school experiment at Deptford. He included in the Act a clause which gave local authorities power to open nursery schools or classes where they were necessary or desirable. Grant would be given to nursery schools which were open to inspection. It was unfortunate that the clause was only permissive. The value of the open air nursery school was not yet generally appreciated and local authorities were extremely slow in taking advantage of this permission. Some of the more progressive authorities began to build nursery schools but as soon as the economy cuts started, they slackened their efforts. The result was that in 1939 there were only 114 nursery schools, of which more than half had been built by private initiative.

The scheme on which Mr. Fisher placed great hopes was the provision of part-time education for all young people up to the age of 18. There is little doubt that he would have preferred to have raised the school-leaving age to 15 but as this was inappropriate at the time, he adopted an alternative plan. He knew full well that in many elementary schools the older pupils tended to 'mark time'. Hence he made it the duty of the L.E.A.s to provide, through central schools or classes, practical instruction suited to the age, abilities, and requirements of the pupils and in addition to organize courses of advanced instruction for older and more intelligent children who remained at school after the statutory age of 14.

There remained the problem of the child who left school at 14 and then secured a job. The Act required L.E.A.s to establish 'a sufficient supply of continuation schools in which suitable courses of study, instruction, and physical training are provided without payment of fees for all young persons resident in their area who are, under this Act, under an obligation to attend such schools.' (sect. 3. i.). This section of the Act was to come into force on the appointed day and would be fulfilled in two stages. At first, continuation schools would be for young people between the ages of 14 and 16. They would be obliged to attend for 320 hours in each year, though in certain cases L.E.A.s might reduce the number of hours to 280. After seven years from the appointed day, the obligation to attend continuation schools would be extended to 18 years of age. In practice, it meant that the pupils who left school at 14 would have to spend one whole day a week or two half-days or the equivalent in a continuation school.[1]

Mr. Fisher realized that the success of the scheme depended upon the co-operation of employers. Indeed, many enlightened employers welcomed it. Others were suspicious and in order to convert them Mr. Fisher toured the great industrial cities and pointed out to directors and managers the value of the scheme. In this way he succeeded in arousing a good deal of enthusiasm but once more the mistake was made of leaving to the discretion of local authorities whether the schools should be started on a compulsory or a voluntary basis. London, Birmingham, Swindon, Rugby, and several other towns immediately decided for compulsory attendance. Other parts of the country chose a voluntary basis. This led to some peculiar anomalies. Some employers did not take the wider view and were able to seize the opportunities offered by this policy. 'For some distance the Edgware Road constituted the boundary between London and Middlesex. Young people applying for posts were often asked where they lived. If their homes were in the London

---

[1] For many years a number of important industrial firms had maintained their own continuation schools, e.g. Rowntrees at York.

area, where attendance at a continuation school was compulsory, some employers refused to consider their application further'.[1]

Then came the post-war slump and the beginning of unemployment on a large scale. In 1921 the Board issued Circular 1190 which brought further expansion to an end. Stratford-on-Avon, Swindon, and Rugby still continued obligatory attendance. Later in the same year the Committee on National Expenditure under Sir Eric Geddes recommended that the cost of education should be reduced by one-third. The result was that all over the country continuation schools began to close. When the second World War broke out, Rugby alone continued the schools on a compulsory basis. The enactments of 1918 were consolidated with the existing law of education by the Education Act of 1921.

One of the most important changes made by Mr. Fisher was in regard to the examination system in secondary schools. The external examination of school pupils dates from the middle of the nineteenth century. At this time there had grown up an almost universal belief in the value of written examinations. It was held that the examiner not only tested the work of the individual and the school but that it provided an incentive, a goal at which to aim and so gave unity and purpose to the studies of the schoolroom. As one witness said when giving evidence before the Schools Inquiry Commission, 'Examination is to the student what the target is to the rifleman. There can be no definite aim, no real training without it'. In 1853 the College of Preceptors started its school examination. The Oxford and Cambridge Local Examinations began in 1858. At the same time H.M.I.s were urging pupil-teachers to present themselves for London Matriculation. Robert Lowe, through the Revised Code, had brought examinations into the elementary school and in 1855 both the Home and the Indian Civil Service began to select their entrants by means of examination. The belief in examinations was almost pathetic. As yet, no critic of the system had arisen and authority was able to assume that if an efficient administrator was required for an Indian province, the way to discover him was by means of a rigorous test in the classics or in mathematics. Pupils who wished to enter such professions as medicine, law, accountancy, or pharmacy, were required by the professional bodies

[1] S. J. Curtis, *op. cit.*, p. 347.

concerned to pass certain preliminary examinations which testified to their general educational standard. There is little doubt that the introduction of the examination system did much to improve both the methods and the standards of the secondary schools but by the beginning of this century the multiplication of examinations became a serious threat to the efficiency of a school. In a small sixth form one might find pupils being prepared for as many as five or six different examinations which varied both in standard and syllabus. Some headmasters, in order to gain distinction for their schools, entered the same pupils for two or three examinations of a similar type. Thus the writer was entered successively for the College of Preceptors examination, the London Matriculation, and the Oxford Senior Local.

The inspectors of the Board of Education frequently reported that external examinations were exerting a harmful influence upon the schools by encouraging cramming and restricting the development of improved methods of instruction. In 1909 the Consultative Committee was asked to investigate the problem. In the report of 1911, attention was drawn to the mischievous practice of presenting pupils for public examinations at too early an age and to the multiplicity of examinations. It was recommended that a school should normally send its pupils in for one examination only. At the same time the Committee considered that measures should be taken to co-ordinate the different examinations. The result of the report was a series of protracted negotiations between the different examining bodies until a common basis of agreement was found. The Board of Education invited the universities to take responsibility for the examinations and asked that the teachers concerned should be consulted. In June 1917, the situation had become sufficiently clarified for the Board to issue a statement in Circular 1002. From henceforth the Board would recognize two examinations only; a first examination called the School Certificate, and a second, the Higher School Certificate.

The original aim of the School Certificate examination was that of a test of reasonable industry and ordinary intelligence for a pupil, who having entered a secondary school, had reached the sixth form. Since most sixth form pupils left at the age of 16, it was essentially a school-leaving certificate. The Board was quite aware of the abuses that might result from the examination system and it therefore set on record that 'the examination should follow the curriculum and not determine it'. Unfortunately an after-thought completely frustrated this wish. Could not the same examination be also a matriculation test which would admit the successful candidate to university studies? Such an attractive proposition gained acceptance and in order to satisfy university entrance requirements, the certificate should be awarded on a group system. The candidate was obliged to select his subjects in accordance with four groups. For university entrance he had to include subjects from Group I to III: Group I included English Language, a fail in which meant that the candidate failed in the whole examination; Group II consisted of classics and modern languages, and Group III included mathematics and the sciences. Group IV consisted of music, art, handicraft, and domestic science, but success in these subjects did not count for matriculation or for the certificate. Thus the academic outlook fostered by Morant was still active. The link-up between the school-leaving certificate and the entrance requirements of universities was to lead to consequences which were not envisaged when the examination was first instituted.[1]

The second examination, which was essentially a sixth form test, was known as the Higher School Certificate examination. The intention was that pupils should sit for this two years after they had obtained the School Certificate. In order to understand the plan of the examination, it will be necessary to consider the Board's action in regard to specialization in the sixth form. Whilst Morant was supreme at the Board, emphasis was placed on a general course of instruction and it was considered that specialization should only commence 'after the general education has been carried to a point at which the habit of exercising all these faculties has been formed and a certain solid basis for life has been laid in acquaintance with the structure and laws of the physical world, in the accurate use of thought and language, and in practical ability to begin dealing with affairs'. This view was built upon the assumption that the majority of grammar school pupils would enter the university or one of the professions, but as the free place system brought into the schools increasingly large numbers of scholars from the

[1] The Board of Education recognized seven examining bodies for the School and Higher School Certificates. These were the universities of London, Bristol, and Durham, the Joint Matriculation Board of the Northern Universities, the Oxford and Cambridge Schools Examination Board, and the Oxford Delegacy and the Cambridge Syndicate for Local Examinations. Later, an eighth was added, the Central Welsh Board.

elementary schools, a growing proportion of pupils ceased to attend after the age of 16. They then entered directly into trade and industry. When Morant left the Board, tentative proposals were made to deal with the new situation. In the report for 1912–13, the Board declared that it was willing to approve schemes of instruction which included specialized work in the higher forms and would allow the school course as a whole, to be biased in a rural, industrial, or commercial direction, dependent upon the types of occupation that the majority of the pupils would be likely to adopt. At the same time, the schools were warned that any scheme of specialization they adopted should not encroach upon the sphere of the technical school.

The report of the following year went a stage further and suggested that pupils should choose a group of related subjects, e.g. mathematics and science, classics or modern studies, and Circular 826 pointed out that grammar schools had a dual function. One was to provide a general preliminary education for those pupils who would pass on to the universities or institutions for higher education. The other was to give a general education, complete in itself, for those who left school at 16 and would enter trade, or industry, or agriculture. Experiments on the lines suggested were being planned when the war put an end to further developments. After the war the problem was re-opened and the Regulations for 1917–18 recognized advanced courses in classics, mathematics and science, and in modern studies. Additional grants were available for advanced courses, the objects being to attract specialist teachers of ability and to encourage the more capable pupils to remain at school until they were 18. The grant for a recognized advanced course was £400 and was intended to be used to augment the teacher's salary and to provide additional equipment. The Higher School Certificate examination was for the pupils who had taken one of the new advanced courses. Candidates could offer one of the three groups; classics, modern studies, or science and mathematics. Co-ordination of the School and Higher School examinations of the different examining bodies was to be the function of the Secondary Schools Examination Council.

Mr. Fisher was convinced that the success of any educational system depends primarily upon the teachers. If men of scholarship and ability were to be attracted to the teaching profession, it was essential that the conditions of employment should bear favourable comparison with those in other professions. Teaching had always been a badly paid profession. In the nineteenth century, salaries had been fixed by agreement between individual School Boards, managers or governors and the teachers they employed. The Education Act of 1902 had resulted in a system in which salaries were fixed by L.E.A.s without consultation with the teachers. Some authorities saw that it was to their advantage to attract better qualified teachers by offering higher salary scales. The natural result was that salary scales differed enormously in different parts of the country and those authorities who could not or would not pay an attractive salary had to put up with inferior teachers. An authority which the writer knew well may be quoted as an example of a salary scale which was typical of a county borough. Men teachers commenced at £85 and women at £70 per annum. The annual increment was £5. An additional increment was given for a university degree and also for a third year of training. There was a salary bar at £120 for men and £110 for women, so that an assistant had to mark time until a higher paid vacancy occurred. The salary of a head-assistant was £160 for a man and £140 for a woman. Salaries of head-teachers varied according to the size of the school. Teachers in the London area received a higher salary but there were many rural districts where the salary was much lower than the example quoted. Uncertificated teachers received salaries averaging £76 and £69 for men and women respectively. Even in the light of the low cost of living, it is evident that most teachers were grossly underpaid. The figures quoted applied to public elementary schools. In grammar schools, salaries were higher, but few grammar school masters received as much as £200 a year.

The acute rise in the cost of living occasioned by the war hit the teachers severely. Local authorities tried to deal with the difficulties of teachers by the award of a war bonus. Nevertheless, thousands of teachers were living under conditions not far removed from abject poverty. The Board gave a supplementary grant of more than £300,000 in 1917, the primary object of which was to improve the salaries of teachers. Mr. Fisher, however, saw that this was merely a temporary expedient and that it was urgent that the situation should be reviewed from a national standpoint. A departmental committee was set up to investigate the principles of constructing salary scales. Some authorities saw the way affairs were going and set to work to revise their salary scales. Others obstinately refused and in some areas teachers were goaded into taking strike action. Following the report of the departmental committee the President of the Board commenced negotiations with the local authorities and the teachers' associations. The outcome was the establishment of Lord Burnham's committee in September 1919 on which the L.E.A.s and the N.U.T. were equally represented. The committee recommended a provisional minimum scale and after further discussions in 1920 three standard scales for different areas, and a fourth scale applicable to London and the Metropolitan district. Similar scales were constructed by the secondary and technical committees which were also under the chairmanship of Lord Burnham. All the scales came into force in 1921. The awards made were not excessively generous but they had the effect of easing the teachers' financial difficulties for a time. Although extra increments were given for a first degree and additional years of training, there was no incentive offered to teachers to obtain further academic or professional qualifications. The salary enjoyed by the average teacher differed but little from that received by his more able and enterprising colleagues. The effect of the Burnham scales was to raise the salary of a trained certificated teacher from the average of £130 for a man and £96 for a woman in 1914 to £310 and £254 respectively by 1923. The scales had no sooner come into operation than the Geddes Committee, in view of the serious state of the national finances, called for reductions in expenditure. In 1922 the teachers agreed to a five per cent voluntary reduction in salary. Other small adjustments were made, such as the abolition of Scale I in 1936, but the principles of the Burnham award were substantially unchanged at the outbreak of the second World War.

The question of superannuation was closely connected with the salary problem. The Teachers' Superannuation Act of 1898 provided a contributory deferred annuity scheme and some local authorities allowed teachers to participate in schemes made after 1902 for the superannuation of their own officials. The Superannuation Act of 1918 applied to all teachers in grant-earning schools with the exception of the universities and other institutions for higher education which had adopted their own federated schemes. The scheme was originally a non-contributory one but the financial difficulties of 1922 made a change necessary and teachers were obliged to contribute five per cent of their salaries towards superannuation. To obtain full benefits under this scheme, a teacher had to have reached the age of sixty and to have spent thirty years in approved service of which at least ten years must have been recognized service. Thus teaching service in a university counted as qualifying but not as recognized service. A teacher who after ten years' service in a recognized school entered university service could only count ten years towards his annuity and lump sum but the amount he received would be based on his average salary during the five years before he retired, i.e. in the university. The benefits of the Superannuation Act were extended to service in Scotland and overseas by further Acts in 1925 and 1937.

We have seen that the need for national economy in expenditure necessitated the cuts effected by the Geddes Committee in regard to teachers' salaries and superannuation, and the continuation school programme. The economy campaign had other consequences. The Board of Education issued instructions that all building expansion except that which was most urgent, such as the erection of schools on new housing estates, should be postponed until further notice. This was a severe blow, as the new programme of building construction had just started. It meant that many of the old-fashioned, gloomy, and insanitary schools which had been on the Board's 'Black List' for years were to be retained for a further period.

The slump, however, was not without its brighter side. When for a moment men's eager aspirations and plans are checked, thought often takes the place of action and it was so in this case. Educationists began to think ahead and to think more effectively than they had done before. The Education Act of 1918 had awakened desires that remained unsatisfied, with the consequence that the whole structure of our educational system became subjected to careful scrutiny. One fact stood out clearly. The elementary school, even when the central school was counted, had to leave a large section of the youth of this country untouched by educational influences. This was especially true of those most precious and formative years of adolescence. Much had been achieved since 1902, but in spite of the numbers to whom secondary education was now open, it was still true that each year more than half-a-million children at the age of 14 passed directly into employment. When the slump had worked itself out, were we to continue from where we had left off in 1922? Ought we not to make up our minds about the functions of both elementary and secondary education and the relations between them?

To some, and these were men of quite different political views, the answers stood out clearly. The elementary school was failing because it was trying to accomplish a task for which it was never intended. Elementary education was in essence preparatory. But preparatory for what? The logical conclusion was that elementary education for all led to secondary education for all. If that conclusion was to be accepted, then elementary education was a misnomer. The kind of education given to children up to 11 would best be regarded as primary. The sequence—primary—secondary was not only a logical one but the abolition of the term elementary, associated as it was with the taint of cheapness and mechanical methods and the slur of patronizing charity, all of which were an inheritance of the early part of the nineteenth century, would be an extremely wise step to take. On the other hand, the idea of secondary education would have to undergo a major change. The academic tradition, so stoutly held by Sir Robert Morant, represented only one form of secondary education, that designed for pupils who remained at school until at least 16 years of age and then proceeded to the university or adopted a profession. There was also the tradition represented by the old higher grade schoools, the existing central schools and the junior technical schools. How did these fit into the picture?

Mr. H. C. Dent, in his recent book, *Secondary Education for All*,[1] has been at pains to investigate the origins of the idea. From the political angle, the Labour Party was first in the field but others outside that fold had been reaching similar conclusions. Some of them were content with the half-way house of the Act of 1918—elementary education for everybody up to 14, followed by secondary education for those who merited it with part-time education up to 18 for the remainder. It is to the credit of the Labour Party that it refused any such compromise and Dr. R. H. Tawney's pamphlet of 1922: *Secondary Education for All: A Policy for Labour* (Allen and Unwin, 1922) stated with the utmost clarity the views that had been held by Labour since 1905. He wrote: 'The Labour Party is convinced that the only policy which is at once educationally sound and suited to a democratic community

[1] Published by Routledge and Kegan Paul. See pages 49 to 59.

is one under which primary education and secondary education are organized as two stages in a single continuous process; secondary education being the education of the adolescent and primary education being education preparatory thereto. Its objective, therefore, is both the improvement of primary education and the development of public secondary education to such a point that all normal children, irrespective of the income, class or occupation of their parents, may be transferred at the age of "eleven plus" from the primary or preparatory school to one type or another of secondary school, and remain in the latter till sixteen. It holds that all immediate reforms should be carried out with that general objective in view, in such a way as to contribute to its attainment. It recognizes that the more secondary education is developed, the more essential will it be that there should be the widest possible variety of type among secondary schools. It therefore looks forward to the time when Central Schools and Junior Technical Schools will be transformed into one part of a system of free and universal education'.[1]

In 1924, the Labour Party came into power for a brief period and one of the first acts of Sir Charles Trevelyan, the new President of the Board of Education, was to give the Consultative Committee the following problems to consider: (1) To consider and report upon the organization, objective and curriculum of courses of study suitable for children who will remain in full-time attendance at schools, other than Secondary Schools, up to the age of 15, regard being had on the one hand to the requirements of a good general education and the desirability of providing a reasonable variety of curriculum, so far as is practicable, for children of varying tastes and abilities, and on the other to the probable occupations of the pupils in commerce, industry and agriculture. (2) Incidentally thereto, to advise as to the arrangements which should be made (a) for testing the attainments of the pupils at the end of their course; (b) for facilitating in suitable cases the transfer of individual pupils to Secondary Schools at an age above the normal age of admission.

The fall of the Labour Government in the autumn of the same year made little difference to the policy of the Board. The new President, Lord Eustace Percy, was content to wait until the Consultative Committee had issued the report and the Government had sufficient time to consider it. The

[1] *Op. cit.*, p. 7.

Report on the *Education of the Adolescent*, generally known as the *Hadow Report* (Sir Henry Hadow was the Chairman of the Committee), was issued in October 1926. The Hadow Report is one of the most important documents ever issued by authority and its interest lies equally in what it did and what it did not recommend. In its suggestions, two different lines of thought appear. On the one hand, it was progressive, that is, it broke new ground. On the other, it looked back to the past, and, perhaps almost unconsciously, allowed the idea of the secondary grammar school to influence its conclusions. It dallied with the present and at the same time reached forward into the future. To those living at the time, it may have seemed, in the words of Mr. John Graves, 'an educational manifesto as authoritative as Morant's famous introduction to the Code of 1904'.[1]

To us who live after the event, the backward and forward pull of tradition and reform is evident. For the moment, let us see how the Hadow Committee approached the problem. In its introduction, the Report indicated the policy it intended to recommend. 'We desire to abolish the word "elementary" and to alter and extend the sense of the word "secondary". The word "elementary" has now become misleading. . . . We propose to substitute the term "primary", but to restrict the use of that term to the period of education which ends at the age of eleven or twelve. To the period of education which follows upon it we would give the name secondary; and we would make this name embrace all forms of post-primary education, whether it be given in the schools which are now called "secondary", or in central schools, or in senior departments of the schools now termed "elementary". If the term secondary is thus given a wider sense, some new term will be needed to denote the schools which have now the monopoly of the name "secondary"; and we suggest that they should be called by the name of grammar schools. If such schools are thus to be re-named, we should propose that the term "central school" (which is neither clear nor particularly apt) should simultaneously disappear, and the term "modern school" should take its place in the future. On such a scheme there will be two main kinds of education—primary and secondary; and the latter of these two kinds will fall into two main groups—that of the grammar school type, and that of the type of the modern school'.[2]

[1] *Policy and Progress in Secondary Education*, p. 124. Nelson, 1943.
[2] *The Education of the Adolescent*, p. xxi–xxii. H.M.S.O. 1926.

It should be noted that the Report envisaged secondary education as falling within the two categories of grammar and modern. Was any place provided for the junior technical school? The recommendations of the Bryce Commission were still ignored. The junior technical school was not included in the secondary class. The Committee considered that within their own province 'they are doing most valuable work and should be developed so far as is possible in accordance with the needs and requirements of certain local industries'[1]

The Report expressed anxiety lest the modern school might come to be regarded as an inferior kind of secondary school but at the same time it took a step which would inevitably lead to such a result. Not only would the curriculum resemble that of the grammar school in general outline but it would be 'simpler and more limited in scope', but the difference between the two types would be accentuated by the fact that in the grammar school pupils remained after the age of 16, whilst in the modern school the utmost that could be expected was a course terminating at 15. In practice the leaving age was still to be 14 and could not be generally extended unless special legislation was effected. Thus from the start the modern school was to be damned as a poor relation. The assumption that the education of the non-academically minded child could be accomplished in less time than that of his brother in the grammar school is a position which seems difficult to sustain. The Report went on to say that the modern school should resemble the grammar school so that the transfer from one type to another would be facilitated. The distinction in the two types would become more apparent in the later years of the school course. In the last year or two of the modern school a practical and realistic bias would be given to the curriculum. The idea that technical studies should be included was anathema. Yet at the same time, the Board's Report of 1912–13 had suggested the inclusion in the programmes of grammar schools certain specialized and vocational courses 'with the object of developing interest in or capacity for the occupations, whether rural, industrial, or commercial, which the majority of pupils are likely to take up'.

The Report looked forward to the provision of a four year course in the modern school but realized that this would be impossible until the school leaving age was raised to 15.

[1] *Ibid.*, p. 66.

For the time being the schools would have to make do with a three year course. This furnishes the real reason for the 'clean cut' at eleven plus between primary and secondary education. Tradition may possibly have influenced this decision. The school leaving age in the elementary school of the mid-nineteenth century was 11 and this had gradually been extended, by the addition of extra standards and ex-standards, until it had been fixed by law at 14 in 1918. This was one of the reasons why the elementary school, admirable as its work was with juniors, failed to cope with the needs of seniors and adolescents. In Circular 1350 of 1925, the Board had suggested a break at 9 or 10 and expressed the opinion that for administrative reasons 9 was the preferable age. In face of the Hadow recommendation the Board kept very quiet about its former view. Anyhow, for better or for worse, the age of eleven plus had come to stay as the dividing line between primary and secondary education. And this despite the facts that the public schools received their entrants at 13 and that north of the Border the age of 12 was preferred. In order to support this recommendation the Report dragged in psychological evidence. Hence the well-known paragraph commencing: 'There is a tide which begins to rise in the veins of youth at the age of eleven or twelve. It is called by the name of adolescence'. Every parent and teacher knows that this is not true. The onset of adolescence is nearer to 13 than to 11. The Report could have made a perfectly good case by emphasizing the value of gathering together children of 11 plus in the same school, so that the emergence of their particular interests and abilities could be studied in view of the special type of secondary education which would be most suitable for them. Also this recommendation of the Hadow Committee was destined to act in a way that at the time was unforeseen; it was to increase the difficulties of bringing the schools outside the State system into closer relations with those within it.

The Board of Education accepted the proposals of the Hadow Report, but with a certain caution and reserve. They were unwilling to commit themselves to the raising of the school-leaving age to 15 by any specific date. There was a good reason for this attitude. The raising of the school-leaving age would necessitate the immediate finding of additional places for about 350,000 school children and there was no means of doing this. Moreover, such a policy would mean the provision of a large number of additional teachers who could not be trained overnight. A surer and safer policy appealed. Before extending the statutory school period, it was more urgent to re-organize the existing schools into junior and senior departments. There were also many schools on the Board's Black List which had to be replaced as soon as possible, and another important consideration was the reduction of the number of classes containing over 50 pupils. The Board felt that it was a question of priorities and when the more urgent problems had been settled, the question of the raising of the school-leaving age would be in the realm of practical politics. In order to forward the work of re-organization the Board issued the pamphlet entitled *The New Prospect in Education* which not only dealt with the problems of re-organization but quoted as examples schools which had already made the change. Nevertheless re-organization was a slow business. Some authorities were not ready to undertake it until they were pushed by the Board to do so. The path of re-organization was beset with a number of administrative difficulties and these had been foreseen by the Hadow Committee.

The first was a consequence of Morant's division of education into the three compartments of elementary, secondary and technical. Each had worked under its own rules and regulations and the inspectorate had been organized according to this classification. This difficulty was the least serious, for many factors existed which were making for greater unity. The tri-partite division of the Board of Education had come to an end in 1922 and in the inspectorate, there was a growing co-operation between inspectors of the different branches. It was anticipated that surviving differences between the three branches would gradually disappear without any active intervention by the Board of Education.

The Dual System represented a more serious obstacle but even in this case the Hadow Report suggested certain developments which were eventually embodied in the Education Act of 1936. The main difficulty which had to be overcome was one created by the Act of 1902, namely, the existence of a number of Part III authorities, responsible for elementary education only, within the areas administered by the county authorities. The most glaring example of this was furnished by the Lancashire County Council, which contained in its area no less than 27 authorities responsible for elementary education only (19 non-county boroughs and 8 urban districts). The problem created by the Part III authorities was an obvious one. The county authorities were responsible for secondary education throughout the county area, i.e. for county grammar schools. On the other hand, a Part III authority in the county area was entitled to establish central and senior schools which in the view of the Committee were in reality schools providing a secondary education. Thus the control of secondary education was split between the county and the non-county borough authorities. The policy of the Part III authority might conceivably run counter to that of the county with the consequence that the latter would be unable to frame schemes for secondary education that would apply to the county area as a whole. 'The smaller the area, the greater were the difficulties. Another Director of Education informed us that there were 13 authorities for elementary education forming enclaves within the area of his county with the result that the education of the county had to be fitted into 13 systems'.[1]

In addition the Part III authorities which administered small areas suffered other disadvantages. 'The position of the Part III authorities has long been unsatisfactory. They are by their very nature small, and in unfavourable instances extraordinarily backward. The populations are not large enough for a proper organization, and their financial resources are slender: they are apt to have no margin, even where their average income over a period is adequate to their needs. They may happen to be very poor, temporarily or permanently, or badly administered. In a word, they are much too small'.[2] In fairness to the Part III authorities it should be remembered that this criticism applied principally to the smaller authorities. Some of the larger authorities were more progressive than certain county authorities.

The Hadow Committee enumerated the possible solutions of this problem. (1) The abolition of Part III authorities with the transference of their powers and duties to the county authorities.

(2) All Part III authorities below a certain minimum standard of population should be merged into the county authority. The remainder should become all-purpose authorities responsible for all types of education.

(3) The merging of Part II and Part III authorities in a much larger regional authority.

[1] *The Education of the Adolescent*, p. 162.
[2] *Report on Education by the Bradford I.L.P. Committee*, para. 459. Thornton and Pearson, 1931.

(4) Increased co-operation between both types of authority so that before the minor authority went ahead with schemes for post-primary education, the county authority should be consulted.

Strangely enough the Committee lacked the courage of their convictions and decided in favour of the last arrangement. This was considered to be a step towards the second but it was thought that the third ought to be the ultimate objective. This decision was defended on the ground that it would reconcile 'a necessary reform with that gradual evolution which is so marked a feature in our constitutional history'.[1] The first alternative was rejected because it was felt that it would lead to major political difficulties. The weakness of this decision became apparent when the threat of war necessitated preparations for evacuation.

When the Labour Party returned to power in 1929, Sir Charles Trevelyan began to speed up the work of re-organization. He introduced a Bill to raise the school-leaving age to 15 and announced that the Government was prepared to pay a maintenance grant to parents who were adversely affected by the measure. One of the considerations which led to the proposal to raise the school-leaving age was the Government's alarm at the rapid rise in the numbers of unemployed. It was estimated that the measure would keep about half-a-million young people off the labour market. When a similar proposal for raising the school-leaving age had been made after the publication of the Hadow Report, the President of the Board of Education had issued Circular 1395, 1928, which emphasized that the statistics in regard to the numbers of children affected by the change showed quite clearly that it was impossible for the local authorities to supply the additional accommodation required. The proposal was for the time being quite outside practical politics and would lead to confusion because of the lack of accommodation, the insufficient number of teachers and the consequent rise in the number of large classes. The Government ignored these figures and proceeded with the measure.

An unforeseen difficulty occurred. This was due to the existence of the Dual System. The managers of voluntary schools complained that however eager they might be to carry out re-organization, they had not the funds to do so. New buildings would be required and State assistance would

[1] *The Education of the Adolescent*, p. 164.

be necessary for their erection. This made the Government pause. A revised Bill was introduced in 1930 which gave power to local authorities to assist voluntary schools to re-organize. In return the managers would be expected to surrender some of their rights as regards the appointment and dismissal of teachers. The Parliamentary session was drawing to a close and the Government decided to proceed with the first part of the Bill and to postpone the problem of the voluntary schools for later consideration. The Bill received the assent of the House of Commons, but it was rejected by the Lords. Before the Government could re-introduce it in an amended form, the country ran into the most serious financial crisis that had yet been encountered. The Government resigned and was followed by a National Government led by Mr. MacDonald.

The cause of the crisis was the deterioration of our export trade, the shrinking of the income this country derived from its overseas investments and the withdrawal of foreign capital. This led to an unprecedented increase in the unemployment figures. The crisis was intimately associated with the worldwide slump in trade and the threat to our financial security was so severe that the Government agreed to set up a committee of seven under the Chairmanship of Sir George May to consider the situation and make suggestions for the reduction of the national expenditure. The National Government accepted the recommendation of the May Committee. As regards education, the Government accepted a reduction of 15 per cent in teachers' salaries which was later reduced to 10 per cent. The 50 per cent Exchequer grant made for buildings was withdrawn. This did not bring all building activity to an end, for it was obvious that the new housing estates would have to be served by schools, but any other building schemes were severely scrutinized. One important change was the substitution of the Special for the Free Place System. Children from the elementary schools competed for secondary school places by means of the Special Place examination. Once a child was selected the income of his parents was taken into consideration. Only those whose income was below certain limits, taking into consideration the number of children in the family, could obtain a free place for their children. All others would be required to pay fees on a sliding scale according to their incomes. The same plan was applied to the assessment of the grant payable to students in training for the teaching profession, and in this particular case the means test is still operative.

The economy measures proved a bitter disappointment to those who were anxious to proceed with the re-organization recommended by the Hadow Report. When the effects of the slump began to disappear towards the end of 1933 prices of materials and the cost of labour had increased considerably and those authorities who had proceeded with their re-building programmes immediately after the Government's approval had been given to the Hadow Report were indeed fortunate. On the other hand it was not all loss. The Government had set a pace which local authorities found themselves unable to follow. Moreover, in the interval efficient bus services between village and village and town and town were being organized and the possibilities of transporting children to senior and central schools were being realized. This was going to have considerable effect upon the schemes of re-organization and meant a reduction in the number of centres in which schools would have to be established.

When it was possible to proceed once more with schemes of reorganization, progress was much more cautious. In the year before the outbreak of the second World War approximately 64 per cent of pupils over 11 were being taught in senior departments and the number of classes containing over 50 pupils had been reduced from 10,017 in 1931 to 2,100. Perhaps these figures give an optimistic view of the progress made. It varied greatly from district to district. Some progressive authorities developed schemes and carried them through with great enthusiasm. Others had scarcely begun to re-organize their schools when war broke out. On the whole rural areas lagged behind urban.

Meanwhile the Consultative Committee issued two further reports—on the junior school in 1931 and on the infant and nursery school in 1933. It was perhaps unfortunate that the Hadow Reports appeared in this order. It would have been more logical to have worked the other way and to have started with the infant school. The actual order of issue was, however, as we have seen, dictated by events. The result was that attention was fixed on the education of the adolescent and the junior school tended to be neglected. It was regarded by some as merely a feeder for the different types of secondary school. Hence its outlook methods and curriculum were influenced by the Special Place examination. It is only just to say that the report on the junior school did much to correct this point of view.

The report on the primary school represents a complete revolution in the English attitude towards education. Implicit in the report on the adolescent, it becomes explicit in this. As Professor Armfelt has often said, it marked the discovery of the child. In the nineteenth century the curriculum had been conceived in terms of the life and work which would await the pupil after he had finished his schooling. The idea of equipment, as Professor Frank Smith terms it, had been predominant. In secondary education, in particular, certain subjects were advocated because of their supposed disciplinary value and the belief that what had been acquired through one study could be carried over to the benefit of other studies or of life in general. The child and his nature received little attention. He was a miniature adult with the emphasis on the adult. Certainly the path of learning must be made easier for him; he could not be expected to assimilate at the same rate as the mature person but this merely meant that the subject matter ought to be simplified, served up to him in smaller helpings, and made more attractive to him by various teaching devices. What really mattered was his future and discussions of the curriculum proceeded on these lines. How far was this or that subject to be pursued because of its value to the scholar in later years? The view that the child had interests and desires and an outlook on life peculiar to himself as a child and which needed satisfaction, was largely ignored.

It is true that certain nineteenth century thinkers such as Pestalozzi and Froebel had tried to focus attention upon the child but they were for a long while misunderstood in England, where attention was directed to the extrinsic features of their teaching rather than its essential spirit. Their influence did indeed improve the technique of classroom teaching but the idea that the child must be fitted to a preconceived curriculum and not the reverse still held sway. In addition, the value of the three Rs, no doubt influenced by the system established by the Revised Code, was vastly over-estimated. If they were the foundation of all future progress in learning, it naturally followed that the sooner one could make a start with them, the better. Hence infants who should have been gaining both pleasure and experience through exercising their senses and expressing themselves in free activity were cooped up in desks and set to learn the beginnings of reading, writing and number before they properly understood what use these skills would be to them. The type of pupil who was considered most satisfactory was the one who sat quietly at his desk, caused no disciplinary trouble, and passively absorbed and mechanically reproduced what his teacher presented to him. It was only on rare occasions that he was allowed to do or say something of his own accord. The writer still remembers how he looked forward to Wednesday mornings when he went into the woodwork shop and was able to move about and do something that interested him. Even then he often felt that he would enjoy making something he really wanted instead of working through a series of graded models.

The first two decades of the present century marked the beginning of the revolt. It was slowly realized that the traditional attitude ran counter to all the fundamental characteristics of childhood. The McMillan sisters owed the success of their experiment at Deptford to their understanding of the nature of the tiny child and their realization of his need for fresh air, sunlight, alternate periods of rest and play and free and unfettered activity. Madam Montessori concentrated attention upon the individual and demonstrated that all education is at root self education. She showed that the repressive atmosphere of the orthodox classroom was unnecessary and that one of the most valuable lessons a child could learn was how to be free and to use his freedom in such a way that it did not interfere with others. Sir John Adams enunciated his now famous dictum that if you wish to teach John Latin, it is as essential to understand John as it is to know Latin. In America, Professor Dewey had emphasized the truth that knowing and doing go hand in hand and that to separate these activities is to introduce a highly artificial and unnatural distinction. Hence his belief in the educative value of suitable practical activities and occupations in school and his emphasis on the use that should be made of the child's everyday experience at all stages of the instruction. The psychologists gave their support to the new outlook. William James's maxim that there should be no impression without expression led to a recognition of the place of expression work in school, although it must be admitted that many of the so-called exercises in expression devised by teachers resembled mechanical repetition rather than free expression. There was also a tendency to forget that before a child can express himself he must have something to express. McDougall was a representative of the revolt against the psychology of the previous century which had given most attention to the intellectual processes whilst ignoring the other aspects of human nature. His teaching brought into prominence the natural endowment of man by showing that the greater part of his behaviour ultimately sprang from his innate tendencies and abilities. The development of mental testing and the work of the psychoanalytic school led to a greater understanding of the individual and of the existence of individual differences. Educationists were not slow to see that this placed definite limitations to the accepted method of class teaching. Individual pupils in the class did not all conform to the same pattern. They differed in intelligence, in interests, in ability, in temperament and character and in their outlook upon life, and no plan of education could be satisfactory that did not take into account these truths. The Dalton and other plans of supervised study were based on the conceptions of freedom, of individual self-learning, and the fact that different pupils progress at varying rates in their learning. The tyranny of the rigid time-table which divided the work of the school into watertight compartments was being broken down; first through the idea of a natural correlation existing between the different branches of knowledge, and later by the adoption of the project method.

Most of these ideas were being discussed in educational circles at the time of the outbreak of the first World War but so far they had not penetrated very deeply. They were the views of the educational progressives and the rank and file of teachers were reluctant to adopt them. Official opinion as expressed in the publications of the Board of Education was cautious and reserved though members of the inspectorate tried with more or less success to enlist the sympathies of the teachers. The ferment of new ideas was beginning to work and when the *Education of the Adolescent* appeared, one of the principal arguments for re-organization was based on the emergence of new characteristics in the adolescent. Unfortunately the argument was also used to support administrative convenience and so the force it might have had was lessened. The *Report on the Junior School* was not restricted in this manner and was therefore able to give full attention to the kind of instruction and training suitable for the child under twelve years of age. The Preface to the Report set the key note when it declared: 'Any education worthy of the name must start from the facts, and the essential facts are, after all, simple. At the age when they attend the primary schools, children are active and inquisitive, delighting in movement, in small tasks that they can perform with deftness and skill, and in the sense of visible and tangible accomplishment which such tasks offer; intensely interested in the character and purpose—the shape, form, colour and use—of the material objects around them; at once absorbed in creating their own miniature world of imagination and emotion, and keen observers who take pleasure in reproducing their observations by speech and dramatic action; and still engaged in mastering a difficult and unfamiliar language, without knowing that they are doing so, because it is a means of communictating with other human beings. These activities are not aimless, but form the process by which children grow. They are, in a very real sense, their education; and the course of wisdom for the educationalist is to build upon them. . . . A good school, in short, is not a place of compulsory instruction, but a community of old and young, engaged in learning by co-operative experiment". (p. xvii).

The remainder of the Report maintained the spirit which the Preface had indicated. After a useful historical chapter on the development of the idea of primary education from the beginning of the nineteenth century up to the time of the Report which was contributed by the Secretary, Dr. R. F. Young, the physiological and psychological approach to the understanding of the primary school child was stressed by the inclusion of two chapters on the physical and mental development of children between the ages of 7 and 11. When the curriculum of the primary school was discussed, the conception of the child-centred school was still dominant. Certain remarks have now become familiar and universally acknowledged maxims, e.g. 'the curriculum is to be thought of in terms of activity and experience rather than of knowledge to be acquired, and facts to be stored.' (p. 153); 'The schools whose first intention was to teach children how to read have thus been compelled to broaden their aims until it might now be said that they have to teach children how to live.' (*ibid*); 'Junior children . . . were little workmen, looking out for jobs to do, and largely incapable of finding them for themselves'. (p. 51).

The Report considered the application of the project method to the work of the primary school and although it encouraged experimentation along this line, it wisely issued some words of caution. 'In its simplest form such a method would be compatible with teaching within the traditional subject divisions, and implies merely that the teaching, instead of imparting knowledge of a subject in logical order, takes the form of raising a succession of problems interesting to the pupils and leading them to reach, in the solution of these problems, the knowledge or principles which the teacher wants them to learn. It is the method which an inquisitive boy is driven to follow, when he wants to find out how a steam engine or an electric bell works'. (p. 102).

The Report made it quite clear that the project method is not an importation from the other side of the Atlantic but is a means which enlightened teachers of all ages have used.[1] It was the method which William Cobbett, distrustful of the bookish education given in the schools of that time, adopted in the teaching of his own children. Hence the Report interpreted the project method on broader principles than the strictly orthodox American exponents. 'Some centre of interest is selected, and for a while the children's studies along many lines converge upon it or radiate out from it. One may, for instance, take up the question of the various ways in which food and other goods find their way into a given city. The pursuit of such an inquiry may first direct the attention of the young researchers to the different modes of transport, by rail, road and now by air, and bring up for solution problems concerning the draught of barges, the way in which the railway engine and the petrol engine do their work, and how aeroplanes can remain in the air.' (p. 103). The danger of the project method, however, lies in over-working it. Hence the teacher was told: 'There is always some danger that a new method, particularly if, within its proper field, it is a strikingly useful one, may be forced beyond its proper limits. While, for instance, music and drama may at times be brought in naturally and usefully in the working out of a project, it is too likely that in many instances they will merely be "dragged in", obediently to the supposed claims of a principle. The teacher in his enthusiasm forgets that both music and drama are activities

[1] The writer possesses a pupils' handbook published in 1667, which was issued for the use of scholars in the Mathematical School for Christ's Hospital. Instead of teaching solid geometry on formal lines, the learner is presented with a number of developments of the solid figures which he has to draw, to cut out and to fasten together by folding along the dotted lines and to discover for himself what kind of solid has been produced.

which contain their own self-sufficient motives; that one may learn a song simply because the song is delightful; and act a play because acting is such good fun. The same thing is true of drawing and handicraft'. (p. 103–4). It was also pointed out that as the child grows older, he is not only able but is anxious to study a subject in a more systematic way than is provided by the project. The teacher was advised not to adopt the method until he had understood it and had come to believe in it. With this proviso, 'the teaching of children in the primary schools should be increasingly informed by the principles of the project method'.

The clean break at 11 plus, as advocated by the Report on the Education of the Adolescent, was approved and the Committee considered that there were two distinct stages in primary education; before 7 and from 7 to 11. Separate schools, wherever possible, should be provided for the younger children. Failing this, the children under 7 should be taught by a mistress with special knowledge of and experience in infant methods.

On the administrative side, the Report considered that the headship of mixed primary schools should be open to men and women but it was advisable for the senior assistant to be of the opposite sex to the head. The value of open-air classrooms, of libraries and of playing fields was emphasized and there should be a sufficient provision of rooms for practical activities. Classes in the primary school should not contain more than 40 children. The Free Place examination should not only include papers in English and arithmetic but also carefully devised group intelligence tests and oral interviews should find a place. The school record of each pupil should be carefully considered. 'We accordingly urge that some form of continuous record of each child's progress should be kept in primary schools. We consider that further inquiry is desirable, in order to determine the most convenient form in which the necessary information may be concisely presented'. (p. 129).

The reports of the Consultative Committee were completed in 1933 by the issue of that on the Infant and Nursery School. The Committee very sensibly considered that if home conditions were good, the best place for children under five was at home. In other cases, children could gain great benefit from attending either a special nursery school or a nursery class within the existing elementary school. The ideal size of a nursery school was one which could accommodate 60 to 80 children but if this was uneconomical, schools of 160 to 180 might be provided if the pupils were grouped in units of 35 to 40. There was no need to change the lower age limit of compulsory school attendance and the Committee thought that the existing practice of paying a grant equivalent to 50 per cent of approved expenditure was satisfactory. The buildings of the majority of existing infant schools came in for severe criticism. Plenty of floor space should be allowed and the classrooms should be constructed to admit as much fresh air, light, and sunshine as possible. Special provision for play, separate from that of the junior and senior department, should be assigned. Attention should be given to a generous supply of hot water, the provision of facilities for drying clothes, and to the furnishings of the classrooms. The walls should be painted in light and bright colours and the rows of rigid desks should be replaced by low chairs and collapsible tables which could be moved when desirable to give ample floor space for free movement.

At last authority had spoken and had set forth the requirements not only of a suitable education for children of varying ages but also the proper conditions under which that education ought to take place. Unfortunately, even now, nearly twenty years after the issue of the Hadow Reports, one cannot truthfully say that everything is satisfactory. An ideal had been presented but it will take a considerable time for it to be attained. When war broke out in 1939, not quite two-thirds of pupils over 11 were attending re-organized schools (63.5 per cent). Moreover there were upwards of two thousand classes containing more than 50 pupils. The war put an end to further progress. Schools which were hopelessly out of date continued to be used and after the war not only had these schools to be replaced but new schools were required to replace those badly damaged by enemy action or to serve the needs of new housing estates. Thus there are, especially in rural districts, many 'through or all standard schools' in use and these are only gradually able to be re-organized since in nearly every case re-organization is impossible without further building. Progress varied greatly in different parts of the country. Some authorities were exceedingly progressive in their outlook whilst others were equally laggard. Besides the schools on the so-called 'Black List' of the Board of Education, there were numerous others which could not possibly carry out the plans which the Hadow Reports envisaged. 'Thus it is that there are primary schools, modern schools and those containing children at both stages housed in buildings which are defective in such basic requirements as heating, lighting or ventilation, or, if not positively defective, lacking the efficiency which is known to contribute to good education. There are others lacking rooms sufficient in number or size for the fundamental purposes which none would question. They are overcrowded, in some cases perhaps with two classes in a room, or with cloakrooms consisting only of porches, rows of pegs and a single basin in a corner. In other cases, they may lack nothing in this respect and yet fall short of the needs. The infant school, or department or class, may, for example, afford space for the children to sit, but none for their movement or play; the junior school may have space inside for "activities" but none outside for a garden; and the new styled secondary modern school might have every amenity which a School Board could imagine and yet suffer for want of a room for science or handwork or art, or any of the other needs which have gained in importance since School Boards passed away'.[1]

Old habits and traditions take a long time to die. There are still many teachers who, having been brought up in the traditions of class teaching, believe that this is the only form that education should take and view with considerable doubt the introduction of modern methods. Their doubts have been strengthened by the excesses of some of those who advocate and practise so-called 'activity' methods. It is true that education is not merely an affair of bricks and mortar and that the human element is the predominant factor but even the most well intentioned and skilled teacher must become frequently disheartened when he has to work in conditions such as Professor Armfelt has described. This picture is not intended to be gloomy and pessimistic. If still a great deal remains to be done, the existence of large numbers of well built, spacious and well equipped schools shows that much more than a beginning has been made. Although international complications and financial difficulties may at times slow up the rate of progress, the ideals set by the Hadow Reports remain as the goal at which English education should aim.

As soon as the economic depression began to lessen, the Government issued its programme of educational reform. In

[1] R. Armfelt. *Education—New Hopes and Old Habits*, p. 83. Cohen and West. 1949.

July 1934 the 10 per cent cut in the salaries of teachers was restored and in view of the election of the following year, the Government, after announcing its belief that 'there never was a time when a well educated democracy was so necessary as it is to-day,' outlined the proposals for a new Education Bill. These were embodied in the Education Act of 1936. The recommendation of the *Report on the Education of the Adolescent* concerning the raising of the school-leaving age was to be put into force. From September 1st, 1939 the school leaving age would be 15. Pressure from industrialists and business men induced the Government to grant certain exemptions. Pupils between the ages of 14 and 15 might be exempted from the operation of the Act if they were offered employment which satisfied local authorities as being beneficial. Non-provided schools found it difficult to proceed with re-organization because of lack of funds. Hence the Act sanctioned the payment by local authorities of grants not exceeding 75 per cent of the cost of the school buildings for senior children. A time limit was fixed before which those managers who wished to avail themselves of the grants should signify their agreement. The grants paid to non-provided schools were to be spent on the provision of increased accommodation which would be needed when the school-leaving age was raised to 15. The principles which should govern the lay-out of the new senior schools were explained in a pamphlet entitled *Suggestions for the Planning of Buildings for Public Elementary Schools*. The number of buildings sanctioned by the provisions of the Act of 1936 was 519 but only 37 of them had materialized at the outbreak of war. Such schools were known as Special Agreement Schools and managers were given a certain time to decide whether or no to take advantage of the offer. The Act of 1944 honoured the agreement even in cases where no active steps had been taken to commence building operations. The religious denominations in return for the 75 per cent building grant agreed to surrender the appointment of teachers to the L.E.A. Denominational teaching could be given to those children whose parents desired it by Reserved teachers. Those who asked for undenominational teaching for their children could avail themselves for instruction based on an Agreed Syllabus.

The Hadow Reports had been concerned with education in the primary school and with that type of post-primary education which is now given in the modern school. So far the problems of the grammar school had not received consideration but in 1933 the Consultative Committee was requested: 'To consider and report upon the organization and interrelation of schools, other than those administered under the Elementary Code, which provide education for pupils beyond the age of 11; regard being had in particular to the framework and content of the education of pupils who do not remain at school beyond the age of about 16.' It was not until 1938 that the Committee under the Chairmanship of Sir Will Spens, Master of Corpus Christi, Cambridge, issued its *Report on Secondary Education with special reference to Grammar Schools and Technical High Schools*. During these five years educational opinion had been considerably modified and the change of view is apparent in the Report.

The Hadow Report on the *Education of the Adolescent* had envisaged two types of secondary education which are at present represented by the grammar and the modern school. The Spens Report advocated a tripartite organization by bringing in the technical high school as the third partner. This tripartite arrangement was subsequently adopted by the Board of Education. It has been severely criticized from a number of different sources. The supporters of the multilateral school formed one group of critics and there were those who like Mr. H. C. Dent regarded the introduction of the technical high school as producing an unnecessary complication in secondary education. Mr. Dent urges with considerable reason that there is nothing in the aims and curriculum of the technical high school that could not be supplied by the grammar school.[1]

The Spens Committee felt that they were justified in going beyond their terms of reference because to investigate their problems thoroughly some review of the whole field of secondary education would be necessary. Thus the question whether the different types of secondary school should exist and develop independently or whether the multilateral school offered a more satisfactory solution, was considered. There were certain arguments in favour of the multilateral arrangement such as the ease with which a pupil could be transferred from one stream to another, the economy in space, staffing, equipment, and supervision that could be effected, and the value of bringing together in the same institution pupils of varying interests, abilities and outlook. Against these the size of the school had to be considered.

[1] H. C. Dent. *Secondary Education for All*, pp. 79–80. Routledge and Kegan Paul. 1949.

The Spens Committee envisaged a multilateral school as containing at least 800 pupils if it was to be run economically. More recent thought is in terms of numbers reaching to 2,000 or even 2,500. A large school of this kind raised a number of practical problems. Would it be possible to find heads capable of organizing and inspiring both modern and grammar streams? It is generally acknowledged that one of the most important influences in a grammar school is that brought to bear on the rest of the school by the sixth form. In a multilateral school the numbers in the sixth would be only a small proportion of the whole since the majority of pupils on the modern side and some on the technical side would not remain at school after 16 years of age. Would not, therefore, the influence of the Sixth Form, to the loss of the school, be greatly diminished? Although parity of esteem for all types of secondary education was desirable, was it not a fallacy to suppose that it could be more readily attained in a multilateral school than under the tripartite system? The grammar school already possessed an acknowledged prestige and there was the risk that this might adversely affect the modern side. Moreover, the Committee had already made up their minds that the technical high school could perform a more valuable service if it was taken under the wing of a technical college.

The Report, therefore, decided in favour of the tripartite organization though it suggested that in particular areas it would be useful to experiment with the multilateral idea. Thus in some rural districts a grammar and central school might be housed in the same building. The essential idea in a reformed system of secondary education was that each pupil should attend the type of school for which he was best fitted. Although the Committee did not actually use the phrase 'Secondary education for all', it is evident that it was uppermost in their thoughts. They considered that as soon as the national finances permitted, admission to grammar and technical high schools should be based on 100 per cent of special places and that all types of secondary school should be administered under a new code of regulations for secondary schools.

The technical high school would recruit its pupils in the same way as the grammar school, namely by means of the Special Place examination but in the former case, school records and oral interviews would be decisive. Mistakes in selection would undoubtedly occur and hence it would be necessary to review all pupils at the age of 13 and to devise machinery for transferring a pupil, when necessary, from one type of school to another. This would entail that in the first two years the curriculum of all secondary schools would be broadly of the same character.

The technical high school would provide a five year course with a scientific and engineering bias for pupils between 11 plus and 16 plus. It is to the credit of the Committee that the view of the Bryce Commission that the idea of secondary education could not be entirely dissociated from technical instruction, was re-introduced and the Secretary, Dr. R. F. Young, in a masterly summary of the development of secondary education in England, very ably defended this decision. In fact the Committee were prepared to take up the extreme position of recommending the introduction of vocational training even to pupils who would be leaving school at 16. As previously mentioned, it was agreed that the technical high school should be accommodated in the premises of technical colleges. It was thought that this would be an advantage because of the pooling of staff and equipment and also that the principal being in close touch with the needs of local industry would be able to guide pupils with regard to employment. A third argument of even more doubtful character was advanced. It was claimed that 'the general atmosphere of the college, which is largely attended by adult students, is a constant stimulant to the pupils of the school. . . . Furthermore, there is much evidence to show that the contact of the pupils of the school with many members of the college staff who are also concerned with teaching adult students has a beneficial effect both on teachers and pupils'. (p. 278). On this argument, it would be a benefit for every type of secondary school to become an integral part of an adult institution, a position which very few would be prepared to support.

The technical high school would have its own headmaster who would stand as a departmental head in relation to the principal of the college. A start might be made by converting a number of of junior technical schools into technical high schools. 'Whilst we do not recommend that every junior technical school should as a matter of course be converted into a technical high school, we do consider that a generous provision of such technical high schools should be made by the conversion of existing schools and the establishment of new schools'. (p. xxx). Trade schools which specialized in training for special industries would not be included in this scheme since the education they gave was too specific. Entrance to them would remain at 13 or 14 and they would be governed by the *Regulations for Further Education*. Curiously enough little was said about the technical training of girls in schools of domestic science, art schools and schools of commerce. These institutions would not be considered as technical high schools.

A special leaving examination should be given to pupils of the technical high schools. 'We recommend that a new type of leaving certificate should be established for pupils in technical high schools on the basis of internal examinations founded on the school curriculum, and subject to external assessment by assessors appointed or approved by the Board of Education. . . . We recommend that these certificates should be given an equal standing with School Certificates as fulfilling the first condition for Matriculation' (p. 373). This idea of an internal examination cropped up again in the Norwood Report and in the deliberations of the Secondary Schools Examinations Council.

The Spens Report criticized the grammar school curriculum on the ground that it was designed for pupils who intended to proceed to a university regardless of the fact that about 85 per cent of the pupils did not remain at school beyond the age of sixteen. The existing grammar school curriculum was 'still coloured by obsolete doctrines of the faculties and of formal training; and the endeavour to teach a wide range of subjects to the same high level to all pupils has led to the overcrowding of the timetable' (p. xxii). In spite of these strictures, the Report disclaimed any suggestion of revolutionary changes in the grammar school curriculum, though, as Mr. Dent points out, 'Having said that, the Committee proceeded to suggest a series of changes which, if their implications be fully considered, cannot be considered other than revolutionary'.[1]

Space forbids a detailed examination of the proposals for the reform of the teaching of the different subjects in the grammar school but there are a few points that should be noted. In the first place, it was considered that up to sixteen, the courses provided should be complete in themselves and it was rightly pointed out that this need not prejudice the interests of pupils who wished to enter a university. As the study of the classics no longer constituted the core round

[1] H. C. Dent, *op. cit.*, p. 75.

which the grammar school curriculum could be based, English subjects should take the place of the classics. Surely this position had not really been thought out in its implications. It has not yet been proved that it is necessary for there to be a core for the curriculum and at present the studies grouped under the generic term 'English studies' are not a substitute for the classics as a means of intellectual discipline. As Professor A. N. Whitehead has reminded us, 'There are three main methods which are required in a natural system of education, namely the literary curriculum, the scientific curriculum, the technical curriculum'.[1]

One outstanding change, however, should be noticed. Board of Education pamphlets had hitherto been extremely reticent in discussing religious education. Even the *Education of the Adolescent* had only mentioned it in the most general terms. Now for the first time, the Spens Report devoted a complete chapter to the consideration of religious instruction which it mistakenly called Scripture, as though the study of Scripture could be equated with religious education. Nevertheless it was a beginning and a few years later we were to see the subject of religious instruction occupy a prominent place in an Education Act.

The Spens Report thought that the School and Higher School Certificate examinations were exercising a harmful effect on the grammar schools. The examination system was controlling the teaching given in the schools, thus having a narrowing and cramping effect on the curriculum. This was partly due to employers who constantly asked for evidence of matriculation from their secondary school applicants. The fault lay in the fact that the same examination served both as a school-leaving certificate and as fulfilling the entrance requirements of the universities. The latter narrowed the choice of subjects already limited by the group system. Accordingly the Committee recommended that an exemption from matriculation should no longer be given on the results of the School Certificate examination. The outbreak of war interfered with these reforms and for a time the original regulations were allowed to remain in force as a special concession.

If the recommendations of the Spens Report were to be put into operation, the Committee saw that certain administrative changes would be necessary. 'The existence of these Authorities (Part III authorities) has entered as a complicat-

[1] *The Aims of Education and other Essays*, p. 74. Williams and Norgate, 1932.

ing factor into our consideration of "the interrelation of schools", and of the desirability of bringing modern schools within the compass of a new Secondary Code of Regulations. The course of our evidence confirms us in the opinion that it is not less urgent now to seek a satisfactory solution of this administrative problem than it was 12 years ago. . . . The problem is one of so great importance and complexity that it should, in our opinion, be remitted to a Departmental or Inter-Departmental Committee, which would not seek any general solution before it has thoroughly investigated the circumstances of individual areas'. (pp. 315–18). The outbreak of war prevented such a committee being formed. Although in a few places, experiments on the lines recommended by the Spens Committee were tried out, the war put an end to progress for the time being. The same fate overtook the Education Act of 1936. The raising of the school-leaving age was to have come into force on the first day of September, 1939. On that day, Hitler had invaded Poland and the evacuation of school pupils in Britain had commenced. On the whole the postponement of these plans proved a good thing, for when the Government was once more able to consider the educational situation it proposed legislation of a more thorough and wholesale character than the measure of 1936.

CHAPTER V

FROM STATE SUPERVISION TO STATE CONTROL

FEW major operations have been characterized by such numerous mistakes as the evacuation of school children from danger to reception areas in the first week of September, 1939. Ever since Munich, it had been realized that if war did come the air power of the enemy would constitute a greater threat to this country than had hitherto been experienced in our long history. Nobody knew how the war would open. Most expected it to begin with air raids of unparalleled severity. For months before the actual outbreak of hostilities, the Government had been preparing a scheme for the evacuation of children and expectant mothers from London and the large cities which were thought to be in the danger area. This was right and proper; it was in the actual execution of the plan that the blunders occurred.

In the first place, if evacuation was considered a necessary safeguard, it should have been made compulsory from the start. The authorities lacked the courage to take this step with the result that initially the scheme was doomed to failure. Even if evacuation was to remain voluntary, the Government should have realized that the greater number of children came from homes where the parents were not accustomed to be separated from their children. In order to bring the parents to accept the scheme, nation-wide publicity would have been necessary and pressed to the point that no parent would think he was justified in exposing his children to the perils that the danger areas might present. Publicity came too late. Moreover, the scheme had been worked out on paper but no general rehearsal seems to have been attempted. A rehearsal would not only have tested the efficacy of the plans but would have been excellent propaganda in persuading parents of the vital necessity of doing all in their power to ensure the smooth working of the evacuation. Although the schools knew their destinations no opportunity was afforded to head teachers for visiting the proposed reception areas to discover conditions for themselves and to establish friendly relations with the schools there. Apparently the plans were delayed so much that there was neither time for a rehearsal nor for visits by the head teachers. The consequence of this policy was that when the time for evacuation came, only a proportion of parents was willing to allow its children to be moved; in some towns, less than 20 per cent of children were evacuated.

In justice to the authorities one must say that practically everybody anticipated heavy air raids which might possibly begin while the evacuation was in progress. Hence the chief concern of the authorities was to get the children to the railway stations, put them on the trains and move them off as expeditiously as possible. Some schools arrived at the wrong destination but this is understandable when the magnitude of the task and the hurry and bustle of the moment are taken into account. The marvellous part of the whole business is that thousands of children were removed without practically any serious accident. Insufficient attention had been given to the co-ordination of railway timetables and the information about billeting facilities in the reception areas was not nearly as complete as it should have been. For example, householders at the receiving end were asked about their preferences but little more seems to have been done than to ascertain if they wished to have boys or girls, children or adults. The mistake was to give the Ministry of Health charge of the evacuation. The local education authorities were accustomed to dealing with children in large numbers and a more rational scheme would have been for the Board of Education to have worked through the local authorities. In fact the responsibility for the operation was divided between the two Government departments. Billeting officers worked in terms of numbers. If billets had to be found for thirty children, then thirty places were allocated without reference to the important factor that children could not feel at home if they were sent to families in which the standards of behaviour and living and outlook on life were vastly different from those to which they had been accustomed. 'The sole consideration was to get everyone under a roof without delay. So slum-bred children were bustled off to lordly mansions and opulent country houses, delicately nurtured youngsters bundled into labourers' cottages, boisterous young "toughs" thrust upon elderly folk of retiring habit, sensitive and introverted adolescents dumped into the midst of loud and hearty families of the "Good Companions" type, pregnant women landed with confirmed spinsters or presented as an additional burden to already overburdened working housewives. Every possible kind of sociological and psychological misfit was made in abundance'.[1] Later came the sorting out but in the meanwhile the damage had been done.

In London the transport authorities added to the confusion by refusing to guarantee that any body of children travelling by rail would arrive at the given destination. Quite naturally a good many parents took the attitude that if you cannot tell us exactly where you are sending our children and are not able to guarantee that they will arrive there, we are not going to send them. Probably the fact that the expected air raids did not start for a considerable period saved the situation from degenerating into one of the utmost confusion and chaos. This allowed time for teachers and voluntary helpers to complete the sorting-out process and one cannot speak too highly of the magnificent work that they accomplished. Teachers, education officials, inspectors and voluntary helpers worked wonders in ensuring that mistakes were rectified as quickly as possible. Most of the teachers went with the children and spent the first few days of evacuation tramping the countryside to find children who had been mislaid and to send them to their proper destination. Mistakes about billeting had to be corrected at once. Some city schools found themselves in rural districts with such scanty accommodation that the children were scattered over half-a-dozen or more villages. As soon as the children were settled in their temporary homes, arrangements had to be made for their schooling. This produced a fresh crop of difficulties since the school accommodation in the reception areas was not adequate for the crowds of new-comers. Thus schools were not only split for billeting but also for instruction. The most common plan was, that of a double shift. The same school buildings were used, say, in the mornings by the original school and in the afternoons by the evacuated children. Sunday schools, places of worship and public institutes were used wherever possible. As these buildings were not designed as schools, their new occupants found them in many ways unsatisfactory. One headmaster of a large grammar school had to use a tiny vestry room in a chapel both for his study and as the office of the school secretary. Speaking of his experience of this restricted space

[1] H. C. Dent. *Education in Transition*, p. 15. Kegan Paul, Trench, Trubner, 1944.

he afterwards humorously remarked that when a boy was sent to him for a whacking, the size of the room seriously cramped his style. Teachers and inspectors worked without thought for themselves to produce some kind of order out of chaos. A good deal of the muddle was caused by the contradictory orders issued by directors of education, especially in areas under the jurisdiction of small Part III authorities. The following example shows the kind of difficulty that had to be faced. Although parents had been issued with a list of the clothes and other articles that children ought to bring with them, yet many arrived without certain essential things. In some cases this was due to the carelessness of parents who had not made themselves fully acquainted with the instructions and in others because the children came from homes where the parents were too poor to supply their children with the requisite clothing. One teacher relates that he found three of his boys tramping the village street with no soles to their shoes. A wet period had begun and the country lanes were thick with liquid mud. He immediately applied to the local Part III education office for authority to obtain some suitable shoes for the boys. The office informed him that it was not within their power to issue the authority but that it must be sought from the major education authority which had sent the boys. This authority in turn denied that it was their responsibility and suggested that he applied to certain voluntary agencies. For a week he was referred from one body to another. At last in desperation he took the boys into the local shoe shop, explained the situation to the shopkeeper and had the boys fitted out with suitable footwear. He expressed his willingness to foot the bill himself if no public body could be found to take responsibility. Fortunately for his own pocket, he found that at the end of a fortnight the bill had been settled by the major education authority.

Eventually by dint of much hard work and improvisation, a tolerable educational organization was constructed. Some children were evacuated overseas. The Dominions and the United States showed their practical sympathy by inviting children to their countries. Many parents who could afford it sent their children out of England especially to Canada and the United States. In September, 1940, the *City of Benares*, which carried a number of evacuee children, was torpedoed in mid-Atlantic during a storm and nearly eighty children lost their lives. This event at once put an end to overseas evacuation.

FROM STATE SUPERVISION TO STATE CONTROL 117

The expected air raids did not materialize and this led to another blunder on the part of the authorities. Parents were given permission to visit their children. The mistake lay in giving this permission too early and allowing too frequent visits of parents. Parents' visits not only unsettled the children but soon there came demands for the children to be sent back home. Thousands streamed back to London and the large cities. When the Blitz started in the autumn of 1940, the movement was reversed and large bodies of school pupils returned to the evacuation areas. Moreover, certain evacuation areas had become unsafe. Hitler had occupied the Channel ports and children previously sent to Kent and Sussex had to be transferred to other parts of England. Still the Government clung to the idea of voluntary evacuation even in those areas which were suffering most from aerial bombardment. In these districts all the schools were closed and the children who remained behind were left to grow up without any kind of schooling. Those teachers who had not been evacuated visited children in their homes to give them what instruction was possible. In Leeds, the Education Department of the University, after pleading in vain for the re-opening of the schools, decided to run a voluntary scheme. In conjunction with many of the local clergy, classes were established at the University and in local churches and the teaching was given by volunteers from the teachers left behind and by the students in training in the Department. This was a help but under the circumstances attendance could not be made compulsory so that only the fringe of the problem was attacked. At length the Government gave way. Air raid shelters were erected at the schools, the windows were covered with gummed paper strips and blast walls were built. The schools started again but thousands of children had lost precious months of schooling.

A further setback was experienced by children in towns where the air raids began in real earnest. The actual number of schools destroyed or rendered useless by bombing was comparatively small and as a considerable proportion of the pupils had been evacuated casualties amongst children were not as heavy as they might have been. In London, children had to spend night after night in shelters during air attacks and it was thought that this would play havoc with their nerves and their work. Strangely enough, they suffered little physical or mental damage but naturally their school work was affected. There was also a shortage of schools, for some buildings had been handed over to the service authorities for billets, stores, or as hospitals and training establishments and it took considerable time to induce the military authorities to part with them.

As at the time of the 1914–18 war, the situation had certain redeeming features. Schools in the reception areas could not take more than a fraction of their equipment with them and often the places which had to be utilized as schoolrooms were practically bare of educational apparatus. Teachers were forced to improvise and many found to their astonishment that they could dispense with many of the aids they had previously thought of as essential. Work in the open air and of a definitely practical character took the place of much of the formal class work. Subjects like arithmetic, geography and history began to have a new meaning for pupils when studied at firsthand. Handicrafts, art, and all types of physical activities came into prominence. Children received benefits from the fresh air and more healthy conditions of life. They came into contact with a kind of life they may have read about but had never before experienced. The impact of town upon country was beneficial not only to town but to country dwellers. There were of course the grumblers who complained about the absence of trams, cinemas and fried fish shops but on the whole the children who had been evacuated led a happy existence.

There is much truth in the saying that one half of the world does not know how the other half lives. Many of us remember stories which revealed the shocking conditions prevailing in the homes of some of the city children. Certainly some of these reports were exaggerated, especially by some selfish well-to-do people who unpatriotically seized upon any excuse to rid themselves of the care of the children who interfered with their time and pleasure. One is not straying far from the truth, however, by stating that the accounts which found their way into the newspapers intensely shocked large numbers of people. One always knew that filthy and verminous children existed; that there were homes in which the sanitary conditions were frightful and in which there was little sense of either decency or discipline. Social workers knew of these defects but the general public did not. Hence the shock when it began to learn from friends in the country and from reports in the daily papers about the low standard of life and behaviour which was characteristic of a large section of the community. Hence, also, the resolve that this state of affairs must be remedied as soon as possible and that a general stocktaking of the whole educational system of the country ought to be put in hand at the earliest possible moment.

Although the crisis of the war had not yet been reached and England was hourly threatened with invasion, attention was already being given to problems of post-war reconstruction and it was realized that one of the most urgent of these was that of education. Professor Lester Smith considers the stimulus was the speech made by the Prime Minister to his old school, Harrow. Mr. Churchill told his audience, 'When the war is won, it must be one of our aims to work to establish a state of society where the advantages and privileges which hitherto have been enjoyed by the few shall be more widely shared by the men and youth of the nation.'[1]

The first active move was made by the religious bodies. The two Anglican Archbishops, the Roman Catholic Archbishop of Westminster, and the Moderator of the Free Church Federal Council joined in drawing up a memorial at the end of 1940, entitled, *A Christian Basis for Peace*, and at the commencement of the following year, Archbishop Temple, Chairman of the Anglican Conference at Malvern, put forward a number of suggestions, some of which found their way into the Education Act of 1944. In August, 1941, Dr. Temple led a joint deputation of Anglicans and Free Churchmen to interview the new President of the Board of Education and lay before him their proposals concerning religious education. Discussion of the proposed educational reconstruction had now become widespread. It has not often happened that educational matters have been regarded with such interest that they have become one of the main topics of discussion, but during this period feeling in all sections of society ran so strongly that the Board of Education was inundated with suggestions for reform coming from bodies of widely different interests. The revelations of the evacuation had so stirred the public conscience that there was a universal demand for a complete overhaul of our social services and it was generally recognized that education ought to be the starting point.

The Government wisely showed itself sympathetic and ready to consider representations that were made. The Board of Education, through its President, Mr. Rams-

[1] W. O. Lester Smith. *To Whom Do Schools Belong?* p. 166. Blackwell, 1943.

botham, made it quite clear that the Government had in mind far-reaching changes in the national system of education. The next step was the preparation of a memorandum on post-war education which was sent as a confidential document to representatives of local authorities, teachers' associations, and to other bodies or individuals who were associated with the service of education. Although it was supposed to be a confidential document, the "Green Book" of 1941 (so called from the colour of its cover) was, in the words of Lester Smith, 'distributed in such a blaze of secrecy' that its contents quickly became public property. This was perhaps unfortunate because through a mistaken interpretation of the President's references to it, everybody thought it was intended as a public document and those who considered that they were entitled to receive a copy and did not obtain one, were disappointed and offended. The 'Green Book' was a questionnaire designed to co lect the views of educationists about every aspect of educational reform. The Government was anxious not to proceed with legislation until it had thoroughly sounded the opinions of those who possessed first-hand experience of the working of the present system.

The publication of the 'Green Book' stimulated lively interest throughout the nation. In civil life, in the Forces, and through the B.B.C., discussion groups minutely examined every aspect of educational reconstruction. The Board received an enormous amount of information contributed not only by individuals but from such important bodies as the N.U.T., the T.U.C., the W.E.A. and the Association of Directors and Secretaries for Education. Although views about details differed considerably, there was a general concensus of opinion about the lines on which reform ought to take place. Mr. Ramsbotham's successor, Mr. R. A. Butler, felt that now the information had been digested, it was time to take a further step. In July, 1943, he issued the White Paper on *Educational Reconstruction* which forecast the contents of the proposed Education Bill. Apart from a few items, the proposals of the White Paper were generally acceptable. The Labour Party wished for the announcement of a definite date for the raising of the school-leaving age to 16 and demanded that in all secondary schools which received grants from public funds, fees should be abolished. Mr. Butler believed that the time was inopportune for fixing a definite date for the raising of the school-leaving age and he was not willing to free all secondary schools from fees.

The favourable reception given to the White Paper encouraged Mr. Butler to go ahead with the drafting of the Education Bill. It was introduced into the House of Commons on December 16, 1943 and received the Royal Assent on August 4, 1944. Its main principles were accepted by all parties and criticisms and discussions were largely directed to administrative matters. 'It was an agreed measure in so far as anything in this world can be agreed. Mr. Butler was fully aware that all the clauses of the Act could not be put into operation immediately and by his description of the day on which the first of its proposals became effective as D Day in education, he negatived the idea that it would be a final solution for all the problems of national education'.[1] Hence the Education Act of 1944, which was avowedly intended as a complete overhaul of the statutory system of education, was designed to come into operation in stages. Thus Parts I and V came into operation at once but Part II which dealt with universal free secondary education was postponed until April 1, 1945.

Acts of Parliament make dull reading for most people so that it is not the intention of this book to examine the Act clause by clause. That has been done elsewhere and many commentaries on the Act have been published.[2] The writer will therefore restrict his discussion to certain of the main changes that were effected.

In regard to administration, central and local, the Act may be considered as fulfilling the recommendations made by the Bryce Commission in 1895. The Board of Education has disappeared and its place has been taken by a Ministry of Education. The Minister has been given the powers which the Bryce Commission considered were necessary. Instead of being responsible to Parliament for the 'superintendence of certain matters relating to education in England and Wales', the Minister has the duty of directing the national policy in education and ensuring that it is carried out by the local authorities. This change was not effected without some criticism. Some members of the House thought that too much power was being put into the hands of the Minister.

[1] S. J. Curtis. *History of Education in Great Britain*, pp. 374–5. U.T.P., 2nd Edition, 1950.
[2] E.g. H. C. Dent. *The Education Act of 1944*. University of London Press, revised edition, 1947; A. E. Ikin, *The Education Act 1944*. Pitman, 1944; S. J. Curtis, *op. cit.*, c.xi., *The Overhaul of 1944 and the Future*.

Mr. Butler's reply was that it was the function of the central authority to provide leadership and to initiate, not to follow timidly. At the same time he pointed out that there was no suggestion of breaking up the partnership between the central and local authorities which had gradually been cemented since 1902. The increased powers of the Ministry were not intended to be used to build up an educational dictatorship but the Minister now has statutory power to compel backward and laggard authorities to carry out their duties.

The Act itself provides safeguards against the abuse of the Ministerial powers. The Minister is ultimately responsible to Parliament for the actions of his department and he is obliged to present an annual report which can be criticized by any member of the House of Commons. He has the power to frame Regulations (Statutory Rules and Orders) but these must be laid before Parliament and may be annulled by a resolution of either House. Any member of the House of Commons may ask a question in the House on any matter concerning the public service of education and members frequently avail themselves of this right. Also every private citizen can communicate with the member representing his own constituency and request him to take up any point about which in the public interest he thinks an inquiry should be made. Everything depends upon the vigilance and sense of public duty of members of Parliament and the citizens of this country. If they are watchful and alive to their responsibilities there should be no fear that an educational dictatorship may grow up.

The Consultative Committee of the Board of Education has also disappeared. In its place there are two Central Advisory Councils for Education, one for England and one for Wales. These councils are entrusted with the powers recommended by the Bryce Commission. They can at any time, as they think fit, advise the Minister on matters connected with the theory and practice of education. This is another limitation of the powers of the Minister. The chairman and personnel of the councils are appointed by the Minister but since he is required to report their composition and proceedings to Parliament, he is liable at any time to become the target for hostile criticism. The councils are to include 'persons who have had experience of the statutory system of public education as well as persons who have had experience of educational institutions not forming part of that system'. A glance at the composition of the councils as announced by Mr. Butler in December, 1944, shows that this principle has been observed. The President was Sir Fred Clarke and the membership of the councils included representatives of primary and secondary schools (including the public schools), Trade Unions, the universities, the religious bodies, industry, science and agriculture, and adult education.

The net result is that the Minister of Education as regards status is now on an equality with those of his colleagues who preside over other Government departments. He possesses increased powers, subject to certain necessary restrictions, and he has at hand a body of expert advisers who can take the initiative by bringing to his notice matters which they think he should consider. Under these circumstances it is to be hoped that a greater degree of permanency may be achieved than happened in the case of the Presidency of the Board of Education. Up to date, there have been four Ministers of Education, Mr. R. A. Butler, Mr. Richard Law (in Mr. Churchill's 'Caretaker' Government), Miss E. Wilkinson, and Mr. George Tomlinson. Taking into account the untimely death of Miss Wilkinson and the special circumstances under which Mr. Churchill formed his administration, the record seems more promising.

The revised scheme for the local administration of education returns to the spirit of the recommendations of the Bryce Commission before they were modified by the Act of 1902. It was this part of the Act which occasioned most debate. The point at issue was the abolition of the Part III authorities. The White Paper had selected two extreme examples to show the kind of anomaly which existed: Harrow U.D.C., which had a population of 183,000 in 1938 but was not an education authority because its population was less than 20,000 in 1901, and Tiverton, Devon, population in 1938 under 10,000, which was still a Part III authority. The Local Authorities (Education) Act of 1931 had prohibited the establishment of any new L.E.A.s but this measure had merely strengthened the Part III authorities in their opposition to absorption. They canvassed their local M.P.s and in many instances were able to demonstrate that they were among the most efficient and progressive L.E.A.s and that some of the county authorities had been extremely remiss in putting forward schemes of re-organization. All this may have been true but they failed to realize that a new educational scheme based on the principle of secondary education for all would mean a complete revision of local administration units.

The White Paper proposed a solution which was afterwards materially modified in the Act. It suggested the abolition of the Part III authorities and the division of the counties for administrative convenience into areas under district sub-committees. This was already the practice of certain authorities, e.g. those for Lancashire, Durham, Cheshire, Kent, and the West Riding. It should be noted that these are large counties and one might say that delegation had been thrust upon them. The reasons advanced for handing the control of education to the county councils were: unification of the educational system; the adoption of larger units would spread the cost, and it would facilitate matters when it came to framing educational policy. The reduction in the number of educational units would also be a distinct advantage for the Ministry. If this policy had been adopted, 146 out of the original 333 L.E.A.s would have been retained.

When the White Paper was discussed in Parliament, the Part III authorities, through their local members, put up a strenuous opposition. It must be admitted that in most cases the driving force was fear of loss of power but this was not necessarily a selfish motive. One may consider the case of a member of a Part III authority who has worked conscientiously for twenty years or more for the cause of education within his district and who has freely given his time and advice with genuine enthusiasm. He has acquired an accurate and detailed picture of his area; he understands its peculiar problems, and he has a first-hand knowledge of the schools, the teachers, and the different bodies of managers. In short, he has his finger on the pulse of his district. The abolition of the Part III authorities might mean the end of his usefulness. He may have been chairman of his particular committee but now, at the best, he would only be a member of a much larger education committee and would lose the power of determining lines of policy which perhaps seemed vital to him. His activities would be largely limited to giving advice. No wonder, as Mr. Dent remarks: 'the controversy over units of educational administration blew up in a white heat on the publication of the White Paper'.[1]

---

[1] H. C. Dent. *Education in Transition*, p. 215. Routledge and Kegan Paul, 1944.

The opposition urged that it was essential to keep local interest alive and this could only be stimulated if there was local responsibility. The member for Swindon said quite frankly that his constituents viewed the loss of power with apprehension. The larger Part III authorities demanded special consideration. Captain Gammans, Conservative member for Hornsey, said, 'What worries many of these authorities is the proposal to delegate their work to district committees appointed by the county . . . these committees are not democratically elected . . . if there is to be delegation, it should be delegation direct to the local authority'.[1]

Mr. Chuter Ede, in replying for the Government, admitted that he was much impressed by the arguments on behalf of the Part III authorities and he hoped that they would send their representatives to discuss the problem with members of the Government. During the five months preceding the introduction of the Education Bill, the case for Part III authorities was very skilfully argued by Mr. Lipson, the member for Cheltenham. His persistence was rewarded, for when the Bill was presented to the Commons the Government had considerably modified the proposals of the White Paper. The Explanatory Memorandum to the Education Bill (Cmd. 6492) contained the following significant paragraphs: 'Instead of the proposal that district committees should be entrusted with the general duty of keeping the needs of their areas under review and of making recommendations to the county education committee, there is substituted a system of delegation of functions to divisional executives representing individual county districts or groups of them.' 'The divisional executives will . . .˙prepare and submit their own annual estimates of expenditure.'

Counties were not obliged to set up D.E.s for all districts. Some counties or parts of counties could continue to be administered directly by the county education committee. The D.E.s were to be concerned with both primary and secondary education and also further education, if the county authority was willing to delegate such powers and the approval of the Ministry was obtained. Altogether, 171 D.E.s were constituted.

The White Paper had also mentioned excepted districts. These may be regarded as D.E.s in which the borough or urban district council constitutes the executive and has the

[1] *Hansard*, vol. 391, No. 98, Col. 2013.

power, after consultation with the county authority, to prepare its own schemes for primary and secondary education. According to the original draft of the Education Bill, the condition for recognition as an excepted district was that the area should either have had a population of 60,000 or over at the census of 1931, or a public elementary school roll of not less than 7,000 on March 31st, 1939. Pressure from Part III authorities produced some modifications in the Act. According to the original criterion, 39 areas could claim excepted district status, some by a very small margin. The bulk of these were in the London area. In the Act, the first condition was altered so that an area could claim excepted district status if its population was more than 60,000 on June 30th, 1939, according to the estimate of the Registrar-General. This alteration was made in the interest of areas which had grown rapidly between 1931 and 1939. Eight more districts, all round London except for Worthing, were brought in. Some areas either did not claim or later withdrew their claims (e.g. Watford) thus leaving 37 excepted districts.

A further provision was made for special circumstances. Sixty-seven authorities applied but only 7 were admitted: Cheltenham, Stretford, Keighley, Solihull, Nuneaton, Wallsend, and Lowestoft. Some of the claims were ridiculous, e.g. Richmond, Yorks., with a population of 7,000. This raised the number of excepted districts to 44. Like the divisional executive, the excepted district has no power to raise a rate or to borrow money but otherwise it has the powers of a Part III authority with regard to primary and secondary education.

Divisional executives vary in composition in different parts of the country. They possess both executive and advisory functions and the actual power they wield depends upon the amount of delegation by the county authority. In general they include three types of member: representatives of the county authority, representatives of local authorities, e.g. an urban district council, and added members chosen because of their special knowledge and experience or representing important interests such as the religious bodies, industry, or a university.

Divisional executives have now been in existence over five years, a sufficient time for one to inquire whether this scheme of local administration is a satisfactory one. The answer, on the whole, is in the negative. Divisional administration is an entirely new experiment in local government. It was frankly a compromise and though the majority may agree, nobody is really enthusiastic about a compromise. The divisional executive is not a democratically elected body. It is true that it contains a large element of representatives of elected bodies but in its constitution it runs counter to the whole tradition of English local government. This fact would not by itself condemn the system of administration provided that it can be shown that it works efficiently. The *raison d'être* of the divisional executive is to permit expression of local views and to foster local interest in the education service. The work that can be accomplished by a divisional executive varies enormously according to whether the county authority is or is not ready to be generous in the matter of delegation. One must bear in mind that a great number of divisional executives were former Part III authorities and though they are prepared to work loyally in the present administrative set-up, they cannot help but feel a certain amount of resentment at their loss of power and responsibility. A generous scheme of delegation will largely overcome this feeling. Some authorities, such as Lancashire and the West Riding, have sensed this and are not only prepared to delegate large responsibilities, but urge divisional executives to make full use of the powers granted to them. On the other hand, some county authorities have endeavoured to force upon the divisional executive a policy which is distasteful to the locality. This has been apparent in regard to the tripartite-multilateral controversy which unfortunately has been complicated by the intrusion of party politics into a problem which should be settled on purely educational grounds. Thus the Middlesex L.E.A. at Enfield rejected the executive's proposal for a tripartite arrangement of secondary education and ruled that the multilateral principle should be accepted. The West Riding tried to force divisional executives to accept the multilateral idea even in places in which local feeling ran strongly against acceptance. In this case the county elections decided the matter and those areas which dislike multilateralism are now free to submit revised schemes for the organization of secondary education. Although the main support of multilateralism comes from the Labour Party, it is interesting to note that several South Yorkshire divisional executives which had Socialist majorities have clung tenaciously to their grammar schools, largely because of the outstanding personalities of individual members of the committee who were unwilling to lose the schools for which in the past they had fought so vigorously.

The divisional executive frequently administers an area which is neither co-terminous with the municipality, the urban district nor the former Part III district. It is in fact a new district which has been carved out for the executive and since it has no traditional unity, this has to be built up, no easy matter for an authority which may cut clean across existing local administrative areas. The executive depends for much of its effectiveness upon its relations with the county authority, the various boards of governors and managers of schools and the teachers. The two latter were at first inclined to be suspicious and ill feeling could easily have been caused by unwise meddling with the administration of the local grammar school. One has to remember that for years the grammar school has been administered by its head, who is responsible to his governors, and that undue interference by the local executive is naturally resented.

Much depends upon the calibre of the divisional executive officer. His position may not be a happy one. 'No man can serve two masters; for either he will hate the one and love the other; or else he will hold to the one and despise the other'. The divisional officer is an employee of the county authority but at the same time he is responsible to his executive committee. To carry out his work successfully demands considerable patience and tact. At the inception of divisional executives, many of the divisional officers were the former Part III directors of education, who were, as a rule, men of considerable ability and experience. These are growing less in number and the present policy is to appoint well qualified graduates with good teaching but not necessarily administrative experience. The right type of man is not easy to find and the low salaries which are usually offered are not calculated to attract him. The danger is that the person appointed may be one who is using his appointment as a stepping stone to an excepted district or a small L.E.A.

Many criticisms have been levelled at the so-called three tier system, that is, county authority, divisional executive, governors and managers of schools. Thus the member for Sutton and Cheam told the House of Commons that he had been at great pains to persuade five authorities which were entitled to be excepted districts, to relinquish their claims and to accept the status of divisional executives. He declared that he now believed that his efforts had been wasted and he added: 'I find that in every case it has brought duplication and it has not brought any simplification. It has caused delay, and is causing delay, and it is a very serious matter to which no doubt the Minister will have to give attention within the next year or two'. Delay often occurs in matters where immediate action is urgent. Thus in mid-winter the school boiler bursts and the rooms are without heat. The governors draw the attention of the executive to the matter and the executive are at once in a difficulty. In many counties, the approval of the major authority has to be obtained before a sum exceeding £50 or perhaps £100 may be spent. The installation of a new boiler or the overhaul of the old one may cost more than the amount permitted. Hence the only course open to the executive is to pass on a recommendation to the county authority. This not only means correspondence between the executive and the county but the incidence of the meetings of the county council and the executive may occasion a delay of as much as four months. In the meanwhile the children sit and shiver. No wonder that some critics have stated that divisional administration is expensive in money and man power.

The error when the scheme was launched was that of creating a new system of educational administration before the existing system of local government was overhauled. The mistake was the outcome of circumstances. The reform of the educational system was an urgent necessity and could not wait until a complete revision of local government had taken place. Hence divisional administration is somewhat of a makeshift scheme. The divisional executives are just as much *ad hoc* bodies as were the School Boards except that the latter had the additional advantage of being elected bodies. There is no reason at all, after five years have passed, why the whole framework of local government of which educational administration is a part should not receive close attention with the object of greater co-ordination and the achievement of increased efficiency.

On what lines may we look for reform in the future? The Local Government (Boundary Commission) Act of 1945 set up a commission to investigate the circumstances of the areas into which counties are divided for the purposes of local government. Although the findings of the Commission were rejected by the Government, some of the suggestions made are relevant to the problem of educational administration.

ᴛʜe Boundary Commission believed that some counties were

too large for efficient administration and they proposed that the larger ones should be divided into more reasonably sized units. They recommended the creation of Most Purpose Authorities in certain areas. The new authorities should be responsible for the local government of districts which should have a minimum population of 60,000 and should be based on boroughs or urban district councils. Such authorities should be given control over the majority of the social services including primary and secondary education. An area of this size would be able to maintain its own primary and secondary schools and possibly its county colleges. Senior technical institutions, schools of art and teacher training establishments might be provided by the county or, in the case of the smaller counties, by a larger regional authority. In practice this would amount to the restoration of the Part III authorities but with a very important difference. The Most Purpose Authorities would be responsible for both primary and secondary education and for a large part of further education. Moreover they would be popularly elected bodies.

How could sparsely populated areas which have no definite centre of population be administered? One answer is that the county should administer them through newly constituted district committees which should have the power of submitting their own estimates of expenditure for the approval of the county. They could be entrusted with much of the detailed day by day administration, e.g. repairs to roof or floors or the redecoration of the interior of the school. Local governors and managers would have to be brought into relation with this scheme. If it be urged that the scheme would entail an increase in the numbers of local education authorities, the answer is: does this really matter? The problem of local administration has been treated in some detail because, in the opinion of the writer, it constitutes the weakest feature of the Education Act.[1]

The overhaul of the national system of education which was the intention of the Act of 1944 was the logical outcome of the lines of thought that we have seen expressed in the Hadow and the Spens Reports. The Act regarded education as a lifelong process organized in the three progressive stages

[1] Recently, Devon and Somerset have suggested the discontinuance of divisional executives. Lancashire has proposed to reduce their number (at present 35 D.E.s and 2 excepted districts) by the amalgamation of smaller districts, presumably granting them additional responsibilities.

of primary, secondary, and further education. It put upon the local authorities the duty of contributing towards 'the spiritual, moral, mental, and physical development of the community by ensuring that efficient education throughout those stages shall be available to meet the needs of the population of their area'. Hence re-organization became compulsory; the initiative no longer remained with the local authority. By April 1st, 1946, every authority was to survey its area in order to ascertain its present and future needs as regards primary and secondary education, and to submit its development plan to the Ministry. Many authorities found that the time allowed was insufficient and on their request an extension of three months was granted. The London County Council was given an extra year for this purpose. Before development plans were submitted to the Ministry, the governors and managers of voluntary schools were to be consulted. When the Minister has approved the development plan, a local education order is issued. A period of two months is allowed during which the authority may submit objections.

The Dual System has been retained in a modified form by the Act. Voluntary schools fall into three categories. The smallest class consists of the special agreement schools sanctioned by the Act of 1936. If the governors or managers of a voluntary school are both able and willing to contribute half of the costs of improvements or alterations to the school buildings to bring them up to the standard required by the building regulations of the Ministry, they can apply for aided status. If this is granted the school retains its right to give denominational religious instruction according to the trust deed and its governors and managers will continue to appoint the teachers. If the governors or managers are unable or unwilling to contribute 50 per cent of the cost of alteration or rebuilding, the L.E.A. will take over the maintenance of the school. In this case it is said to be controlled. Two-thirds of the governors or managers will be appointed by the authority and the religious instruction will be based on an agreed syllabus. Parents who request religious instruction to be given to their children on a denominational basis can obtain their wish on not more than two periods a week. The denominational teaching is given by reserved teachers except in those schools where the staff (including the head teacher) is less than three. This means that in many small villages the whole of the religious instruction provided by the school will be based on an agreed syllabus. All schools maintained by a local education authority are known as county schools; county primary or secondary as the case may be.

The above compromise was reached after consultation with the religious denominations. From one point of view, the retention of a modified Dual System marks the State's recognition of the part the religious bodies have played in education for many centuries and the connection they have with it at the present. On the other hand, it has saddled them with a heavy burden. Few voluntary schools conform to the standards laid down by the building regulations; in fact many of them had been for years on the 'Black List' of the Board of Education. Hence the majority will have to be drastically altered or entirely rebuilt. When the L.E.A. has received the Ministry's approval of its development plan, the governors or managers of the voluntary schools are informed. They have six months to decide whether they wish the school to be aided or controlled. The Churches have been taking stock of the situation. The Roman Catholics suggested a scheme on the lines of the Scottish solution of the dual control problem but this has been rejected by the Ministry. In the Anglican Church, each diocese has explored the situation in its area and has decided what schools it can afford to keep as aided. A certain amount of assistance is available from diocesan funds and the National Society has recommended the Barchester Scheme to enable managers to accumulate a building fund. In spite of this, it is evident that the Church will be unable to keep many secondary schools as aided and the number of primary schools which are aided will be seriously reduced.

Religious instruction and worship are now obligatory in every school, county or voluntary. The parent retains his right of withdrawal and no teacher is compelled to give religious instruction. The Act prescribes that every school day must begin with a collective act of worship attended by all the pupils. If a school has no assembly hall, worship may take place in the classrooms. In county schools the worship may not be distinctive of any particular denomination and the religious instruction is based on an agreed syllabus. The earliest agreed syllabus was the Cambridgeshire which was published in 1924. Other authorities followed suit and soon there were many agreed syllabuses available. The earlier syllabuses were little more than outlines but it soon became evident that teachers would welcome detailed guidance with regard to teaching method, illustration, and background material. To meet their needs, most authorities revised their syllabuses and added to their contents.

The Fifth Schedule of the Act lays down the procedure for bringing an agreed syllabus into operation. The local authority convenes a conference consisting of representatives of the Church of England, the Free Churches, the teachers' associations and the education authority. The conference has the choice of recommending the adoption of a syllabus prepared by some other authority or of drawing up its own. When the syllabus has been completed it has to be approved by the conference. Each of the four panels constituting the conference has one vote and all four must be unanimous in recommending the syllabus. If the conference fails to agree or the authority does not adopt a syllabus, the Minister may appoint a conference to draw up a syllabus.

The religious instruction provided by the agreed syllabuses differs vastly from the Scripture teaching of the earlier part of the century. Dissatisfaction with Scripture teaching had been rapidly growing and in the words of Mr. Chuter Ede, most parents 'desire that their children shall have a grounding in the principles of the Christian faith as it ought to be practised in this country'. Most agreed syllabuses concentrate on presenting the fundamentals of the Christian religion. Some people have expressed doubts whether in the present divided state of Christendom a syllabus which has been approved by all the denominations can give any doctrinal teaching which is sufficiently definite to be of value. An examination of the best known agreed syllabuses reveals the astonishing fact that the body of doctrine about which there is dispute is comparatively small when compared with the bulk of Christian belief which is accepted by all denominations.

Religious instruction is no longer limited to the beginning of the school session. In county schools it is open to inspection by H.M.I.s. This is an innovation which should do much to impress both children and teachers with the importance of the study. The religious instruction in aided schools and that given by reserved teachers in controlled schools is inspected, as in the past, under arrangements made by the denominations. For many years to come the difficulty will be to obtain a sufficient number of teachers who are both anxious and qualified to give religious instruction. Much has been accomplished by the training colleges and the vacation courses held by the Ministry. The Institute of Christian Education has provided lectures and courses and publishes each term the journal entitled *Christian Education* which contains articles designed to assist the teacher. Some of the Institutes of Education organize special study courses on the agreed syllabuses for teachers in the area they serve. All these efforts lead one to hope that there will be an appreciable rise in the standard of religious instruction in our schools.

The principle of secondary education for all has been established by the Act. All fees were abolished in maintained secondary schools after April 1st, 1945. The Act says nothing about a tripartite or any other form of organization for secondary education. It contents itself by stating the fundamental principle that the education given must be in accordance with 'the age, ability, and aptitude' of the pupil. It is the parent's obligation to see that this is carried out as regards his own children. Previously, Lord Sandon's Act of 1876 had defined the parent's duty as that of causing 'his child between the ages of 5 and 14 to receive efficient elementary instruction in reading, writing and arithmetic'. As ideas about the scope of education have become much broader, so the obligation placed upon the parent has developed. Contrary to general belief, there is no such thing in this country as compulsory school attendance. If the parent has the time, the knowledge and the skill, he is at liberty to undertake the instruction of his children himself. Alternatively he can provide a private tutor for his child or pay fees to have him educated at an independent school. Failing these, he must avail himself of the education provided in the State schools. An important innovation in the Act was the section which enabled parents to obtain the benefits of a boarding school education for their children. Some authorities have experimented by placing pupils in independent or grant-earning boarding schools, and Middlesex has recently built its own maintained boarding school. In some areas the L.E.A. has taken over grammar schools which already possessed boarding attachments, e.g. the grammar schools at Ripon, Skipton and Drax in the West Riding.

It was the failure to make certain clauses mandatory in the Act of 1918 which ultimately caused them to become inoperative. The Act of 1944 remedies this defect. It is no longer the option but the duty of a local authority to supply nursery schools or classes wherever they are deemed necessary. The continuation schools are to be revived under the name of county colleges. It is now the duty of L.E.A.s to establish county colleges for the part-time education of those pupils of 16 years of age who do not remain at the secondary school or enter an institution for higher education. The date fixed for the opening of county colleges was to be not later than 1950. Education authorities have for some time been busy with their plans for further education but because of the problems connected with the supply of buildings and teachers and the financial position of the country, it is likely that the establishment of county colleges will be delayed for some time.

One of the essential features of the Act was the raising of the school-leaving age to 15. This was to have become effective on April 1st, 1945, but as we were still at war, this was postponed for two years. As soon as conditions permit the leaving age will be raised to 16. The Labour Party pressed Mr. Butler to name a definite date for raising the school-leaving age to 16. In view of the fluidity of the situation, he very wisely refused to do so. He stated that only just over half the schools had carried out the Hadow re-organization and in rural districts the proportion was not more than 20 per cent. When the school-leaving age was raised to 15, about 391,000 additional school places would be required. To raise it to 16 would entail another 406,000 places and neither buildings nor teachers were available. Moreover the schools had lost 150,000 places as the result of enemy action and the first task was to replace these.

The raising of the school-leaving age has had consequences that were probably unforeseen. For more than a quarter of a century, strenuous efforts had been made to ensure that secondary school pupils remained at school until at least 16. These efforts had been partially successful. Parents who accepted a special place for their children signed an agreement that they would keep them at school until 16 years of age. Only in special cases of hardship were they allowed to break this agreement. Immediately the school-leaving age became 15, an increasing number of parents were anxious to remove their children from school as soon after their fifteenth birthday as possible. It is a problem that many governing bodies of grammar schools are now facing. In some cases the children who leave constitute more than a fifth of the

15-year-old age group. There is now no statutory obligation for a parent to keep his child at a grammar school after the end of the term in which his fifteenth birthday occurs. Some authorities have passed bye-laws fixing the grammar school-leaving age at 16. Curiously enough some secondary modern schools have been affected in a slightly different way. A few authorities had taken advantage of the powers conferred on them by the Act of 1918 to raise the school-leaving age to 15. As soon as the Act of 1944 passed, the school-leaving age for the whole country became 14 until it was raised in 1947.

Space forbids mention of such important topics as the extension of special school facilities, the school medical service, and the increased provision of school meals and milk. One important feature of the Act, however, cannot be omitted viz. the position of independent schools. The term 'independent school' includes all those institutions which are outside the national system and do not receive grants from the Ministry. They range from private and proprietary schools to the larger public boarding schools such as Winchester and Eton. Private schools, or as they were frequently termed, 'private adventure schools', had for many years presented a difficult problem. There was, in the nineteenth century, no legal obstacle to prevent any person from setting up a private school in part of his house. The Newcastle Commission of 1858 was seriously concerned about the large number of inefficient private schools. The Report of the Commission informs us: 'When other occupations fail for a time, a private school can be opened, with no capital beyond the cost of a ticket in the window. Any room, however small and close, serves for the purpose; the children sit on the floor, and bring what books they please; whilst the closenesss of the room renders fuel superfluous, and even keeps the children quiet by its narcotic effects. If the fees do not pay the rent, the school is dispersed or taken by the next tenant'.[1]

The Report of the Newcastle Commission contains many examples of crowded, insanitary and inefficient establishments, some of which were so bad that one is tempted to ask why parents should choose to send their children to be educated in such wretched places. The Commissioners were quite alive to the main reason. It was the belief of parents that to pay fees for one's children's education was a mark of respectability. In other words it was snobbery which

[1] *Newcastle Commission Report*, vol. I, p. 94. H.M.S.O., 1861.

accounted for the existence of these institutions. Although the Report passed severe censure on the private adventure schools and the ill-qualified people who taught in them, it did not recommend any drastic action. Hence when in 1870 the Government instructed Sir J. Fitch and Mr. Fearon to investigate the state of education in the four towns of Liverpool, Manchester, Leeds and Birmingham, the reports they made on certain private schools showed that the situation had not improved.[1] The expansion of the Board Schools had a salutary effect on the private schools. The very worst examples disappeared through lack of patronage but even in the present century many private schools lag far behind those in the national system as regards amenities and standards of instruction.

One should not jump to the conclusion that all private schools are inefficient. Many are excellent and in the past took advantage of the offer of inspection made by the Board of Education and so were able to include in their prospectuses the words, 'Inspected by the Board of Education'. This was a guarantee to parents that the school was an efficient establishment. There was, however, no compulsion on a school to open its doors to the inspector and the machinery for closing an inefficient school worked slowly and cumbrously. No register of private schools was kept so that it was only possible to guess at their number. It was estimated that there were nearly 10,000 such schools, of which over 4,000 had never been inspected. The Education Act of 1918 had laid down that all private schools were to be registered and inspected, but this clause was not enforced.

The Education Act of 1944 did not aim at the destruction of independent schools. Mr. Butler was convinced that a variety of institutions for the education of children was an advantage to the nation and that the parent ought to have the right of choosing the school to which he desired to send his children and of paying fees for them. On the other hand, it was a manifest duty of the State to guarantee to the parent that the school he selected gave a sound and efficient training. Hence the Act required all independent schools to be registered and open to public inspection. The Ministry was unable to bring this section of the Act into operation immediately because of the shortage of H.M.I.s and because the difficulties in regard to building materials made it unreasonable for a school to improve its deficiencies within a fixed

---

[1] S. J. Curtis, *op. cit.*, pp. 273-5 contains typical instances.

time. The situation is now slightly eased and the inspection of independent schools began in March 1949 and has continued at the rate of about 150 a month.

The Act requires an independent school to apply for registration and in the first instance, until inspection has taken place, the school is placed on the register provisionally. If the report of the inspector is satisfactory, the registration is confirmed by the Minister. Schools may be refused registration on the grounds of the unsuitability of the buildings, insufficient accommodation, an unsatisfactory standard of instruction, and the unsuitability of the proprietor or the staff. In such cases the proprietor is served with a 'notice of complaint' which allows him six months to remedy the defects of the school. He has also the right of appeal to an Independent Schools Tribunal which consists of two panels, the legal panel being appointed by the Lord Chancellor, and the educational by the Lord President of the Council. Officials, whether of the Ministry or of a local authority, cannot be appointed to the tribunal. Any person who keeps an unregistered school or who, having been disqualified to act as a teacher, accepts employment in a school, is liable to severe penalties.[1]

Mr. Butler secured that certain schools or classes of schools would be exempt and would be automatically registered. He had in mind the schools which had been reguarly inspected and had been found to be efficient. Some members of the Labour Party objected to this on the ground that certain schools were being favoured. Mr. Butler replied that this was merely a labour-saving device. The Ministry would have sufficient to do in inspecting schools which had never been visited before. It would be a waste of time and money to inspect schools which were already known to be efficient. Some critics objected to the existence of schools outside the State system. A strong argument in favour of these schools is that they possess opportunities for carrying out educational experiments which would be difficult, if not impossible, to conduct in maintained schools. The experiments in school discipline and government and in regard to the curriculum which are being tried out in the so-called

[1] It is interesting to note how conditions have become reversed. Before the nineteenth century, schoolmasters had to be licensed by the Church, which exercised full responsibility for education. This power has now passed to the State, which now takes responsibility for the recognition both of schools and teachers. The licensing of grammar school masters was discontinued in 1869, as a result of the Schools Inquiry Commission.

'progressive schools' are a case in point. The independent public schools form a special category which will be discussed in the following chapter.

Contrary to expectations, the legislation of 1944 has not so far appreciably lowered the number of private schools but has rather made for their increase. Many parents have discovered that the Act has faced them with a difficult problem. They wish to obtain a grammar school education for their children but this is not possible unless the children have been selected by means of the tests used for grammar school entrance. The other possible avenue for obtaining a traditional secondary school education is that of the public and direct grant school. Most of these schools have long waiting lists and competition is so severe that a boy or girl who failed to pass the test for grammar school selection would have little chance of satisfying the entrance requirements of a public or direct grant school. Hence a number of private schools, fashioned on the pattern of the grammar schools, have come into existence. The provisions as regards registration and inspection guarantee their efficiency.

Although the Education Act of 1944 contains a number of provisions which are open to criticism, it may justly be said that, taken as a whole, it constitutes the most important single advance ever made in English education. Already certain misunderstandings have been cleared up and obscurities more clearly defined by the Acts of 1946 and 1948 and no doubt other minor modifications will occur in the future. The Act has completed the revolution that has been taking place in the conception of national education. For the first time the nation will possess a fully co-ordinated system of schools based on the idea that education is a progressive development through the successive stages of primary, secondary, and further education. The provision of free secondary schooling for all children has been secured. One may have doubts whether the provision of part-time further education in the county colleges is the most adequate solution of the problem, but most people would acknowledge that it is at least a definite step in the forward direction. The most serious difficulties are of a practical kind, namely, those which are being encountered in making the Act operative in the fullest sense. It is one thing to legislate but quite another to ensure that the enactment is implemented in the spirit in which it was intended. Therefore it is essential for the nation to insist that those clauses which have not so far been carried out do not suffer a fate similar to those of 1918.

For many years one of the most serious problems is that caused by the shortage of building materials and of labour. This has been temporarily complicated by the raising of the school leaving age and the 'bulge' which is the result of the increased birthrate after the war. At present the first priority is housing and until the nation has been fully supplied with a sufficient number of houses, the building of schools cannot proceed at more than a very modest pace. The uncertainties of the international situation which call for a partial rearmament are not likely to help matters. The post-war financial condition of the country is another adverse factor. The Ministry of Education has already discovered that the scales laid down by the Regulations prescribing Standards for School Premises, 1945, are at present too ambitious and costly and modifications have been introduced to reduce the cost per school place. Other changes in the direction of greater economy may be forced upon the Government in the near future.[1]

Looking at the situation as a whole, one is driven to the conclusion that certain ideals must be temporarily shelved and that the most effective means of securing progress will be that of deciding upon a system of priorities. Doubtless there will be great differences of opinion about which things should come first, so that the following suggestions are merely tentative. One principle, however, seems to be an overriding one; flesh and blood are more important than bricks and mortar. In other words, although a well trained enthusiastic teacher can produce wonderful results in an inadequate environment, yet an indifferently qualified teacher or one who is discontented will be nothing more than a drag upon progress. Thus the first priority seems to be concerned with the teaching profession. It is essential that the supply of teachers should be maintained. During the war, various estimates ranging from 50,000 to 120,000 were made in regard to the numbers required for the reorganized schools. The Ministry decided that 70,000 was the minimum and the Emergency Training Scheme was launched in 1943 to obtain men and women teachers from the Forces and from others engaged in national service. In co-operation with the local authorities emergency training colleges were opened in different parts of the country. Those

[1] See Appendix, p. 311.

who wished to enter the teaching profession by this route were interviewed and if they were approved as satisfactory they were awarded a place in one of the new colleges. The course lasted for one year only but it was more intensive than that of the two-year training college. After its completion, the young teacher was required to follow a programme of directed reading to extend his academic background. It should be noted that many of the successful applicants had not attended a secondary school. Local authorities arranged special courses of instruction for their emergency teachers.

The type of individual obtained by this means was admirable as regards character, personality, and enthusiasm. Many had taken an active part in Service education and they brought to their teaching a mind filled with new ideas and unrestricted by the fetters of tradition. The weakness of the scheme lay in the short period allowed for training and the lack of an adequate academic background. It was hoped that these deficiencies would be made good by attendance at suitable refresher courses. The Emergency Training Scheme has now come to an end. Some of the colleges have been retained as normal two-year training colleges but the majority have been closed. Even now the supply of teachers, especially that of women in nursery and infant schools, and science graduates in secondary schools, is a source of anxiety. Training colleges and university departments have been urged by the Ministry to admit students up to their full capacity.[1]

The supply of teachers is only one factor that has to be considered. The other is an economic one but nevertheless one of outstanding importance. In order to attract the right type of man and woman to the profession, salary conditions should be at least equivalent to those in other walks of life. Since the war, the Burnham scales had been twice revised but even then teachers justly complained that they were hardly treated in comparison with other professions. The danger that threatens is twofold. On the one hand, there is a growing shortage of well trained science graduates. A graduate student who has obtained a good honours degree in a science subject finds that the rewards offered by industry

[1] A full account of the Emergency Scheme for the Training of Teachers in England and Wales is given in *Challenge and Response*, Ministry of Education Pamphlet No. 17. H.M.S.O., 1950. Out of 124,000 applicants, 54,000 were accepted for training. Taking into account withdrawals and transfers to two-year training colleges, the scheme has provided about 35,000 teachers, of whom 23,000 are men.

are more adequate than those to be gained by teaching. The consequence is that many of the best qualified men never contemplate teaching as a career. The tendency will be for the teaching profession to become the refuge for those who are not sufficiently qualified to be offered well-paid posts in industry or in the administrative services. If this continues over a number of years the result will be the recruitment of mediocrities. The other danger is the discontented frame of mind of those already in the profession. The rising cost of living and the incidence of high taxation have seriously affected many teachers, especially those who have to maintain dependants. Some have taken up part-time work of a non-educational character in order to make ends meet.

The Government expressed sympathy with the teachers but at first decided against any modification of the present Burnham scales. As a result of repeated representations made by the teachers through their professional associations, a new award was announced by the Burnham Main Committee, November 1st, 1950. The basic salary scales for qualified teachers which date from April 1st, 1951 are as follows: Men: £375–£18–£630 and Women: £338–£15–£504 as compared with the previous scale of Men: £300–£15–£555 and Women: £270–£12–£444. Additions for experience gained prior to qualification remain as under the old scale. Graduates now receive an addition at the minimum and maximum of £60 for men and £48 for women as compared with £30 and £24 respectively. The additional increment for a first-class honours degree has been discontinued. Certain modifications have also been made in regard to the salaries of head teachers. The allowances paid to teachers awarded posts of special responsibility have been completely changed. They are now based upon a formula which was used in the 1948 revision for determining the amount of head teachers' allowances and which depended upon the 'unit total' for the school. In addition the Burnham Committee recommended the establishment of a pool from which 'to supplement special allowances to assistant teachers in cases where the authority considers the amount provided by the formula to be inadequate to meet the needs of the school'. Teachers' associations have accepted the revised scales, though not without considerable criticism. It remains to be seen whether the flow into industry of highly qualified graduates will be arrested.

The next priority seems to be that connected with the size

of classes. There are still classes with over 40 and even over 50 pupils. Modern psychology has emphasized the necessity of individual treatment of pupils but this recommendation can only be an idle dream until large classes are abolished. The natural solution seems to be that of reducing the size of classes in stages, first to a maximum of 35 and then to 30. As regards buildings, the first necessity is to see that the new housing estates are supplied with schools and that those buildings which are hopelessly out of date are replaced. Apart from this we shall have to grow accustomed to the idea that the completion of local authorities' development plans will be an operation extended over ten, fifteen, or even twenty years.

Re-organization in rural districts brings with it additional financial burdens. When an all-standard village school becomes a primary school, the pupils over 11 are directed to the appropriate grammar or modern school. This may entail a journey of as much as ten or fifteen miles. The transport of children by bus and in some cases by taxi is a very expensive item, though costs may be reduced when more secondary schools are available and the school bus services become more effectively co-ordinated. When the children have reached school, they have to be supplied with a mid-day meal. In large schools which possess their own kitchens, the meal can be cooked on the premises, but in the case of many rural schools, heavy expense is incurred by transporting cooked meals in containers. Again, the cost will fall as central canteens become more numerous and a reduction of the distances meals have to be carried becomes possible.

While the provisions of the Act of 1944 were being debated in Parliament, two committees were engaged in making recommendations which have since exerted a profound influence upon our educational system. The first of these was the Committee of the Secondary Schools Examinations Council appointed in 1941 under the chairmanship of Sir Cyril Norwood. The Norwood Committee reported in 1943. Its terms of reference were, 'to consider suggested changes in the Secondary School curriculum and the question of School Examinations in relation thereto'. It was the Norwood Committee which in the words of Mr. H. C. Dent, 'transformed tripartism from a proposal into a doctrine'. The Report called for a broadening of the conception of secondary education which would include many types of secondary school. 'At the beginning of the century secondary education meant grammar school education; forty years later secondary education officially so recognized and named means the education provided in secondary schools which inherit the grammar school tradition. In these years, however, secondary education has gradually altered its meaning so as to denote a stage in the educational process rather than a type of educational programme. This alteration has been brought about, partly, by change in educational theory and ideals, partly, by the increased demand for a stage of education which would go beyond the "elementary" or primary stage'.[1]

The Report decided upon somewhat flimsy evidence that the tripartite organization of secondary education was both rational and natural. Thus it says: 'The evolution of education has in fact thrown up certain groups, each of which can and must be treated in a way appropriate to itself. Whether such groupings are distinct on strictly psychological grounds, whether they represent types of mind, whether the differences are differences in kind or in degree, these are questions which it is not necessary to pursue. Our point is that rough groupings, whatever may be their ground, have in fact established themselves in general educational experience, and the recognition of such groupings in educational practice has been justified both during the period of education and in the after-careers of the pupils'.[2]

Seldom has a more unscientific or more unscholarly attitude disgraced the report of a public committee. One would imagine that the very questions raised in the above quotation and which are then thrust aside as being of little consequence, were the essentials about which answers should have been secured before planning a re-organized scheme of secondary education. The argument of the Report is a purely empirical one. Past experience seems to suggest certain groupings; irrespective of psychological evidence, we have made up our minds what they are, and having adopted this classification, our next business is to devise secondary schools to fit our pre-conceived scheme. The Report then proceeds to describe the characteristics of the grammar, technical and modern school pupil and to allot a different kind of curriculum to each type. The suggestion of the Committee seems to be that the Almighty has benevolently

[1] *Curriculum and Examinations in Secondary Schools*, p. 14. H.M.S.O., 1943.
[2] *Ibid.*, p. 2.

created three types of child in just those proportions which would gratify educational administrators. The problem is not such a simple one as the Norwood Report would have us believe. There are good grounds for making a rough and ready distinction on a bipartite basis, but if one wishes to be more accurate and to base conclusions on psychological evidence, one would discover that more than two or even three types would have to be considered. The fact is that the tripartite arrangement of secondary education had been implicit in our administration ever since the Taunton Commission recommended three grades of secondary school. It began as the outcome of the social and economic stratification of nineteenth century society, and becoming more firmly lodged as educational administration developed, it was an easy matter to adopt it and then to look for reasons to bolster up what had become an established practice.

The simplest and most natural classification is a broad division between those pupils who are bookishly inclined and those in whom practical interests are predominant. Even this twofold division becomes an unreal architectonic if one does not allow for considerable overlapping between the types. A bipartite scheme would have gone a long way towards securing parity of esteem for the modern school. As it is, one embarks upon the rather hopeless task of persuading pupils and parents that the modern school is something more than an establishment which caters for those who are considered not to be good enough for the grammar or technical school. All educationists know that the modern school stands for something very different from this but the difficulty is to bring this home to parents and pupils. The differences between the so-called grammar and technical types seem to be those of degree rather than of kind and there appears to be no reason whatsoever why the grammar school in its higher forms should not provide courses biased in an academic, technical, or commercial direction. In fact, before the war, many grammar schools possessed flourishing engineering departments. The decision had been made but it is significant that the Ministry in the pamphlet entitled *The New Secondary Education* (H.M.S.O. 1945), whilst adopting the tripartite arrangement recommended by the Spens and Norwood Reports, relents so far as to admit that experiments in other forms of organization could profitably be made.

The Norwood Committee considered the feasibility of multilateral schools but like the Spens Committee they thought that the technical high school would lose much if its relations with local industry were severed. 'Nothing should interfere with that relationship, and it is very doubtful whether it could be maintained unless the technical school were free to direct its own destiny.'[1] Hence, in the absence of relevant evidence to the contrary, the combination of the grammar and technical school was pushed aside, though it was admitted that 'a two-type school combining grammar school and modern school seems to be satisfactory in certain circumstances.'

The Norwood Report accepted the age of 11 plus as the most suitable for transfer from primary to secondary education but it suggested two modifications of importance. The age 11 plus was described as a convenient administrative term to denote children of 10 plus to 12 plus 'in whose interest transfer to secondary education should be accelerated or delayed'. Many psychologists had pointed out that 11 plus is often too early an age for discovering the special aptitudes and abilities of pupils. Hence it was to be expected that mistakes would be made however careful the process of selection. It would follow, therefore, that some machinery for rectifying mistakes should be devised. Hence the Report recommended 'that for an average two years after entry to the secondary school the pupil should belong to a "Lower School", placed in the general control of a master or mistress responsible to the head master or head mistress. This master or mistress would be charged with special oversight of the work of the forms comprising the lower school; besides co-ordinating the teaching, in which he would share, he would have the special duty of observing the progress and development of the individual pupils; he would recommend that after due allowance of time pupils for whom the higher forms of that school could not offer a suitable curriculum should be transferred elsewhere.'[2] In short, the first two years in the secondary school would be a period of diagnosis. This was a fruitful recommendation but its full value would not be realized if any member of the school staff were selected to take charge of the lower school. The teacher in charge should be a person who had received special training for the purpose so that he possessed the necessary psychological knowledge for carrying out the diagnosis effectively. Furthermore, the lower school

[1] *Ibid.*, p. 19.
[2] *Ibid.*, p. 18.

should not be considered an integral part of the main school; it should be looked upon for what it is, a diagnostic school and a kind of clearing house for the different types of secondary school. The Ministry did not encourage the idea of a diagnostic school, so that although most local authorities undertake a review of 'misfits' at 13 plus, very few have established anything further. In the following chapter the problem of bringing the public schools into relation with those in the national system is discussed. The reader will see that the suggestion of a diagnostic period would be valuable in regard to the problem of overcoming the discrepancy between the ages of entry to the public schools and the maintained grammar schools.

The other fruitful suggestion of the Norwood Report was that of a break of six months 'in which boys and girls between the ages of 18 and 19 years would render public service interpreted in a broad sense. . . . Before this break comes, pupils going on to universities and other places of advanced study would have taken the examinations necessary to secure admission and financial aid, and would take up residence after the period of service.'[1] The need for building up an adequate defence system in post-war England has necessitated the retention of conscription for boys after the age of 18. Boys who propose to enter a university are usually deferred until they have completed the university entrance requirements. At present they are allowed to choose between performing their national service before entry or of deferring it until they have completed the university course.

At first the general opinion was that the former alternative was preferable. It was urged that some small loss as regards academic subjects would be inevitable but that this would be compensated for by the greater maturity of mind and the deeper knowledge of the world and of human nature that the young person would bring to his university studies. Experience of men who have returned from national service has caused this view to be modified and at a recent universities' conference many speakers considered that national service should be deferred until the student has completed his university course. It was argued that this would be to the benefit of both the universities and the Services. Much was said about the sense of frustration experienced by boys during their period of service for which both the Army and the attitude adopted by some parents would have to accept

[1] *Ibid.*, p. 16.

responsibility. A boy of 18 enters the university at a very impressionable age at which his studies will exercise a strong influence upon his mind and character. He will leave the university as a grown man who will enter upon his service with a greater understanding of what it involves. It is obvious that no hard and fast rule can be laid down. Much depends upon the individual boy and it would be unwise to try to secure uniformity in this matter.

The Norwood Committee considered very carefully the problems of school examinations. The Report recommended that 'in the interest of the individual child and of the increased freedom and responsibility of the teaching profession, change in the School Certificate Examination should be in the direction of making the examinations entirely internal, that is to say, conducted by the teachers at the school on syllabuses and papers framed by themselves'.[1] As this change would be a drastic one, it was felt advisable to recommend a transitional period during which the School Certificate Examination would be carried out by the existing examining bodies and supervised by a standing committee of eight teachers, four members of local authorities and four university members with four H.M.I.s as assessors. The schools should be free to submit their own syllabuses and no restrictions as to choice of subjects, as under the group system, would apply. The transition period should be seven years and when it came to an end, the whole problem could be reviewed and if feasible, a change to a wholly internal examination could be effected.

To meet the requirements of the professions and of university entrance, a school leaving examination should be conducted twice a year for pupils over 18. This would take the place of the Higher School Certificate examination. Pupils would offer for examination the subjects they required for their particular purpose. As regards university scholarships, the Committee felt that the aid given to students was both inadequate and unevenly distributed. The view expressed was that 'the winning of a college scholarship at Oxford or Cambridge or a University scholarship elsewhere should in itself constitute a claim upon public funds for assistance towards the cost of living at the university, subject to evidence that such assistance is necessary. The cost of living should be so estimated as to cover all the expenses incidental to full participation in the many-sided life of

[1] *Ibid.*, p. 140.

the university. There should be no need for a successful candidate to search round for means of supplementing the college or university award. Such scholarships should be awarded for three years and should be extended on sufficient cause being shown'.[1]

It was therefore recommended that State and Local Authority scholarships should be awarded, in the first instance, on the results obtained by candidates in the examination held in March by the university examining bodies. The latter would recommend to L.E.A.s and special boards would be constituted to interview these candidates. Considerable weight would be attached to the school record of the candidate. The Ministry of Education would then make the awards. In addition to State Scholarships, L.E.A.s would have the power of making further awards to suitable candidates. The State would pay half the cost of the local authority awards. Many L.E.A.s had for some years past granted loans to assist university entrants. The Committee did not favour this practice because the repayment of the loan threw a heavy burden on the student.

Finally the Report suggested that the time was ripe 'to change the name by which the inspectorate is known, since that name carries with it from far-off days associations which the teaching profession does not welcome'.[2] The reference was to the antagonism between teachers and inspectors which had been created by the Revised Code. It was considered that the inspectorate should be named 'His Majesty's Educational Advisory Service' since 'such a title would then more closely correspond to their true function and the change of name only represents the change which has taken place in practice in the last two generations'.

The Ministry carefully examined the recommendations made by the Norwood Report in regard to the public examination system and as a result, the Minister of Education, Miss Ellen Wilkinson, reconstituted the Secondary Schools Examination Council to make it more fully representative and asked it to advise on the future of examinations in secondary schools. The Council met under the chairmanship of Sir Philip Morris and issued its report in 1947. Certain principles that should govern future examinations were suggested. The secondary school curriculum should be

[1] *Ibid.*, p. 37.
[2] *Ibid.*, p. 53.

designed with appropriate variety of subjects and treatment to suit the ages, abilities, and aptitudes of pupils. In the higher forms, the school course should bear some relation to the kind of career chosen by the pupil. Those pupils who showed that they were able to profit by further full-time education should be encouraged to stay at school beyond the age of 16. Excessive or premature specialization should be deprecated and the valuable conception which was expressed by the term 'Sixth Form work' should be retained.

The practical proposals of the Council were as follows. On leaving school, the pupil should be given a school report which should contain as complete information as possible about his work, his abilities, and his potentialities. Objective tests should be periodically given within the school and the results should be recorded in the school record and used to guide the pupil towards a suitable course of study or type of employment. As recommended by the Norwood Report, the School Certificate and Higher School Certificate examinations should be discontinued and their place would be taken after 1950 by a new examination for a General Certificate of Education. The papers should be set at three levels—ordinary, advanced and scholarship—and the group system should be abolished. The certificate issued to a successful candidate would record the subjects and the level at which he satisfied the examiners. The Pass at the ordinary level would become roughly equivalent to the credit standard at the School Certificate examination and a Pass at the advanced level would approximate to a pass in a principal subject at the Higher School Certificate. It was desirable in view of university awards that the results of the examination should reach the Ministry of Education by August 1st. This would mean placing the examination earlier than had been customary, probably in May. The original recommendation was that candidates should not be allowed to enter for the examination before the age of 17 but when the Minister (Mr. G. Tomlinson) approved the findings of the Council, he took into account the comparatively small numbers of pupils who remained at school until 17. Accordingly, as a provisional measure, he fixed the minimum age at 16. The Minister's decision provoked much criticism on the grounds that the minimum age requirement would unduly handicap the brilliant pupil who had the ability to pass the examination before he reached the age of 16. The claim that the new examination system will tend to eliminate cramming and premature specialization is one that can only be substantiated after some years of experience of the change. The subjects offered by candidates who intend to proceed to a university will be governed by the entrance requirements of each institution.

The second important Committee which met during the latter period of the war was that under the chairmanship of Sir Arnold McNair. It was concerned with the training of teachers and youth leaders and it reported in 1944. Until 1930 the examination for the Teachers' Certificate had been conducted by the Board of Education. In that year a change was made and the training colleges were organized in groups, each group being associated with its appropriate university or university college. The idea of this scheme was to develop a closer relationship between the universities and the training colleges. Joint examination boards containing representatives of the university and its associated training colleges were established. Boards of studies, on which both the university and the training colleges were represented, were set up. Their business was to draw up and approve syllabuses and to appoint the examiners. The Board of Education continued to examine practical teaching, physical training, and other practical subjects. The high hopes entertained with regard to the new scheme did not materialize, and the McNair Committee came to the conclusion that the joint board system was not working as intended. It neither brought about the desired co-operation between the universities and the training colleges nor between the training colleges themselves. Hence it was proposed to appoint a Central Training Council for England and Wales consisting of three to five members with the duty of advising the Board of Education about bringing into existence that form of training service which the Report should recommend and which the Board would decide to adopt.

Although the Committee agreed to the proposal for constituting area training organizations, the exact form these should take produced a definite divergence of opinion. One half of the Committee favoured what is generally known as Scheme A which involved the establishment of University Schools or Institutes of Education. The supporters of this view admitted that this involved a 'major constitutional change' in the organization and administration of the education and training of teachers. They realized that the institution of University Schools of Education 'will demand of the universities a richer conception of their responsibility towards education: it will also involve additional staff, both teaching and administrative. On the other hand, we are not proposing that the universities should burden themselves with detailed administration, but rather that they should accept responsibility for the general supervision of the training of teachers and that in that task they should have the active partnership of those already engaged in the work and of others who ought to be engaged in it'.[1]

Some universities were seriously concerned about the major constitutional change involved in accepting Scheme A and preferred as an alternative the extension and modification of the joint board system which has come to be known as Scheme B. In this arrangement, the university department of education and the training colleges maintain their separate identity, but their work is integrated by a joint board. The majority, however, adopted Scheme A but since conditions in different universities varied considerably, minor differences exist in the arrangements adopted. The general plan has been to establish a University Institute of Education to which is given the function of co-ordinating in the university area the work of teacher training and of promoting and providing facilities for study and research in education. The governing body of the Institute is the Board of the Institute on which the university, the training colleges, and the local education authorities are represented according to a scheme specified in the ordinance which constitutes the Institute. The actual day by day work is the function of the Professional Committee and discussion of syllabuses of instruction is carried on in the boards of studies. The teaching profession is represented on the Board of the Institute and on the Professional Committee and two assessors are appointed by the Ministry of Education. They can contribute to the discussions but they have no voting power. The Board and the Professional Committee have numerous sub-committees which deal with such matters as lectures and courses, the Institute library, research, apparatus, and school text books.

The Institute awards certificates in education to candidates from member institutions who have satisfied the examiners and it is responsible for recommending the successful candidates to the Ministry for the award of the status of 'qualified teacher'. In accordance with the recommendations of the

Report on Teachers and Youth Leaders, p. 50. H.M.S.O., 1944.

McNair Committee, the Ministry of Education now only recognizes one grade of teacher, namely, that of qualified teacher. The Institute organizes refresher courses for acting teachers and also provides instruction of a more advanced nature which leads to various diplomas, such as the diplomas in infant or religious education, or in educational administration. In order to carry out its functions effectively, it is essential that the Institute should be housed in a suitable building equipped with library and conference rooms. So far, because of lack of accommodation, this has rarely been possible and the Institutes have had to make do with what buildings are available at the time and then to move into more commodious quarters as these become vacant.

The McNair Report suggested that the diploma in education, issued to graduate students in university education departments, should disappear and that the award of a diploma should be resumed for candidates who seek an advanced qualification following the initial one. This suggestion has caused a good deal of discussion in university education departments. It has been argued, with considerable justice, that the course of the graduate student differs widely from that given in the two-year training college and that the three-year degree curriculum possesses a particular value for the work which most of these students will undertake. In other words, the academic side of the training college student's course is so different from the normal degree studies of the university that it is impossible to equate the two and that a grave injustice would be committed if the same professional qualification was awarded to both types of candidate. On the training college side it is urged that the existence of two different professional qualifications would split the unity of the teaching profession. A compromise has been suggested to the effect that the graduate's certificate should be inscribed 'graduate' or 'post-graduate certificate'. As regards splitting the unity of the profession, this compromise would seem a distinction without a difference.

The McNair Committee considered at length the problem of the recruitment and supply of teachers in the post-war period. It was thought that not only would it be an advantage if the work and prospects of the teaching profession were more widely publicized in the upper forms of the grammar school, but that older men and women should be attracted. Their initial salaries ought to be based on their age and previous experience. The conditions of service should be improved and there should be a simple basic scale of salaries for teachers in all types of schools. Special qualifications and experience ought to be recognized by additional increments to the minimum and maximum salaries, and allowances for posts of responsibility should be more widely distributed than at present. The 'Pledge' system, under which entrants to training colleges or universities received a two or four years' grant on the condition that they declared it was their bona fide intention to take up teaching as a profession, should be discontinued as soon as possible. The Ministry urged upon local authorities the advisability of making more general use of local authority awards. It was felt that the undergraduate when entering upon his degree course should not be earmarked for a particular profession. The local authorities asked, on financial grounds, for a postponement of the abolition of the pledge, but it is the intention of the Ministry that the four year grant system should come to an end as quickly as possible. [1]

The recommendations of the McNair Committee regarding salaries were considered by the Burnham Committees and a new scale of salaries came into force on April 1st, 1945. Its main principle was the single basic salary for all qualified teachers irrespective of the type of school in which they taught. Extra allowances were granted for additional qualifications and experience. Graduate teachers and heads of grammar schools were not satisfied with the increases because they felt that their special qualifications and experience were not sufficiently rewarded. The rising cost of living necessitated further revisions of the salary scales in 1948 and in 1950.

The McNair Committee paid special attention to the development of the Youth Service. Like so many important movements, the Youth Service started in the Nineteenth Century under the stimulus of voluntary effort. Thus the Y.M.C.A. was founded in 1844, the Y.W.C.A. in 1853, the Boy Scout Movement was founded by Lord Baden-Powell in 1908 and the Girl Guides originated in 1910. These voluntary organizations, together with youth clubs associated with the religious denominations, did most valuable work but they were restricted in their influence to a limited section of the adolescent community. It was not until the period of

[1] The four year grant has been abolished for candidates entering in 1951 and after.

the first World War that the State began to concern itself with youth organizations. The increase in juvenile delinquency during the war years induced the Home Secretary to institute a Standing Committee to investigate the problems involved and to review the work of the voluntary associations concerned with the welfare of young people. This was in 1916, but the amount of work involved delayed the publication of the report until 1920. The Education Act of 1918 empowered education authorities to make grants to youth organizations and in 1920 the Board of Education took charge of the Juvenile Organizations Committee. Local J.O.C.s were also formed but the post-war slump had a very adverse effect on the youth movement. In 1935 King George's Jubilee Trust was constituted to commemorate the Silver Jubilee and it accumulated funds to purchase playing fields for young people. The Government began to make grants for physical training and the provision of recreational facilities, and in 1937 the work of the central J.O.C. was transferred to the National Fitness Council which was sponsored by the Board of Education. At the outbreak of war, the National Fitness Council was replaced by the National Youth Committee.

From this time the development of the Youth Movement was rapid. The King, in a speech, roused considerable enthusiasm and the result was the publication of Circular 1486 of 1939, entitled *The Service of Youth*. The Board of Education urged local authorities to set up Youth Committees to survey, encourage, and co-ordinate the youth services in their areas. This was followed by Circular 1503 of March, 1940, in which the Board announced its decision to make grants covering 50 per cent of the expenses incurred by L.E.A.s in organizing their youth services. Another Circular (1516) of June, 1940, entitled *The Challenge of Youth*, definitely recognized the youth service as part of further education. The Board wisely declined to create a compulsory youth service and maintained the policy of supplementing the resources of existing voluntary organizations. Yet another Circular (1577) of December, 1941, entitled *Registration of Youth*, was concerned with boys and girls who became liable for registration by the Ministry of Labour and National Service. When boys and girls were interviewed by the Youth Committees of L.E.A.s, those who were not already associated with some youth organization or some form of Service were encouraged to join.

Various forms of pre-Service training were now available for boys and girls. During the nineteenth century, universities had organized volunteer companies and when Lord Haldane created the Territorial Force in 1907, the Officers' Training Corps had been formed. The Senior Division was attached to universities and the Junior Division to certain public and secondary schools. Junior cadets were prepared for Certificate 'A', and the Seniors for Certificate 'A' and 'B'. The aim of the O.T.C. was to supply officers for the Territorial Army and the Special Reserve. During the first World War, many O.T.C.s were expanded into officer training units, one of the best known being the Inns of Court O.T.C. In 1940, the O.T.C. was re-organized and greatly extended. The two divisions were known as the Senior and Junior Training Corps respectively, and all university students of military age and who were medically fit were required to join the S.T.C. The different establishments for universities were increased to include units other than infantry, and students were given a preliminary training to enable them to pass to an O.C.T.U. if they were suitable. When compulsory service for students ended in November, 1944, the numbers of the S.T.C. fell rapidly. The S.T.C. (now the University Training Corps) has been brought into line with the National Service scheme. Since April 1st, 1948, the U.T.C. has been an integral part of the Territorial Army and undergraduates who join are eligible for the same benefits and bounties as other members of the T.A. Students who have been members of the U.T.C. and have completed their National Service can, if they wish, carry out their Territorial obligation by returning to their university unit. The most recent development has been the formation of W.R.A.C. units in connection with the universities.

The O.T.C. had been mainly restricted to undergraduates and pupils of certain schools. As the war continued, the demands for pre-Service training increased and in 1941 the Air Training Corps was formed. This expanded rapidly since it appealed to the mechanical interests and the love of adventure, such prominent features in adolescence. Other bodies were constituted, such as a junior section of the Home Guard with a lower entrance age of 16 or 17, the Sea Cadets, and the Army Cadets. Girls could take up pre-nursing courses provided by the St. John Ambulance Brigade Cadets and the British Red Cross Society probationers.

By 1942, the President of the Board of Education decided

that the National Youth Committee had completed its work in initiating different types of youth service, and that what was needed now was an advisory council to co-ordinate the various people who were working in the service of youth. The Youth Advisory Council took the place of the National Youth Committee. The function of this body was to advise on problems submitted by the Board of Education and also to bring new suggestions to the notice of the Board. One of the first problems which had to be considered was the training of those who, for want of a better name, have been called Youth Leaders. This received special attention from the McNair Committee. Youth leaders could be broadly divided into those who gave their whole time to the work and received a salary, and the part-time workers who might be either paid or unpaid for their services. The Committee highly praised the voluntary workers and expressed the hope that the growth of a large number of professional youth leaders would not lead to a decrease in the number of part-time workers. A special three-year course was recommended for candidates who wished to take up youth work as a full-time occupation. Those who had already some experience of the work might enter upon a shorter course of training but this should not in any case be less than one year. Suggestions were made for a close association between those who were engaged in youth work and the teachers in the schools. In order to bring this about, it was considered that the salaries paid to youth leaders should be comparable with those of teachers and that the service should be pensionable. Arrangements should be made to facilitate the transfer from one kind of service to the other.

CHAPTER VI

THE PUBLIC SCHOOLS

DURING the war years the public schools formed a popular topic for discussion and seldom have such ill-informed and unintelligent opinions been expressed by supporters and opponents alike. The views which were put forward roughly fell into four groups. The first was a small group mainly composed of ex-public schoolboys who resented any kind of criticism and who honestly believed that the type of education provided in the public schools was the most perfect form that had yet been achieved. The public schools were sacrosanct and the State should not meddle with them. Any government which attempted to interfere was exceeding its authority. Some members of this group were ready to admit that minor improvements might be effected but on the whole there was nothing radically at fault with the public school system. Any criticisms levelled at it originated in envy, malice, or ignorance.

A second group asserted that the public school system was indefensible in a democratic community. It would have to go. The influence exerted by the public schools was out of all proportion to the number of pupils who were educated in them. When it came to the question of appointments to important positions, the boy from the State school was generally passed over in preference to the product from the public school. Statistics were prepared to show the relative numbers of public and non-public schoolboys who obtained key positions or lucrative appointments. The more extreme members of this group loudly expressed the opinion that there was only one remedy; the public schools should be abolished. Others would retain them but make them part of the State system.

Another small group whose views were as antagonistic as the second talked incessantly about the bad moral influence of the public schools. They asserted that the public schools gave a false sense of values. Boys were taught to regard prowess at games as the most important thing in life. The public schools were hot-beds of snobbery and in the public boarding schools even more disagreeable vices flourished. It rarely occurred to these critics that home influences might be more instrumental in causing snobbery than anything that took place in the schools. Hence they concluded that the public schools were so useless to the nation that the best policy would be to ignore them and leave them to their own devices. They would inevitably decrease in numbers and influence. The incidence of taxation upon the wealthy would see to that. Any school of outstanding merit would survive but the disappearance of the remainder would cause little loss to the nation.

Apart from these extremists, there existed a large body of opinion which was convinced that the public schools had something of great value to offer to the nation. Nothing would be gained but, on the contrary, much would be lost if they were destroyed, or handed over to the State, or left to their own devices. This party was less noisy but more constructive in thought than the other three. Many of the members of this party were public school men themselves and although they were quite ready to criticize some aspects of the public school life and curriculum, yet they believed that on the whole these institutions represented a noble tradition which stood for a type of education and training which had no counterpart anywhere else in the world. In some respects this tradition had lagged behind the times but in the past the schools had contributed their best to England and they were able to do the same in the future. At the same time, they felt that it was a serious weakness in English education that it was split into two parts, those schools which belonged to the national system and those which were outside it. Some means ought to be found for bringing the two systems together: for constructing a bridge between them without destroying that which was of value in either system. Opinions were divided as to how this might be accomplished and it was emphasized that certain links between the two systems already existed. The practical problem was how these could be strengthened and extended. In reply to the objection that the existence of a large number of schools which charged fees was a contradiction in a democratic community and represented a privilege which should not belong to any section of society, they asserted that if parents were willing to husband their resources in order to provide their children with the kind of education they wished them to have, to forbid them to do so would be an intolerable restriction upon the liberty of the individual. Donald

Hughes admirably summarized this view when he wrote, 'The public school system is part, and no insignificant part, of that decent British life and society which has been slowly and patiently built up, and I cannot believe that we shall allow it to be swept away in the days when our need for enlightened and effective education will be so urgent. We shall want, in future, not fewer, but more and better public schools'.[1]

The parties which aimed at the destruction of the public schools were guilty of committing two glaring mistakes. In the first place they spoke of the public schools as if they all conformed to a homogeneous pattern. Nothing could be more contradictory to the facts. Much greater variety existed among the public schools than in the State system. Indeed it is a pertinent criticism of the schools in the national system that there is a marked tendency to reduce them to a pattern so that each school should approximate to the impressions which result from the application of the same rubber stamp. Naturally the practice of different local authorities varies considerably but it should be a cardinal principle that the individuality of a school is at least as precious as that of the individual himself. It would be nearer to the truth to maintain that no two public schools are alike. They differ in regard to their origin, their history and traditions and in their particular purpose, and yet, in spite of these divergences, there are certain things which are common to all of them. One of the essential preliminaries to discussion would seem to be that of discovering the actual meaning that the term 'public school' possesses at the present day.

The second error of the opponents of the public school system consisted in their neglect of history. To understand the public school of the twentieth century, one would find it necessary to go back to the nineteenth and then the eighteenth centuries. Even this would be insufficient and very soon the inquirer would find himself immersed in the history of the Tudor period and after that of the Middle Ages. He would discover that the origin of the public school differed in no way from that of the endowed grammar school, in fact that the term 'public school' had undergone some significant alterations in connotation through the ages and that social changes, of which the Industrial Revolution was not the least, exerted a considerable influence upon the

[1] *The Public Schools and the Future*, p. 71. C.U.P., 1942.

development of the schools. Only when these inquiries had been made and satisfactory answers obtained, could he hope to reach conclusions which would have a direct bearing upon the controversy. As the reader has by this time discovered, this is the view taken in the present work and to justify it one must regress a long distance from the beginning of the present century.

When the public schools are considered from a purely chronological point of view, that is with regard to the date of their foundation, one finds a wide diversity. One group originated in the Middle Ages. The chief examples are, of course, Winchester and Eton, but there are also some pre-Reformation grammar schools which are now reckoned as public schools, e.g. The King's School, Canterbury, St. Peter's School, York, the King's School, Ely, Oundle, Giggleswick and Sedbergh. A large number originated in Tudor and Stuart times, either as new foundations or as re-foundations of existing grammar schools. Amongst these are such schools as Harrow, Rugby, Shrewsbury, St. Paul's, Westminster, Merchant Taylor's, Charterhouse and Christ's Hospital. The older schools passed through a period of depression in the eighteenth and early nineteenth centuries when one may truly say that the conditions of the public schools had reached their lowest. Numbers declined, recovering for short periods when a particular school came under the rule of a capable and energetic head. Thus at Winchester, although the number of scholars, i.e. boys on the foundation remained at the original figure of 70, the Commoners, i.e. pupils for whom fees were paid for their commons or residence, fell to eight in 1751. It is said that when Dr. Samuel Butler became headmaster of Shrewsbury in 1798, there were only two boys in the school. The revival of the public schools was the consequence of the work of a group of outstanding headmasters among whom were Thomas James and Thomas Arnold of Rugby, and Samuel Butler of Shrewsbury. Arnold's reforms at Rugby are perhaps the most widely known because they have been popularized in *Tom Brown's Schooldays*, and the reputation he acquired had such a far-reaching influence. Not only did a number of schools model themselves upon the principles of Rugby, but members of Arnold's staff and old boys of the school were appointed to the headships of other schools and handed on the tradition. The social changes brought about by the Industrial Revolution were another important factor. In addition to the landowning class, another social group emerged consisting of the well-to-do manufacturers and merchants. The latter sought a first class education for their sons and to meet the demand a considerable number of proprietary schools sprang up. At first, these were day schools but through the spread of Arnold's influence and the development of the railway system, which made all parts of the country easily accessible, the later schools were of the boarding type. On the whole these schools were much less expensive than the older foundations and their curriculum was more varied. In a very short space of time they developed a prestige almost equal to the ancient public schools. Amongst the nineteenth century foundations were such schools as Cheltenham (1841), Marlborough (1843), Wellington College (1852) and Epsom (1855).

The outspoken criticisms of the public schools which appeared in the *Edinburgh Review* and the *Westminster Review* resulted in the appointment of the Clarendon Commission (1861–4) which investigated conditions in nine of the best known schools, and the inquiry into the remaining endowed schools was continued by the Taunton Commission (1864–8). These Royal Commissions were followed by the Public Schools Act of 1868 and the Endowed Schools Act of 1869. By this legislation, the governing bodies of the schools were re-constituted and the new schemes of government indirectly raised the efficiency and prestige of the schools. At the beginning of this century, the public schools had achieved a position of great prosperity and popularity. They were fortunate in possessing a number of headmasters of striking personality and character of whom the most influential were Edward Thring of Uppingham (1853–87) and Sanderson of Oundle (1892–1922). As the work of the latter falls within the period under review, a more detailed account of his achievements will be given later in the chapter. The curriculum of the schools had expanded. It began with the adoption of a Modern Side at Harrow in charge of Edward Bowen. Other schools followed this example with the result that the narrow classical curriculum of the early part of the nineteenth century had disappeared and adequate treatment was being given to modern subjects such as English, history and geography, modern languages, mathematics and science.

The contributions made by ex-public schoolboys during the war of 1914–18 did much to raise the prestige of the schools. In spite of the industrial depression and the financial slump which followed the war, there was an unprecedented demand for more school places. Existing schools were enlarged and new ones were established, e.g. Rendcombe, Gloucestershire, in 1920, Stowe and Canford in 1923, and Bryanston in 1928.

The date of foundation is not the only factor which is responsible for the great variety of type to be found amongst the public schools. Many were developed through the instrumentality of the religious denominations and this circumstance affected their curriculum, traditions and general character. In this connection the schools of the Woodard foundation may be mentioned: Lancing, 1848, Hurstpierpoint, 1849, and Ardingly, 1858. These were Church of England schools. Roman Catholic schools included Stonyhurst College, 1794, Ampleforth College, 1802, Downside, 1814, and Douai, 1903. There were also schools belonging to other denominations, in particular the Methodist, such as Kingswood School, Bath, founded by Wesley in 1748, and Woodhouse Grove School, West Riding, Yorks., and the schools of the Society of Friends which included Ackworth, Bootham School, York, and Leighton Park School, Reading. Hence it is quite true to say that there is no uniform pattern to which the public schools conform. There is to be found in them a greater variety than in the schools of the national system, and further differences have developed in recent years because of the financial circumstances of the schools. Whilst the larger number is independent, some schools receive direct grants from the Ministry of Education and there are also a few maintained schools amongst them.

The changes which have occurred in the meaning of the term 'public school' can only be understood after a historical inquiry and the main lines along which the development in meaning has taken place have been summarized in the admirable appendix printed in the Fleming Report (*The Public Schools and the General Educational System*, Appendix A., H.M.S.O., 1944). It is sufficient to say here that the name 'public school' was rarely employed in the Middle Ages and on the occasions it was used its meaning was not fixed. Public was sometimes used in contrast to private to indicate the difference between private tuition and the instruction given in the endowed grammar schools which were supported by local endowments and governed by a public body such as a cathedral or monastic chapter or by feoffees or trustees appointed by the will of the founder. This meaning survived the Reformation. Thus in the *Constitutions and Canons Ecclesiastical* issued in 1603 it was ordered that 'No man shall teach either in publick School, or private House, but such as shall be allowed by the Bishop of the Diocese or Ordinary of the place'. (Canon 74).

Another meaning, however, gained currency during the later Middle Ages. Some endowed grammar schools, because of conditions stated in the founder's will, limited their entrants to boys belonging to a specified class such as those who came from the neighbourhood of the school or who were descendants of the founder. Thus the schools at Kinoulton, Yorks., were open to parishioners only: 'all other clerks and strangers whatsoever being kept out and by no means admitted to the schools'. (York Episcopal Registers, June 1289). On the other hand, the charter of Giggleswick (founded 1512) ordered the master 'to teach indifferently (i.e. impartially) the poor as well as the rich, the parishioner as well as the stranger'. The latter was a public school in the sense that it was open to the public, i.e. to boys from any part of England and not merely to those belonging to a particular class or to a restricted district. According to this meaning, schools like Winchester and Eton, and in Tudor times Harrow and Rugby, were public schools. The contrast is seen by the distinction made in the Minutes of the Committee of Pious Uses at Leeds between the Free School at Leeds and the 'private grammar school at the North-end of the Great Stone Bridge'. Charles Hoole, late master of the Free School at Rotherham, when he published his book entitled *A New Discovery of the Old Art of Teaching School* in 1660, described himself as 'Teacher of a Private Grammar School in Lothbury Gardens, London'.

In the seventeenth and early eighteenth centuries, the larger public schools were usually known as the 'great schools'. By the end of the eighteenth century the term 'public' began to be applied in a restricted sense to a few of the larger endowed grammar schools. Thus Edgeworth in his *Practical Education*, 1798, advised parents to send their sons 'to large public schools, to Rugby, Eton or Westminster; not to any small school: much less to one in their own neighbourhood'.[1] This usage was officially sanctioned by the Clarendon Commission which by its terms of reference confined its investigations to the seven boarding schools, Win-

[1] *Op. cit.*, chap. xix, p. 502.

chester, Eton, Shrewsbury, Westminster, Rugby, Harrow and Charterhouse, and to the two day schools, St. Paul's and Merchant Taylors'. When the Taunton Commission was appointed, Edward Thring of Uppingham was alarmed at what he considered the danger of Government interference with the independence of the endowed grammar schools. To combat this threat, he initiated the Headmasters' Conference in 1870. The early members of the H.M.C. were Uppingham, Repton, Sherborne, Tonbridge, Liverpool College, Bury St. Edmunds, Richmond (Yorks.), Bromsgrove, Oakham, the King's School (Canterbury), Felsted, Lancing and Norwich. They were soon joined by Winchester, Eton and the older schools and as soon as new members began to ask for admission, it was thought advisable to draw up rules of membership. Conditions of membership of the H.M.C. have varied from time to time but at present if a headmaster wishes to be elected, his school must satisfy the following criteria: The School must be satisfactory as regards its freedom. As a rule it must be either an independent school or a direct grant school though certain maintained grammar schools have been accepted because they have been granted a satisfactory degree of freedom by the L.E.A. and their history and traditions compare favourably with those of other members. The school must also be satisfactory from an educational point of view, i.e. there must be a sufficient number of boys over 13 and in the Sixth a sufficient number of pupils must be prepared for the Higher School Certificate. Finally the school must each year send an adequate proportion of its scholars to the universities. At first membership was limited to 150 schools but in 1937 this number was increased to 200. At the time of the Fleming Report the H.M.C. had 182 members.

In 1941 it was thought expedient that the governing bodies of schools should form an association in which matters of common interest might be discussed. Much of the business would involve problems which were outside the sphere of the H.M.C. To meet this need the Governing Bodies' Association was formed which at the time of the Fleming Report had 149 members including the governors of nine aided secondary schools. The existence of these two associations, the H.M.C. and the G.B.A., was the occasion which produced the modern definition of a public school. When Mr. Butler was asked in July 1942 to define a public school, his reply was that the name included all those schools which are in membership with the G.B.A. or the H.M.C.

The historical inquiry also shows that the origin of the public school was in no way different from that of the endowed grammar school. The present older public schools began as grammar schools. Even before the close of the Middle Ages, certain grammar schools by reason of the scale of their foundation and the number of pupils they possessed, had acquired a position of pre-eminence. Winchester and Eton are the notable examples. To these were joined post-Reformation foundations or re-foundations such as Harrow and Shrewsbury and, later still, other grammar schools, because of the distinguished work of their headmasters, were added to the list, e.g. Uppingham owed its prestige to the achievements of Thring. In spite of Mr. Butler's definition, the ordinary person, when he hears the name public school, at once associates it with a group of about thirty large schools, either of ancient foundation or established as proprietary schools at some time in the nineteenth century. One can, therefore, on the basis of popular usage, draw a rough distinction between the larger and the smaller public schools.

It would be a mistake to assume that the public schools have no links with the secondary grammar schools which are within the national system. Christ's Hospital had always recruited its entrants from those who had attended primary schools. Most public schools possessed a scholarship scheme by means of which children from the elementary schools were given an opportunity of entrance. The late headmaster of Winchester, Canon Spencer Leeson, instituted a very generous scholarship scheme at his school. Rendcombe College, Gloucestershire, admits boys from primary and preparatory schools in almost equal numbers and at Giggleswick nearly a third of the intake is from the locality and is admitted on the results of a scholarship test. The Royal Naval College, Dartmouth, admits pupils from all types of school.

Another link was forged by the Board of Education Act of 1899 which permitted the Board to 'inspect any school supplying secondary education and desiring to be so inspected'. At first the public schools were slow in coming forward. Up to 1914, only nine had been inspected but by 1921 nine others had been included, Harrow and Rugby being amongst them. Eton and Shrewsbury were inspected in

1936 and Oundle in the following year. The institution of the School and Higher School Certificate examinations also extended the common ground. Pupils from the public schools and from the maintained grammar schools entered for these examinations and began to compete for open scholarships at the universities. A further link is afforded by the governing bodies of the public schools. Although most of these schools are controlled by independent governing bodies, in most cases public representatives including those from L.E.A.s are to be found on their boards of governors.

The public schools have also influenced the schools of the national system. Practically every grammar school has adopted the prefect system, which although it was not the invention of Arnold at Rugby, yet owes its modern development to him.[1] Most schools are organized into houses for work and games, on the model of the boarding houses of the older public schools. The development of organized games in our secondary schools received impetus from the same source and the various school societies which have now become so marked a feature in both grammar and modern schools had their prototypes in similar societies which had been deliberately encouraged by heads of boarding houses. The public schools have also had an effect on the curriculum and the teaching methods of grammar schools, e.g. the influence of Sanderson's experiments at Oundle and those of Dr. Rouse and his colleagues at the Perse School, Cambridge, in connection with the direct method of teaching modern and classical languages. Mr. Caldwell Cook of the latter school did much to popularize the Play Way method in the education of younger pupils. All these are ways in which the public schools have to a greater or lesser extent affected the schools within the national system. The present problem is how to enlarge and extend these points of contact so as to bring the two systems into a more intimate relation. This was the problem which the Fleming Committee set out to solve in 1942 and in the Report of 1944 a number of fruitful recommendations were offered.

[1] Prefects were employed in certain mediæval schools. The statutes of William of Wykeham provided that in each dormitory three older boys were to keep watch on the younger and report offenders to the master. Præpostors and monitors at Eton had regular duties assigned to them by at least as early as the 16th century. Colet's statutes for his re-foundation of St. Paul's used the system of form presidents, and prefects were a regular institution at Manchester Grammar School. Arnold's name is associated with the prefect system because he used it as an essential part of his policy for running the school.

The views of the Fleming Report on the subject of the public schools are of similar pattern to those already set forth in this chapter. The conclusion of the Committee was 'that the education given by the public schools includes elements of a very high educational value, especially but not entirely on the boarding side. It would, therefore, be wrong to destroy them, as the more extreme of their critics desire (by the appropriation of their endowments and the diversion of their buildings to other purposes) or to refuse to associate them in any way with the general system of education, provided that the number of boys admitted to them from primary schools is sufficient to avoid the dangers which have been discussed (e.g. the fear that boys from poorer homes would be uncomfortable and fail to adjust themselves). The problem of providing boarding education for all who can benefit will only be partly solved by this means, but the contribution of the public schools, though relatively small in numbers, would be very far from negligible in other respects. The public schools have been giving a boarding education for generations, and some for centuries, and thus they have experience in a matter where experience is of the highest importance, and they have also, in most cases, sufficient and suitable accommodation and equipment to make a sound start. Above all, they are willing and anxious to play their part and they can begin without delay. We see the risks and difficulties, but these are not sufficient to persuade us that proposals cannot be framed which will be to the immediate educational advantage of thousands of children and will be a first step towards a much greater measure of social and educational unity in the nation' (p. 56).

The last but one sentence in the above paragraph refers to an incident which is not nearly as widely known as it should be. In 1919 the H.M.C. made an offer to open their doors to elementary schoolboys. Mr. Fisher carefully considered it and expressed his gratitude for the spirit which prompted it but he regretted that at the moment he was unable to accept it because of the lack of demand for places in the public schools for ex-elementary school children. The Board of Education intimated that if, in the future, the need arose, they would avail themselves of the proposal.

The Fleming Report considered in detail how the policy it recommended could be carried out. The first step would be for the Board of Education to compile a list of schools which were not maintained by local authorities and which would be willing to play their part in association with the national system. Such associated schools would be grouped under one of two categories—Scheme A or Scheme B. Both schemes should apply equally to boys' and to girls' schools. Scheme A would consist of the present direct grant schools.[1] and although some of these were boarding schools, the majority were day schools. To be admitted as associated schools, they would either be required to abolish tuition fees or 'if tuition fees are retained, to grade them according to an approved income scale which shall provide for total remission if a parent's income requires it; and that boarding charges shall be similarly graded in all schools participating in the Scheme' (p. 64). Local education authorities should have the right to reserve at the schools a number of day or boarding places. The exact number, which would vary from school to school, would be decided by an agreement between the governing body of the school and the local authorities concerned. The tuition fees of the pupils selected would be paid by the local authorities and in the case of boarders the local authority would pay the boarding charge to the school and recover the appropriate amount from the parents according to the fixed income scale. The Board of Education would pay direct grant to the remainder of the pupils. Some of the schools in this category had been paying salaries in excess of the Burnham Scale in order to attract more highly qualified staff. They would still be allowed to do so. The teaching staff would come within the Government Superannuation Act so that their pensions would in most cases be more generous than those usually paid in independent schools. In day schools, at least one-third of the governors should be nominated by the L.E.A.s which sent pupils to the school. In boarding schools which received pupils sent by the Board of Education, the nominated

---

[1] In 1926 grant-aided schools not maintained by local authorities were given the option of receiving a capitation grant in respect of children over 11 direct from the Board of Education instead of through the L.E.A. In 1949 there were 165 direct grant schools containing 81,673 pupils in England, and in Wales four schools containing 1,541 pupils. The number of boarders in direct grant schools was: England, 7,490, Wales, 490. Direct grant schools were required to accept a minimum percentage of free or special place pupils. When fees were abolished in maintained secondary schools, all direct grant schools were asked to re-submit their claims. Some were rejected even when they had previously enjoyed direct grant status. A certain number of schools which had sufficient endowments were, by raising their fees, able to continue as independent schools.

governors would be chosen partly by the Board and partly by the L.E.A.

Scheme B would be open to such schools as the Board might accept and 'should apply only to Boarding Schools or schools having a substantial number of boarders, recognized by the Board as efficient and not conducted for private profit' (p. 65). The Board of Education would grant bursaries to qualified pupils who had spent at least two years at a grant-aided primary school, to enable them to proceed to boarding schools. The bursaries would cover tuition and boarding fees and the amount would be graded according to an approved income scale with total remission where necessary. Schools under this scheme would be required to offer a minimum of 25 per cent of their annual admissions to pupils from primary schools. The scheme of admission should be reviewed every five years. Local authorities, as in Scheme A, would be able to reserve places at particular schools for pupils from their areas. Parents desiring a bursary would apply to the Board of Education through their local authority. They would be free to apply for any boarding school in the country which had accepted the scheme and if they wished to apply for more than one, they could indicate their order of preference. The candidates would be seen by Regional Interviewing Boards, who would send their recommendations to a Central Advisory Committee which would make the final recommendation to the Board of Education. The regional boards should consist of about four members and should include the head of one of the public schools which participated in the scheme, a head teacher of a primary school, and a representative of a local education authority.

The Fleming Committee had to consider a further problem. The age for transfer from primary to secondary education had now been fixed at 11 plus. This, however, was not the practice of most of the public schools, which generally accepted their entrants at 13. Parents who wished to send their children to a public boarding school entered them about the age of eight at a preparatory school. Some of the public schools have their own preparatory schools but as a rule the preparatory school is a separate establishment, and is in private hands. The preparatory school, as its name implies, undertakes to prepare its pupils for the Common Entrance Examination which was established in 1903. As the preparatory schools depend for their existence on the successes they obtain, most of them are highly efficient and many are inspected and recognized by the Ministry of Education. Many are boarding schools and since they do not receive a grant from public funds, they are obliged to charge high fees. The larger public schools had always set a high value on classical studies with the consequence that the normal 'prep' school course includes classics, modern languages, mathematics and science, subjects which are not taught in the State primary schools. The Fleming Committee realized that the factors mentioned above constituted a very real difficulty. Two methods of dealing with the problem were suggested. On the one hand, the decision to send a pupil to a public boarding school might be delayed until 13. He would spend two years in the lower forms of a State grammar school. If, however, the decision for transfer was made at 11, the pupil could be sent to one of the preparatory schools. The school selected should not be one which was run merely for profit and it should be recognized by the Board of Education as efficient and be approved for the purpose of receiving bursars. The problem would not have existed if the recommendation of the Norwood Report about the establishment of a lower school to every secondary school had been accepted, and these classes used for diagnostic purposes, as was suggested in the previous chapter. Two useful results would be achieved by adopting this method. In the first place, the child who was provisionally accepted by the regional interviewing board would enter a diagnostic school where he would be closely watched by experts in order to discover his special abilities and aptitudes, and at the end they would be able to report if he was the type who could profit from a public boarding school education. Recommendations from the diagnostic school would be valuable in helping the regional board to come to a final decision. Secondly, the pupils who were provisionally accepted could be given a course of instruction in the additional subjects required for public school entrance.

The Fleming Report was naturally a compromise and few people are enthusiastic over compromises. It certainly did not satisfy the extremists who wished to destroy the public school system. On the other hand, it was received rather coldly by many heads of State grammar schools. They complained that it would be a grave injustice to the grammar schools to 'cream' them of their best pupils. This attitude is somewhat selfish. Surely the good of the individual pupil is as important as that of the institution. Moreover, it is not merely the ablest pupil intellectually who is best suited to a public school. Other qualities have to be taken into account and of these character, personality and capacity for leadership may be considered quite as important as intellectual ability. It seems a valid argument that the boy who possesses these qualities should not be prevented from receiving that kind of education which is likely to foster his growth and which would accrue not only to the benefit of the individual himself but to the good of the nation as a whole. In these days of tests and examinations, a premium is apt to be placed on intelligence so that other qualities tend to be thrust into the background. It may be that intelligence and attainment are less difficult to test than the other characteristics of the individual. The Fleming Report is valuable, because although its recommendations may not meet with universal acceptance, they indicate a possible approach to the problem of bringing the public schools and those in the national system into line. Only the future can say whether the solution suggested is at once acceptable and workable.

The Fleming Report had some interesting points to make on the subject of girls' public schools. Before 1850 there were few opportunities for a girl to receive a secondary education. Most girls in well-to-do families received their education at home, either at the hands of their parents or from private governesses. Some attended private boarding schools in which they were taught deportment and such accomplishments which the Victorian age considered were likely to attract a husband. The movement to establish secondary schools for girls and to gain admittance to the universities and other institutions for higher education began in the middle years of the nineteenth century. Its pioneers are well known: Miss F. M. Buss, Miss Dorothea Beale, Miss Emily Davies and Miss A. J. Clough. The result of their efforts was the foundation of high schools for girls and the admission of women to certain courses and examinations at the universities. The effect was cumulative. Once it became possible for girls and women to receive secondary and higher education, the careers open to the sex were considerably extended. Previously a woman who did not marry had only the choice between becoming a governess or training for the nursing profession. As more and more professions became open to women, so the demand increased for the establishment of a greater number of secondary schools for girls.

The first public boarding school for girls, which was modelled on the lines of the corresponding boys' schools, was St. Leonard's School, St. Andrews, which was opened in 1877. During the following thirty years, a considerable number of similar schools were established. Some were sponsored by the religious denominations. Day schools also multiplied and one of the chief agencies which founded schools similar to the proprietary schools which had been opened for boys, was the Girls' Public Day School Company. In some cases, the Charity Commission, working with the powers conferred on them by the Endowed Schools Act of 1869, divided the endowments of certain large grammar schools so as to enable a corresponding girls' grammar school to be established. Two typical examples were those of the Leeds and the Bradford Grammar Schools. A division of the endowments and a new scheme of government made possible the foundations of the Leeds Girls' High School and the Bradford Grammar School for Girls. Following the example of the boys' schools, the Association of Governing Bodies of Girls' Public Schools came into existence in 1942. At the time of the Fleming Report, the Association comprised 80 independent and 59 direct grant schools.

The Fleming Committee considered that the scheme for associated schools would be much less difficult to initiate in the case of girls' schools. The reasons given were: (1) a girl does not gain the same advantages and social privileges as a boy from the fact of having attended a public school. (2) A much freer interchange of staff and pupils between day and boarding schools has been customary. This has been assisted by the fact that all secondary school mistresses had but one association (the Association of Head Mistresses, founded by Miss Buss and Miss Beale in 1874) whilst headmasters were split between two bodies, the Headmasters' Conference and the Headmasters' Association. (3) The girls' schools being of more recent origin than most of the boys' schools, did not possess the same strong classical tradition. There was no Common Entrance Examination and the curriculum was usually more flexible and varied than in the corresponding boys' schools. They had been accustomed to receiving girls at different ages with a previous education which varied greatly in character. Hence the Report considered that although Schemes A and B should apply to both boys' and girls' schools, in the case of the latter there was no necessity to send girls to preparatory schools.

The Report also included an interesting historical chapter on the development of secondary education in Wales together with a review of the endowed schools which had remained outside the county scheme set up by the Welsh Intermediate Education Act of 1889. It was noted that the proportion of schools which were wholly or mainly boarding was much less than in England. Another important factor was that of language. Until the latter part of the last century, the policy had been that of forcing the use of the English language upon the Welsh schools. Llandovery School, founded by Thomas Phillips in 1848, could be regarded as the reaction of Welsh nationalism to that policy. Phillips had expressly stated in the foundation deed that the school aimed at the study and cultivation of the Welsh language and literature. In the latter part of the same century, the Education Department had turned a more kindly eye upon the teaching of Welsh in the elementary schools and in 1927 the Report of the Board of Education on Welsh in Education and Life showed a warm appreciation of the language, literature and history of the Principality. All educational advance in Wales, whether in the elementary, secondary, or university spheres, had come about in response to a popular demand. Hence it was important in considering the application of the associated school scheme to Wales to ensure that the schools should not become segregated from Welsh social life. Associated schools in Wales which participated in Schemes A or B and accepted bursars from Wales should make arrangements to continue the pupils' Bilingual instruction. Otherwise, the same recommendations made with regard to English schools should apply to Wales.

It is perhaps fitting that this chapter should conclude with a brief account of the work of Sanderson of Oundle, one of the outstanding public schoolmasters of the present century. Mr. F. W. Sanderson was appointed as headmaster of Oundle school in 1892 and in the thirty years he spent there he completely changed the character of the school. Oundle School was an old foundation. It originated in the bequest of Joan Wyatt in 1485, who left property for the maintenance of a master to teach grammar. In 1556, Sir William Laxton, Lord Mayor of London and Master of the Grocers' Company, gave considerable property into the charge of the Company to support a grammar school in his native town of Oundle. When the Company found that a grammar school already existed in Oundle, it was decided to take over and develop the Wyatt foundation. The school had a somewhat chequered history. The Grocers' Company were not ideal guardians of the fortunes of a grammar school and, moreover, the proximity of the school to Rugby and Uppingham tended to restrict its development.

In the time of Sanderson's predecessor the number of boys had fallen to less than 100 and there was little to distinguish Oundle from other country grammar schools of a moderate size. It had a strong classical bias and regularly sent its best pupils to the older universities. Mr. H. G. Wells provides a vivid picture of Oundle as it was before the coming of Sanderson. He writes, 'Even in the seventies and eighties these smaller "classical" schools had a quaint old-fashioned air amidst the surrounding landscape. They were staffed by the less vigorous men of the university-scholar type; men of the poorer educated classes in origin, not able enough to secure any of the prizes reserved for university successes, and not courageous enough to strike out into the great world on their own account. They protected themselves from the sense of inferiority by an exaggeration of the value of the schooling and disciplines through which they had gone, and they ignored their lack of grasp in a worship of the petty accuracies within their capacity. Their ambition soared at its highest to holy orders and a headmastership, a comfortable house, a competent wife, dignity, security, ease, and a certain celebrity in equation-dodging or the imitation of Latin and Greek compositions. Contemporary life and thought these worthy dominies regarded with a lofty scorn'.[1]

This was true of Oundle when Sanderson was appointed. The boys led 'the normal life of boys in any small public school in England. Most of them were frightfully bored by the teaching of the bored masters; the wonderful classical master lashed himself periodically up to the infectious level of enthusiasm for his amazing exercises; there was cribbing and ragging and loafing, festering curiosities and emotional experimenting, and, thank heaven! games a fellow could understand. If these boys learnt anything of the marvellous new vision of the world that modern science was unfolding, they learnt it by their own private reading and against the wishes of their antiquated teachers. They learnt nothing in school of the outlook of contemporary affairs, nothing of contemporary human work, nothing of the social and

[1] H. G. Wells, *The Story of a Great Schoolmaster*, pp. 23-4. Chatto and Windus, 1924.

economic system in which many of them were presently to play the part of captains'.[1] This was the state of affairs that Sanderson set out to remedy when he was appointed to Oundle.

Sanderson entirely changed the character of the school, and at the time of his sudden death in 1922, it had become one of the foremost public schools of the country, containing over 500 pupils and possessing a long waiting list of applicants for entry. The increase in numbers was matched by the growth of the material equipment of the school. New boarding houses and classrooms were added but these by no means exhausted the additions made by Sanderson. New laboratories for chemistry, physics and biology were built. More significant of the change of attitude introduced by Sanderson was the provision of workshops for engineering and joinery, the erection of a machine shop, a forge and a foundry, the addition of art rooms, a museum and an observatory and experimental farm. All these were but the outward and visible signs of the new spirit which Sanderson brought into the life and studies of Oundle School.

Sanderson was not a psychologist or a student of educational theory. Like most of the great headmasters who have transformed our public schools, he was essentially a practical teacher. In this he was like Butler, Arnold and Thring. He thoroughly understood boys and the things and activities which interested them and he used this understanding in the reforms which he introduced at Oundle. On the other hand, there were certain defects in his understanding of educational aims. Thus we find in him a violent dislike of classroom studies. He often contemptuously referred to classrooms as tool sharpening rooms, necessary at a certain stage in the educational process but always subsidiary. This attitude sprang from his lack of experience of the class teaching which had developed in English elementary and secondary schools. He was also a scientist and this fact led him to stress science as affording the best example of creative thought in the service of mankind. Later in life he began to appreciate more fully the value of the cultural studies. Even science, unless it was studied from the point of view of its service to humanity, was in his eyes of little value as a school subject. It was not so much the subject that mattered but the spirit in which it was studied. Sanderson's watchwords were work, service and co-operation. He often said that the

[1] *Ibid.*, p. 27.

traditional spirit of school learning was individualistic, acquisitive and possessive, whereas it ought to be social, co-operative and creative.

Before his appointment to Oundle, Sanderson had held the post of senior physics master at Dulwich and it was while he was there that the ideas which governed his work at Oundle began to shape themselves in his mind. When he came to Oundle, neither the boys nor the staff were willing to accept his views. At first he met with strong opposition from the boys, who were encouraged in their attitude by the masters. The climax came when the pupils acted a play which contained all the bitter and insulting references to the new headmaster which presented themselves to their ingenious minds. The calm dignity with which Sanderson reacted turned the tables in his favour and from that time a different attitude to him slowly developed in boys and masters alike. Sanderson was not always so dignified and self-controlled. By nature of a choleric disposition, his indignation at what he considered the unmerited treatment afforded him would cause him to explode in a violent outburst of temper during which he would flog unmercifully. 'He was often simply and sincerely wrathful with them, and in his early years he thrashed a great deal. He thrashed hard and clumsily in a white-heat of passion—"a hail of swishing strokes that seemed almost to envelop one". A newspaper or copybook at the normal centre of infliction availed but little'.[1] A member of his staff once told the writer that Sanderson was equally enraged at the shortcomings of his assistants. He would frequently stride into a room and listen to the teaching of a master and when something occurred of which he disapproved he would shout for all to hear that he gave immediate notice to the member of his staff. Fortunately his bark was worse than his bite and after a master had been ‘sacked’ half-a-dozen times in a fortnight, he ceased to take much notice of outbursts of temper that disappeared as quickly as they came. As Sanderson grew older, he mellowed considerably and towards the end of his rule at Oundle, corporal punishment was extremely rare.

Sanderson's personal enthusiasm and his obvious sincerity enabled him to win over both staff and boys and one of the monuments to his memory is the book *Sanderson of Oundle*, a personal tribute written by members of the school staff. Like Thring of Uppingham, Sanderson believed that every boy

[1] *Ibid.*, p. 34.

had an interest in something and could do something. The problem was to find out what these things were. Hence his maxim was, 'Education must be fitted to the boy, not the boy to Education'. He realized that boys came to school to do rather than to learn and he therefore thought that the job of the school was to introduce them to practical work which must be real work and not make-believe. With these ideas in his mind, he introduced workshops, a foundry and a farm. It was not that he wanted the training received at Oundle to be vocational in the narrow sense. His pupils would rarely be farmers or engineers. He believed that these subjects appealed to the interests of boys and would therefore be a powerful medium for education. In his last lecture at University College, London, a lecture which was followed by his sudden collapse and death, Sanderson explained his aim. He told his audience, 'When I became a headmaster I began by introducing engineering into the school—applied science. The first effect was that a large number of boys who could not do other things could do that. They began to like their work in school. That led on to introducing a large number of other sciences, such as agricultural chemistry, horse-shoeing (if that is a science), metallurgical chemistry, biochemistry, agriculture; and of course, these new sorts of work interested a large number of other boys of a type different from the type interested by the old work, so we got an exceptional number of boys, curiously enough, unexpectedly liking what they had to do in school. Then I ventured to do something daring; it is most daring to introduce the scientific method of finding out the truth—a dangerous thing—by the process of experiment and research. We began to replace explicit teaching by finding out. We did this first with these newly introduced sciences. Then we began to impress the aims and outlook of science on to other departments of school life. History, for instance: we began to replace the old classroom teaching and learning by a laboratory for history, full of other books and other things required in abundance, so that boys in all parts of the school could, for some scientific purpose (not to learn; to go into schools to learn was egotistical), find out the things we required for to-day. We set them to find out things for the service of science, the service of literature, modern languages, music'.[1]

The outbreak of war in 1914 was a great blow to Sander-

[1] *Sanderson of Oundle*, p. 351. Chatto and Windus, 1924.

son. Very soon, however, he had the satisfaction of seeing the school make a signal contribution to the war effort. Oundle had the equipment to help in turning out the shells and other munitions so badly needed by our hard-pressed troops. Each form was sent in rotation into the workshops for a week and the boys not only had the satisfaction of doing something they liked but the greater joy of knowing that what they were doing was hastening on final victory. The war seemed to inspire Sanderson. He went about the country telling audiences what he was trying to do at Oundle and emphasizing the spirit of service and co-operation which he felt was so badly needed by the nation. He told the textile manufacturers of Bradford: 'One of the main aims of a good school is to see that each boy and girl is cared for, that each one has every opportunity for development. We must not cast out or send our weak ones away, we must keep them in school—we must find out what kind of work will appeal to them, so that they too may move upwards, gain in self-respect, and love their life. And we claim that this is what we would have done in all factories, or in any occupation. It is the essential duty of every nation. We are anxious that no worker should be stunted mentally or physically by the kind of work he has to do'.[1] He told the Reconstruction Council in London, 'A new type of school buildings and requirements will arise. No longer buildings comprised only of classrooms, but large and spacious workrooms. . . . Spacious engineering and wood-working shops, well supplied with all kinds of machine tools, a smithy, a foundry, a carpenter's shop, a drawing office—all carried on for manufacturing purposes. Plenty of work which will employ boys of all ages will be found to do. There will be a corresponding spacious literary and historical workshop with a really spacious library full of books: books on modern subjects as well as reference books. . . . Another block will be a science block with an engineering laboratory, machinery hall, physical, chemical, and biological laboratories—well supplied with apparatus and plant for applied science; plant, too, to lead to the investigations of the day; testing machine, ship tank, air tunnels; a miniature standardizing laboratory; and with this a botanical garden and an experimental farm. Another would be an art-room, music-room, theatre, a home of industry for studying industrial development and industrial life'.[2]

[1] H. G. Wells, *op. cit.*, p. 96.
[2] *Ibid.*, pp. 100–102.

Sanderson's projects were carried out in the environment of a large public school where money was no object, but his work has its lessons for other types of school. The grammar schools of to-day can learn much from the example of Oundle. The secondary modern school may find many of its problems answered through a study of what Sanderson accomplished.

CHAPTER VII

UNIVERSITY EDUCATION, 1900-50

IT was emphasized in the previous chapter that there is no one pattern to which the public schools may be said to conform. Each school has its own individuality which has developed as the result of its origin and history so that considerable caution should be exercised in making generalizations about the public schools. The same is even more true of the English universities. In the case of the public schools, however, it was found convenient to consider them in groups, either according to the period at which they were founded, or according to some other criteria such as whether they are day or boarding schools. If similar treatment is accorded to the universities, it will be found that they fall into three types: the ancient universities of Oxford and Cambridge; the University of London and the provincial universities and university colleges. The Scottish universities will be considered separately in Chapter IX. A certain amount of overlapping is inevitable in adopting this classification. Thus the University of Durham is a modern provincial university as regards its date of origin, but since one part of it was modelled on the pattern of the older universities, it can be thought of as belonging, in some senses, to the first and the third types.

At the end of the nineteenth century, all the modern universities were of the federal type which was represented by the University of Durham, the Victoria University, and the University of Wales. The university colleges at Birmingham, Sheffield, Nottingham, Southampton, Bristol and Reading, some of which were destined to achieve university status during the present century, really set the pattern which all the modern provincial universities, with the exception of Wales, were to follow. In addition there was in Wales St. David's College, Lampeter, which had a distinct origin and development.

Until the second decade of the nineteenth century, Oxford and Cambridge had been the only English universities. Although the mediæval period had long passed away, the older universities were, at the beginning of the nineteenth century, very largely bound by the customs, traditions and forms of government which they had inherited from the Middle Ages and had retained long after they ceased to possess value or meaning. The history of Oxford and Cambridge during the greater part of the last century centres upon the events by means of which the two universities became adjusted to the demands of the modern world. A convenient starting point from which the development can be traced is the year 1800, when the Public Examinations Statute at Oxford introduced the practice of written examinations and established the distinction between pass and honours. The story of the transformation of Oxford and Cambridge from semi-mediæval institutions to universities fitted to take their proper place in the modern world is a long and complicated one and does not belong here. It is a story which includes a period of bitter controversy both within and from outside the universities, a struggle for the abolition of religious tests and the admission of women undergraduates to degrees and it is punctuated by the activities of two Royal Commissions which bore fruit in special Acts of Parliament.[1] As a result the universities and their colleges received new statutes; additional honour schools and triposes sprang into existence; mediæval customs which had become obstacles to progress were abolished; new colleges were founded, e.g. Keble at Oxford in 1870 and Selwyn at Cambridge in 1882, and the whole system of awarding fellowships and exhibitions was completely revised.

The opening years of the present century produced a fresh set of problems which the ancient universities were obliged to face. The Education Act of 1902 had produced a rapid growth in the number of maintained secondary schools, whose pupils soon began to enter for the same university scholarship tests as members of the older public schools. The free place system made it possible for pupils from the elementary schools to enter secondary schools and then, by means of scholarships, to proceed to the older universities, to the University of London or to one of the provincial universities. As many of these undergraduates came from poorer homes, the expenses of residence at Oxford or Cambridge often prevented them from taking up a scholarship and forced

[1] Royal Commission on the Universities of Oxford and Cambridge, appointed 1850, reported 1852; followed by the Oxford University Act, 1854 and the Cambridge University Act, 1856. Also the Royal Commission on the Universities of Oxford and Cambridge, appointed 1872, reported 1874. Followed by the Oxford and Cambridge University Act, 1877.

them to accept places in the newer universities. It was for this reason that in 1907, Dr. Gore, then Bishop of Birmingham, moved in the House of Lords the appointment of a Royal Commission 'to inquire into the endowments, government, administration, and teaching of the Universities of Oxford and Cambridge, in order to secure their best use for all classes of the community'. The outbreak of war postponed the appointment of the Commission until after the Armistice but certain changes had already been occurring at Oxford through the reforming zeal of Lord Curzon, who had been chosen as Chancellor in 1907. He worked strenuously to obtain full university membership for women. This was not secured at Oxford until 1920. Cambridge admitted women to titular degrees in 1921 and accorded them full membership of the university in 1948. Lord Curzon also strove for the abolition of compulsory Greek. Cambridge was the first to abolish it in 1919 and Oxford followed a year later.

Post-war conditions brought about the appointment of the deferred Royal Commission. Before the war, Oxford and Cambridge had not received specific grants from the Treasury, though the Board of Education had paid certain sums in connection with the training of teachers and the Board of Agriculture for instruction in agriculture and forestry. The actual occasion of the appointment of the Commission was an application from the newer universities to the Chancellor of the Exchequer and the President of the Board of Education for an increase in the grants from public funds. Their plans for post-war reconstruction involved the appointment of additional teaching staff to cope with the greatly increased number of students. The sharp rise in the cost of living necessitated a revision of the salary scales and the heavy cost of materials and labour restricted schemes for reconstruction and expansion. In fact, under the changed conditions of the post-war world, the newer universities found themselves unable to carry out their task effectively without a much more generous assistance from the State. The President of the Board of Education suggested that representatives from Oxford and Cambridge should be added to the deputation. The suggestions made by the deputation were sympathetically received and the Government asked the universities, Oxford and Cambridge included, to submit to the Board of Education estimates to cover their immediate needs.

This was done but the Government felt that Parliament

needed to be convinced that the universities were unable from their own resources to find the necessary money. Hence the desirability of appointing a Royal Commission to inquire 'into the resources of the universities and colleges and the uses made of them'. It was also considered that as the problem of university government was closely allied to that of finance, this should be another object of the inquiry. The result of the negotiations was the appointment in 1919 of the Royal Commission on Oxford and Cambridge Universities, the report of which was issued in 1922. Meanwhile, as a temporary expedient, the sum of £30,000 a year was paid to each of the Universities of Oxford and Cambridge.

The recommendations of the Royal Commission were embodied in new statutes which came into force in 1926. No drastic changes were suggested. It was recommended that the numbers of the staffs at both universities should be increased so as to meet the needs of research and teaching. The Commissioners spoke very highly of the Tutorial system at Oxford and the corresponding Supervisory system at Cambridge. 'With all its characteristic difficulties, drawbacks and exceptions, which are on the increase, the system of College instruction is largely accountable for the educational achievement of the two senior Universities. The teaching of the undergraduate, man to man, by his Tutor or Supervisor, who is very often resident in college alongside of his pupil, gives to the education at Oxford and Cambridge something scarcely to be got elsewhere in such full measure'.[1] The shortage of staff was causing the college tutors to be much overworked. 'It is interesting to note that whereas the earlier Royal Commissions were concerned with providing against the indifference and want of conscientiousness of some of the Fellows, the charge now made in some quarters is that the Fellows overwork themselves at teaching and administration. However this may be, they have their reward in supplying the country with a system of higher instruction which perhaps gives more attention to the individual student than is given anywhere else. If complaint is made that education at Oxford and Cambridge costs more per man than elsewhere, one reason is that the undergraduate gets more teaching in return for his money, over and above the peculiar residential advantages'.[2]

The Commissioners were quite satisfied that if the older

[1] *Royal Commission on Oxford and Cambridge Universities*, p. 38. H.M.S.O., 1922.
[2] *Ibid.*, p. 39.

universities were to be adequately equipped to meet the responsibilities thrust upon them by a changing world, more money would be needed for libraries, museums, lecture rooms and laboratories, and the development of women's colleges and extra-mural activities. The present staff was quite inadequate to cope with the increase in the number of undergraduates and the variety of subjects demanded constituted a very grave danger to the time that could be given to research. It was essential that any increase of staff should include a proportion of professors and readers whose duties would be mainly those connected with research. Opportunities should be available for the best students to remain at the university for a period of research after graduating. The Commission felt very strongly about this point. They said, 'While, however, freely admitting the great value of all that has been accomplished, we desire now to urge upon the universities the need for making still further provision for advanced teaching and research. Without such provision, we fear that, in view of the rapid growth of knowledge, the position of Oxford and Cambridge as centres of intellectual and learned life will be considerably imperilled'.[1]

Certain changes in the government of the universities were recommended. At Oxford the power of Convocation should be reduced and membership of Congregation should be limited to those who were engaged in teaching or administrative work in the university. There was no body at Cambridge which corresponded to Congregation at Oxford and it was thought that a similar House should be established.[2] The administrative work of the universities ought to be overhauled and placed on a modern footing. Salaries and pensions also received attention. It was essential that the salaries of the staff should be materially increased and that retiring ages should be introduced for professors and other members of staff, and that the Federated Superannuation scheme in existence in the newer universities should apply also to Oxford and Cambridge. The number of women students at Oxford was not to exceed one fourth of the men and at Cambridge it was limited to 500.

[1] *Ibid.*, p. 95.
[2] Convocation consisted of those graduates of the university who had kept up their membership of the university by paying the fees for the Master's degree and the College charges for retaining their names on the books. The actual attendance at Convocation for voting purposes was limited to residents who were members of Congregation. A statute of 1913 restricted membership of

The University of London has always presented a number of peculiar problems. It originated in the protest against the restriction of membership of Oxford and Cambridge to adherents of the Anglican Church and because of the desire to establish a university which would serve the middle classes and break the monopoly enjoyed by classical and mathematical studies. Thus University College, Gower Street, was founded in 1827 and as a counterblast, the Anglican party established King's College. The latter received its charter in 1829 but the Gower Street College had to wait until 1836. In the same year the University of London was created as the body which was empowered to grant degrees. In this way the anomalous position was created of a university which was merely an examining body and had no constituent colleges whilst the two colleges, University and King's, which taught the candidates who entered for the examinations, were not integral parts of the university. From 1858 the University of London began to confer degrees solely on the results of examination. The demand for a teaching as well as an examining university caused violent controversy which led to the investigations of two Royal Commissions and finally, in 1898, to the University of London Act which reconstituted the university and appointed a committee to draft new statutes for it.

The ultimate result of all this was that on its teaching side, the University of London became a federation of a large number of dissimilar institutions. Its troubles, however, did not come to an end with the passing of the nineteenth century. During the earlier years of its existence, the university had no permanent headquarters. It moved from one set of Government buildings to another, until eventually it was offered a home in the Imperial Institute at South Kensington. This building was originally intended as a memorial of the first fifty years of Queen Victoria's reign. It proved to be a 'white elephant' and when it sought Government assistance to support its dwindling income, the Government proposed to hand over the greater part of the building as an administrative headquarters to the University of London, leaving the remainder to the Imperial Institute for carrying on its work of research and propaganda. This decision, which was made in the year 1900, was to prove a momentous one

Congregation to persons who were engaged in teaching or administrative work in the university or in the colleges. Hence it was important to define the functions of Convocation to prevent overlapping with those of Congregation.

for the university. When the university moved into its new headquarters it found itself surrounded by a group of institutions for higher education which had been administered by the Science and Art Department, but now, as the consequence of the Board of Education Act of 1899, came under the superintendence of the Board of Education. Amongst these institutions were the Victoria and Albert Museum, the Science Museum and Library, the Royal College of Science, the Royal College of Art, the Royal School of Mines, the Royal College of Music, the Royal School of Art Needlework, the Natural History Museum, and the City and Guilds of London Institute for the advancement of Technical Education.

The events of the next ten years were extremely complicated and only a general sketch of the main developments can be given.

In 1907 the Imperial College of Science and Technology was established and granted a Royal Charter. At the same time, the Board of Education transferred the control of the Royal College of Science and the Royal School of Mines to the governing body of the Imperial College. The City and Guilds of London Institute, now renamed the City and Guilds (Engineering) College, was associated for administrative purposes with the Imperial College. The buildings on the South Kensington estate were extended until every square yard available was occupied and it was ironically said that 'almost the only science which has not been practised at South Kensington is town planning'.[1]

These developments were to prove significant for the University of London. The establishment of the Imperial College was the outcome of a movement, which started in 1903, to provide for teaching and research in applied science at South Kensington. Lord Rosebery had proposed the erection of a new college of applied science to work in close co-operation with the existing science colleges and the L.C.C. promised an annual grant of £20,000 to the new institution. Lord Rosebery, in writing to the Chairman of the L.C.C., concluded his letter with the words, 'Should this scheme be successfully carried through, I am not without hope that it may be possible to follow it up by taking further steps towards developing the University in such a fashion as to make it worthy to be the University of the metropolis of the

[1] T. L. Humberstone. *University Reform in London*, p. 80. Geo. Allen and Unwin, 1926.

Empire'. In the following year, a Departmental Committee of the Board of Education under the chairmanship of Lord Haldane adopted Lord Rosebery's scheme and recommended that the new college of applied science should be a member of the federation of colleges on the South Kensington site. The Board of Education seems at first to have agreed with the recommendations of the Departmental Committee but to have modified its policy at a later stage. As related in the previous paragraph, the new college, which was named the Imperial College of Science and Technology, was not only amalgamated with the existing science colleges but they were subordinated to the Imperial College in a single scheme of administration. One can trace the hand of Sir Robert Morant in this arrangement, for it was a scheme that would appeal to him because of its administrative tidiness. The administrator, however, frequently ignores the human factor and it was so in this case. The colleges brought under this common scheme bitterly resented the loss of their individuality and complained of the emphasis placed upon applied science to the detriment of the study of pure science.

The next step was in 1906 when negotations began to incorporate the proposed Imperial College with the University of London. Mr. Birrell, the President of the Board of Education, favoured this policy but his successor, Mr. McKenna, advocated the grant of a Royal Charter to the Imperial College as an independent institution. He suggested, however, the advisability of appointing a Royal Commission 'to consider whether the amalgamation of the new institution with the university is desirable and feasible, and, if so, on what lines it can best be carried out'. This idea did not appeal to the staff and students of the Imperial College, for immediately it received its charter they began to agitate for its transformation into an independent university.

The Royal Commission was appointed under the Chairmanship of Lord Haldane and it issued its Final Report in 1913. The Commission was given very wide terms of reference. It was charged 'to inquire into the working of the present organization of the University of London, and into other facilities for advanced education . . . existing in London for persons of either sex above secondary school age; to consider what provision should exist in the metropolis for University teaching and research; to make recommendations as to the relations which should in consequence subsist between the University of London, its incorporated colleges, the Imperial College of Science and Technology, the other schools of the university; and the various public institutions and bodies concerned; and further to recommend as to any changes of constitution and organization which appear desirable'.

The Haldane Commission thought that the best means of bringing unity into the very varied collection of institutions which constituted the University of London was to adopt a faculty organization. The Government agreed with this principle and the University of London Act, 1926, created a new constitution for the university. The various institutions which comprised the university were recognized as 'schools of the university' in one or more faculties. All the medical schools are included in the faculty of medicine. The women's colleges such as Bedford, Royal Holloway, and Westfield are schools in the faculties of arts and science. The other constituent colleges such as University and King's, the Imperial College of Science and Technology, the London School of Economics, Queen Mary College, Birkbeck College and the remaining institutions are also schools in the different faculties. This organization was possible because of the specialist teaching given in the different institutions. Eight faculties were recognized: arts, science, technology, economics, medicine, laws, theology, and music.

The Haldane Commission realized that the South Kensington site was inadequate and considered that one of the essential needs of the University of London was a permanent central headquarters. 'London as a whole,' said the Report, 'cannot be made a university town like Oxford or Cambridge, where the university dominates the town and may consist of many separate colleges without losing its unity and identity. But we think it is quite possible to create a university quarter in London, in which the university life and interests would grow and develop, and students and teachers alike would find themselves in the atmosphere of a great seat of learning'.[1]

The Commissioners were not prepared to make recommendations with regard to all the purposes for which accommodation should be provided in the central buildings of a reconstituted university. Obviously rooms and offices would be needed for the Senate and its committees, the Principal

[1] *Final Report of the Royal Commission on University Education in London*, p. 44 H.M.S.O., 1913.

and the officers of the university, and for meetings of Convocation. 'The graduates of the university should have a place of their own within the university walls'. Adequate buildings would also be required for developing the social and corporate life of the university. These were, at the time, entirely wanting. Laboratories for advanced work, lecture halls, and a central library were also essential requirements. 'But about some things there can be no doubt. A great hall will be required for university ceremonies and for the many important occasions—such as the meetings of International Congresses and other great educational gatherings—when it is fitting that the university should act as host. The McEwan Hall in Edinburgh and the Whitworth Hall in Manchester are worthy of the universities to which they belong, and even in so comparatively small a town as Reading a spacious hall for academic assemblies was built in 1906. But for the University of London, founded in 1836, the only accommodation of the kind at present available is a temporary wooden structure erected in 1887 for the opening of the Imperial Institute by Her Majesty Queen Victoria. It appears to us totally unfit for the uses it has to serve'.[1]

The problem of choosing a new site for the university produced a violent controversy. In 1920 the Government offered a site of 11½ acres situated to the rear of the British Museum. This land was to be given to the university but the state of the national finances would not permit the buildings to be erected at the expense of the public. King's College had long complained about the inadequacy of its buildings in the Strand and it was proposed that it should be moved to the site in Bloomsbury. Although the Government offered £375,000 as compensation for the old site, King's obstinately refused to move and at first it was feared that this attitude might wreck the whole scheme. It is now to be hoped that the large administrative centre at Bloomsbury will draw together the varied institutions that constitute the University of London and that in future one will not be able to say as Flexner did in 1930, 'If a university is, whatever its type or form, a highly vitalized organism, vitalized, not by administrative means, but by ideas and ideals, with a corporate life, I confess myself unable to understand in what sense the University of London is a university at all'.[2]

The University of London is unique in being the only

[1] *Ibid.*, p. 210.
[2] A. Flexner, *Universities*, p. 231. O.U.P., 1930.

British university which is organized to grant degrees to candidates who are not resident members. This policy has been repeatedly criticized on a number of grounds. It is urged that the different institutions, e.g. university colleges and technical colleges, which prepare candidates for London University examinations have little control over the syllabus. In addition, a large number of candidates are not members of any recognized educational institution but prepare by means of private study and correspondence courses. Hence they are unaffected by two of the most important influences that a university brings to bear upon its students, namely, the close association with teachers of rich and varied experience and the daily contact with students from other faculties which is so vital in the development of a wide outlook and many-sided interests. On the other hand, one must admit that the external degree system possesses two advantages which in the opinion of some people outweigh its disadvantages. In the first place, had it not been for the external degree system, many of the provincial universities which pride themselves on being residential would never have come into existence. It was only because at the time they were university colleges they could enter their students for the degree examinations at London, that they could fill their halls and lecture rooms. Secondly, one should remember that the external degree system has made it possible for many individuals to obtain a university qualification which otherwise would have been permanently beyond their reach. Whether the system has now outgrown its usefulness in these days when facilities for university education are more numerous is a matter of opinion but the external examination still has the merit of making considerable contributions to the funds of the University of London. It has been stated that many candidates are ill prepared for the examination test and that this accounts for the large percentage of failures amongst external students. The authorities of London University have paid attention to this fact and in recent years have instituted a scheme for guiding external candidates in their reading. Nevertheless it is true that no other university has been willing to adopt the external degree system and the provincial universities, which attach such high value to residence (though this often means nothing more than attendance at a limited number of lectures), are always ready to contest any proposals which seems to open the door to an external degree system.

The oldest member of the confederation known as the Victoria University was Owens College, Manchester. John Owens was a prosperous Manchester business man who, in 1845, willed the sum of £97,000 for the foundation of the college which bears his name. It was opened in 1851 but for some years it had a strenuous struggle to maintain its existence. Eventually the college triumphed over its early difficulties and settled down to make slow and steady progress. In 1871 it received a new constitution which empowered it to admit women students but the proposal was contested on the grounds that it was in direct opposition to the conditions of John Owens' will. In 1874 women were admitted but on the condition that adequate provision was first made for all men who wished to enter the college. Owens College looked forward to incorporation as an independent university in 1875. These hopes, however, were frustrated by events which had occurred on the other side of the Pennines.

In 1874 the Yorkshire College of Science was established at Leeds. After a somewhat precarious existence in hired buildings, the position of the college was strengthened by the accession of the university extension work which had been established in Leeds by the University of Cambridge. A working arrangement had also been made with the Leeds School of Medicine and the college was taking steps to acquire its own premises. As courses in the arts subjects were now being provided, the word 'Science' was dropped from the title of the college. When the news was received that Owens College was seeking incorporation under the name of the University of Manchester, the Yorkshire College made a counter proposal in 1878. The memorial it presented to the Lord President of the Council prayed that the Queen should be advised not to grant a charter to Owens College but to create a new institution in which Owens College and similar colleges might be incorporated as soon as they could fulfil the necessary conditions. The new university ought not to be named after a city nor should it bear the name of a local person. Both Leeds and Liverpool possessed flourishing schools of medicine and therefore they strongly objected to degree courses in that subject being held at Manchester. There should be no religious tests in the new university; women as well as men should be eligible for degrees, and full-time attendance at a college of the university should be necessary for graduation. Thus the idea of adopting the external degree system of London was definitely rejected. After negotiations between Owens and the colleges at Liverpool and Leeds, a basis of agreement was reached and in 1880 the Victoria University received its charter and Owens College was immediately incorporated in it.

University College, Liverpool, was founded in 1881 with strong support from the Corporation of that city. Its avowed object was to seek incorporation in the Victoria University. It made rapid progress and in 1884 it became the second constituent college of the Victoria University. The Yorkshire College developed more slowly. An important step was its amalgamation with the Leeds School of Medicine in 1884. Both institutions realized that by themselves neither would be able to fulfil the conditions for incorporation. In 1887 the Yorkshire College was admitted as a member of the confederation.

Under the federal scheme the three colleges prospered, growing in numbers and material resources, and it was not until the close of the century that any misgivings about the nature of a federal university began to arise. The first signs of a rift occurred when a proposal for the establishment of a faculty of theology was mooted. Although this only affected Owens College, both Liverpool and Leeds were strongly opposed to it. The proposal was defeated but it was made again in 1900. Once again Liverpool and Leeds were in opposition and controversy was still continuing when the news came that the University of Birmingham had been created by Royal Charter as the first English university to bear the name of a provincial city as its title.

The University of Birmingham, although it was the result of the amalgamation of two separate institutions, the Mason Science College and Queen's College which was at first a theological and medical school, really owed its origin to the generosity of Josiah Mason. The latter had an astonishing career. He started by selling cakes in the streets of Birmingham, and after trying his hand at a multitude of ventures, he retired as a millionaire. He was the founder of a successful pen factory. In later life, Mason turned himself to philanthropy and after founding a combined orphanage for girls and almshouse for elderly women, he conceived the idea of establishing a college for the teaching of science. At first he excluded all humanistic teaching but when the college opened in 1880, he consented to the inclusion of other subjects in the curriculum. He took this step because he hoped that the college would become a constituent member of either the Victoria University or the University of London.

As the college prospered, it began to fix its eyes upon the achievement of independent university status. Its ambitions were ably supported by Mr. Joseph Chamberlain and when in 1898 Andrew Carnegie subscribed the sum of £50,000, it was thought that the time was now ripe to petition the Privy Council for the grant of a charter. The success of Birmingham raised the question in the minds of the members of the Victoria University, 'If Birmingham has become an independent university, why should there not also be separate universities for Manchester, Liverpool and Leeds?' Liverpool was the most anxious to be independent. The City authorities authorized the levy of a penny rate to assist the college and a fund of £170,000 was raised by subscription. Leeds wished to remain in the federation so that the outcome depended upon the decision taken by Owens College. The latter took some time in making up its mind but in 1902 the Court considered that it was now opportune to claim independent status. One of the arguments in favour of dissolution was that since all board meetings were held in Manchester, the representatives of Liverpool and Leeds wasted a great deal of time in travelling. Manchester and Liverpool obtained their charters in 1903 and it was agreed that Leeds should also be the seat of a university though whether it should be a federal university for Yorkshire, including Sheffield, or a separate university, was not at once decided. The Privy Council was not agreeable to the former plan so that in 1904 the University of Leeds received its charter. The sole remnant of the federal institution to-day is the Joint Matriculation Board for the Northern Universities.

The University of Sheffield owes its origin to the beneficence of Mark Firth, a wealthy iron-master who in 1879 gave a site, a building to the value of £29,000 and an additional endowment of £10,000 for the foundation of Firth College. The early years of the college were a grim struggle but the assistance it derived from the medical school, the corporation, and from its university extension work enabled it to carry on. At one time it considered applying for membership of the Victoria University, but as the latter was already in the throes of dissolution, Firth College decided to aim at indedendent status. The University of Sheffield received its charter in 1905.

The remaining English federal university was in the north-east. During the Commonwealth, a college was established from the revenues of the Chapter of Durham Cathedral but it was short-lived and at the Restoration the Dean and Chapter were reinstated. In 1832 the Dean and Chapter of Durham obtained an Act of Parliament which gave them authority 'to appropriate part of their church to the establishment of a university in connection therewith'. The charter was issued in 1836. Thus, in its origin, the University of Durham was an ecclesiastical foundation and its students were housed in the precincts of the bishop's palace. As an Anglican foundation it had its religious tests like Oxford and Cambridge. The university was of the residential type modelled after the pattern of the older universities. It had a somewhat chequered career at first and in 1857 the number of students had so decreased that its closure was seriously contemplated. The situation at Durham had grown so bad that in 1862 Parliament passed a Durham University Act to appoint a Royal Commission to inquire into the prospects of the University. The Commission issued a scathing report on the government and curriculum of the university and drafted a set of ordinances which introduced drastic reforms.

In Newcastle, a school of medicine and surgery had been opened in 1834 and a college of science in 1871. The medical school became a constituent member of the university in 1872 and the college of science was associated in 1874. As in the cases of the Yorkshire and Mason's Colleges, the science college at Newcastle began to develop an arts faculty. It received additional endowments and from 1904 it became known as Armstrong College. Thus at the beginning of the present century, the University of Durham was of the federal type. It consisted of three practically autonomous institutions, each of which controlled its own finance, appointed its own staff and took responsibility for its teaching and discipline. The older section of the university, situated in Durham, had strong classical and arts elements and in its system of residential colleges resembled Oxford and Cambridge. The Newcastle section, which included Armstrong College and the Medical College, was more akin to the provincial universities of northern England. The only other university of a similar pattern in Britain is St. Andrews with its more modern section at Dundee.

The federal constitution was not on the whole successful. The government of the university was in the hands of the Dean and Chapter and although there had been little friction with the Senate it was widely felt that the scheme of administration was out of date. Moreover, there had been considerable differences of opinion between the Durham and the Newcastle sections. In 1895 a memorial was drawn up by certain members of the Senate and presented to the Visitor, the Bishop of Durham. The document gave a number of reasons why it would be beneficial to transfer authority from the Dean and Chapter to the Senate. It would have been possible for these points of difference to have been the object of the inquiry of a Royal Commission, but another procedure was adopted. A Bill was presented to Parliament for the appointment of a body of Commissioners who would have power to draft statutes which would provide a new constitution for the university. The provisions of the original Bill aroused opposition from all quarters and in view of this its proposals were modified. The University of Durham Act of 1908 reconstituted the university in two divisions. The Durham division contained University College, Hatfield, St. Chad's and St. John's and the Newcastle division Armstrong College and the College of Medicine. The government of the university was radically changed by means of a series of statutes drawn up by the Commissioners appointed by the Act.

The changes effected did not secure the unity of the university. Difference of opinions between the two divisions grew so serious that a Royal Commission was appointed in 1937. The Commissioners found many points of criticism; for example, the constitution of Armstrong College as a limited liability company was not an arrangement suited to an institution of university status. The result of the Commission was the abolition of the federal constitution of the university. All its constituent members were grouped under a single control for administration and finance. Another consequence was that Armstrong was renamed King's College.

The federal University of Wales was founded in 1893 by the amalgamation of the university colleges of Aberystwyth, Bangor and Cardiff. The foundation of the University of Wales lies outside the period suggested by this book. It was the result of a national movement which began in the middle of the nineteenth century and which was inspired by the same personalities who played such a prominent part in the development of secondary education in the Principality. The later phases of the movement owed much to the support of Lord Aberdare and Viriamu Jones. The Technical

College at Swansea and the National School of Medicine at Cardiff eventually became constituent members of the federation.

University College, Bristol, founded in 1876, became an independent university in 1909. The two latest recipients of university status were Reading in 1926 and Nottingham in 1948. Both Reading and Nottingham present some unique features in their development. The University of Reading originated in the University Extension College which was opened in that town in 1892. The college made steady progress and when at the end of the century it became recognized as a university college, it received considerable assistance from local benefactors, and by 1912 it was looking forward to the achievement of university status. The outbreak of the first World War postponed the grant of a charter, which was not secured until 1926.

As a university college, Reading had attached great importance to the idea of a completely residential institution. This was largely forced upon the college authorities because Reading was one of the smaller university towns and being situated in an agricultural district with no large towns near at hand, was unable to supply the number of students which would guarantee the growth of the college. Hence the college adopted the policy of receiving its entrants from all parts of the country and was therefore obliged to develop halls of residence. The result has been that, with the exception of Oxford and Cambridge, the University of Reading is the most fully residential of the English universities. The second noteworthy feature of Reading has been the development of agricultural and horticultural studies. This again was the result of its geographical position.

The University of Nottingham sprang from the university extension work carried on in that city by Cambridge. The college which developed from this was opened in 1881. University College, Nottingham, is the only English institution of its kind which grew up under municipal control. In this respect it may be compared with Edinburgh. The support of the corporation ensured the success of the venture but as the college grew the governing body felt acutely the need for controlling their own affairs. The achievement of freedom was impossible until it possessed adequate endowments. The generous benefaction of Sir Jesse Boot (afterwards Lord Trent) supplied this need and the college was able to erect its new buildings in 1928. From this time it looked forward to obtaining university status. It received a charter in 1938 which changed its constitution and freed it from municipal control. The final step was in July, 1948, when it obtained recognition as an independent university.

The remaining institutions of university rank are the university colleges and it is to be presumed that their advancement to university status is only a matter of time. They provide a full university course for their students who sit for the external degree examinations of the University of London. The older institutions are the University College of Southampton, 1902 (which developed from the Hartley Institution) and Exeter, 1901, which sprang from the university extension work carried on in that city. University Colleges were founded at Leicester and Hull in 1918 and 1927 respectively but they were not in receipt of Treasury grants until 1945. The latest comer is the University College of North Staffordshire, Stoke-on-Trent, which has recently opened. This college wished to experiment with a curriculum less specialized in character than that of the degree courses in other universities. It was felt that the external degree system of London would not permit such an experiment and the college obtained a charter enabling it to grant its own B.A. degrees.

The modern universities were all seriously handicapped by lack of funds during the early stages of their development. Some were more fortunate than others in securing large gifts from local benefactors, e.g. Owens College, Mason College, Firth College. The Yorkshire College began its life in hired rooms and it was not for some years that it was able to purchase land and erect its own buildings. In 1889 grants of public money became available. In that year the Government authorized the sum of £15,000 per annum to be distributed among the university colleges. The condition for participation in the Treasury grant was that the applicant performed 'an appreciable amount of advanced university work', and this has generally been understood as provision for post-graduate research as well as undergraduate teaching. When the day training colleges were attached to universities and university colleges, the Board of Education paid a grant for the training of students for the teaching profession. Many colleges participated in the grants for technical education made available through the 'Whisky Money' and in some cases county and borough councils levied a small rate to assist the college in their areas.

The annual Treasury grant continued to increase until in 1911 a body known as the University Grants Committee was constituted. Its present terms of reference are: 'To inquire into the financial needs of university education in Great Britain; to advise the Government as to the application of any grants made by Parliament towards meeting them; to collect, examine and make available information on matters relating to university education at home and abroad; and to assist, in consultation with the universities and other bodies concerned, the preparation and execution of such plans for the development of the universities as may from time to time be required in order to ensure that they are fully adequate to national needs'. Earlier in this chapter we saw how Oxford and Cambridge came to participate in the Treasury grant.

The members of the University Grants Commission are chosen because of their wide experience of the work and needs of the universities. All institutions of university rank are visited by members of the Commission, who discuss with the governing body and heads of departments the needs of the particular institution and its plans for development. The annual grant is of two kinds—one to meet current expenses and the other—a non-recurrent grant—for capital expenditure. The grant is given without prejudice to the authority of the universities. Every university is free to decide what it will teach, the details of its syllabuses and the organization of its own examinations for degrees and diplomas. This arrangement has worked very well and it has avoided the unhappy results, due to over-centralized control, that have been a feature of many universities on the Continent.[1]

The war of 1914–18 dealt a very heavy blow at the work of the universities. They were almost denuded of men students and a large proportion of the younger members of staff served with the Forces. Nevertheless the universities contributed materially to the war effort and the research work they were able to do was a very considerable help towards final victory. Although many colleges and hostels were requisitioned for military needs or for Government services, the universities suffered no damages as regards their

---

[1] The following figures show the increase in the grant paid to universities:

1932–3	..	£1,680,000
1947–8	..	£9,775,000
1949–50	..	£17,564,500
1950–51	..	£23,184,150
1951–2	..	£23,234,625

buildings. After the Armistice, they had to cope with the problem of a sudden increase in the student population, swelled by the return of large numbers of ex-service men. Needless to say, all schemes for development were postponed during the war years and when they were resumed after the war, all kinds of difficulties occasioned by the rising costs of living, the scarcity of materials and the shortage of labour had to be surmounted.

The second World War, from one point of view, did not cause so much dislocation in the work of the universities. The Government had adopted a planned scheme for the call-up of university students and staff so that there was not the sudden fall in numbers that occurred in 1914. In all universities and university colleges, Joint Recruiting Boards were established. Each student was considered individually and those with specialist technical knowledge were either deferred or posted to that type of national service in which their knowledge or experience could be utilized. Full-time members of the teaching staffs were at first reserved at 25 years of age but later, the age of reservation was raised to 30, and in some categories to 35 years of age. The three years degree course was reduced to two years and three months and the standard of attainment was maintained by adopting a four term arrangement which practically cut out the whole of the summer vacation. Men in the arts faculty and others who were not deferred were attested, placed on the reserve, and allowed to complete three terms at the university before their call-up, on the condition that they trained with the Senior Training Corps or with the Air Training Corps.

Some universities suffered severely during the intensive air bombardment. London University was perhaps the worst case. University College was extensively damaged; Bedford College lost nearly one-third of its buildings; Birkbeck College was damaged by fire, and the medical schools and other institutions of the university suffered varying degrees of damage. One of the most unfortunate incidents occurred at the London School of Medicine for Women a few weeks before the war in Europe ended. The new wing of the school received almost a direct hit by a rocket. It was completely wrecked and in addition three laboratories were put out of use for a considerable time. Bristol and Liverpool Universities also received heavy damage. In the former, the Great Hall and the anatomy wing were entirely gutted by fire. At Liverpool the engineering laboratories were badly damaged. Other universities were either untouched or received comparatively slight damage.

The University of London was considered the most vulnerable to air attack and during the months preceding the outbreak of war, plans had been made for evacuating the whole of the university as soon as hostilities commenced. The operation was complicated by the large numbers involved. No one area was capable of receiving all the students; in fact, the faculties of University College were dispersed among no less than eight different institutions in the provinces. There must have been many students who had been accepted by a college and who had never seen the buildings of the institution to which they belonged. It is amusing to read of the principal of one London college who took his evacuated students on a personally conducted tour of the college buildings. The move back to London was carried out piecemeal and was not completed until the session 1946-7. The delay was caused not only by war damage but because many buildings had been occupied by Government departments which could not be moved until some other accommodation was found for them.

In the post-war period the universities have many serious problems confronting them. The most immediate is that resulting from the huge increase in the numbers of university students. The increase from 50,246 in 1938-9 to 76,764 in 1947-8 was largely due to the return of ex-service students but as the flow of these ceased, their places were filled by other candidates. The experience of war had convinced the nation of the value of university-trained men and women with the result that there is now an ever-increasing demand from all quarters for graduates. At the same time, the re-organization of school education brought about by the Education Act of 1944 has begun to make itself felt, with the consequence that the number of school-leavers who are qualified to enter an institution of university rank is much greater than in pre-war years.

In 1946 the Committee on Scientific Manpower (Barlow Committee), issued its report. The Committee was chiefly concerned with the supply of trained scientists and technologists and after a careful review of the present situation, they concluded that the national interest demanded a doubling of the output of graduates in science and technology at the earliest possible moment. The Percy Report in 1944 had considered the needs of higher technological education in

England and Wales and had recommended that the output of engineering graduates should be at least half as large again. In the same year, the Report of the Inter-Departmental Committee on Medical Education (Goodenough Committee) was issued and although it did not recommend anything like the expansion proposed by the Barlow and Percy Reports, it considered that some increase in the intake of the medical schools was desirable. The Ministry of Education has asked for more trained graduate teachers; the professions—dentistry, architecture, and law—want more graduates; finally, the civil service and the local government services have made similar requests. The University Grants Committee admitted that: 'These recommendations involve changes at the universities which can only be described as revolutionary. The desired increase of numbers by something like 80 per cent within a decade represents an expansion out of all proportion to anything which has previously been attempted in the universities of Britain. The accompanying needs for the rapid expansion of staffs and for the building of new accommodation impose upon the universities a task which is unparalleled in their earlier development'.[1] The outcome of these demands is that the total number of students in the universities is likely to be permanently fixed at about 90,000.

The increase in the intake of students only gives part of the picture. When the entrants into the different faculties are considered, the disquieting fact emerges that some faculties and departments are expanding more rapidly than others. This could have a very serious effect upon the balance of university studies. If, for example, the engineering department in a certain university expanded at a rate out of proportion to the increases in other faculties and departments, a decided bias would be introduced. Some foresee another danger. They emphasize that it has been too lightly assumed that there exists a large reserve of potential entrants which so far has been untapped. This assumption has yet to be proved and it may well be that if the number of entrants to the universities increases beyond a certain limit, the proportion of failures and undistinguished pass students will correspondingly increase. They think that there is a real danger in offering a university education to people who would receive more benefit from some other form of training.

All the universities had realized that a great expansion in

[1] *University Development from* 1935 *to* 1947, p. 28. H.M.S.O., 1948.

university education would occur after the war and they had allowed for it in their post-war development schemes. University expansion involves a large increase in the teaching and administrative staffs and that in turn means the adoption of better scales of salaries in order to attract the most highly qualified men and women. On what the University Grants Committee term the 'physical side', university expansion has to be thought of in the light of more lecture rooms and laboratories, libraries and halls of residence. All this requires a much larger income than was received by the universities in pre-war days. This has been met by increased Treasury grants. In 1920-1 the grant was £800,000. This had grown to nearly £17,600,000 in 1949-50 and it will much exceed this figure in the future. The grants paid by local authorities have increased by nearly 50 per cent. Two important issues are raised by the increase of income. Money is not everything. As the Nuffield College Survey states: 'Money is necessary, and more money will accelerate the expansion, but by itself it will not produce the teachers and research workers on whom everything else depends'.[1] This is a grave warning that should not pass unheeded.

The second issue becomes clear when one looks at the increased participation in public funds from quite a different standpoint. In 1920-1 the universities received only 29 per cent of their income from the state. When Oxford and Cambridge accepted a Treasury grant the percentage rose to 32. In 1947-8 it had risen to 60 per cent and it is estimated that for 1951-2 it will be 65 per cent. The rest of university income is derived from fees, endowments, gifts, and grants from local authorities. The significance of the above figures lies in the fact that at present more than half of the income of the universities comes from the state. The following questions at once arise: how long will the State be content to respect the autonomy of the universities? Can the delicate adjustment which has worked so well since 1911 be maintained? It is to be hoped that it can, for if the freedom of the universities gave way to Government control, much of their value to the community would be lost. More than a merely theoretical issue is involved. There are extremists in the Socialist ranks who are always ready to hunt out what they believe to be examples of privilege. They have not realized that the autonomy of the universities has

[1] *The Problem Facing British Universities*, p. 88. O.U.P., 1948.

nothing to do with privilege. The good health of the universities is bound up with their retention of academic freedom. The evil results of state control of the universities are only too apparent in the examples of Germany and Italy in the last generation and of Russia in this. In recent years a new body, the Standing Committee of Vice-Chancellors and Principals, has come into being. It performs the most valuable function of a close liaison between the different universities and the Government departments. Strictly speaking, it is an unofficial body but its work may be regarded as supplementary to that of the University Grants Commission.

Closely connected with the general financial position of the universities is that of the finances of the students themselves. At the present time the number of parents who are able to pay the whole cost of a three or four years' course for their sons is rapidly decreasing. The incidence of unprecedented rates of taxation coupled with the never-ending rise in the cost of living has pressed heavily upon the middle and professional classes in the community. Hence the tremendous growth in the numbers of students who are dependent upon state or local authority grants for their university education. Roughly 68 per cent of students are receiving grants of one kind or another. Until recently the majority of the grants were those paid to ex-service students (Further Education and Training), but when these were coming to an end, the Ministry of Education called a Working Party to consider what type of grant should be paid in future. A large increase in the number of state scholarships and in the aid given towards university scholarships and exhibitions was recommended. The Ministry of Education is anxious to abolish the 'pledge' for intending teachers and with it the four years training grant and to substitute in its place a system of local authority awards. (See note on p. 154.)

Another problem is that of hostel accommodation for the larger numbers of students. Before the war, the modern universities, with the exception of Reading, were deficient as regards halls of residence. Students who lived in the neighbourhood were obliged to spend much time in travelling between the university and their homes and many of those who came from a greater distance had to be accommodated in lodgings. At first the University Grants Committee gave little attention to this problem and even as late as 1936 they thought that it was possible of solution by the universities themselves or by the gifts of private benefactors. Post-war increase in student numbers made the problem even more acute. At the older universities a large proportion of undergraduates were forced to live in lodgings because of the insufficient accommodation in the colleges and hostels. The University Grants Commission have now realized the seriousness of the situation and have earmarked large sums of money for the building of halls of residence.

The universities are also confronted with what may be termed fundamental intellectual and moral problems of a kind so grave that Sir Walter Moberly has entitled his recent book *The Crisis in the University*. Sir Walter brings to the discussion the results of his long experience as Chairman of the University Grants Commission. He believes that it is imperative for the universities to examine themselves to discover how far they have failed in giving the moral leadership which the world now needs so urgently. Hence it is essential that 'all the familiar questions of university policy—questions of clientèle, of curricula, of ways of living, of forms of government, of relation with the outside world—require to be rethought in the new perspective'.[1]

Sir Walter considers that the universities are doing nothing to meet the crisis. He says, 'Beneath the facade of development and hopefulness, the British universities to-day share with the universities of the world a peculiar malaise and impotence. They have little inner self-confidence, because they lack, and are increasingly aware that they lack, any clear, agreed sense of direction and purpose. At this moment they cannot give an effective lead because they themselves share, and have shown small signs of transcending, the spiritual confusion of the age'.[2]

Before coming to the consideration of the remedies he proposes, Sir Walter reviews the three conceptions of the task of the university that have been held during the last century. In the earlier years of the nineteenth century, the prevailing view was what he terms 'the Christian-Hellenic'. This conception appears in Newman's *Idea of a University*, in Whewell's *Principles of English University Education*, and in J. S. Mill's *Rectorial address to the students of St. Andrew's*. Its successor was the 'Liberal conception' in which investigation was thought to be more important than instruction. Its chief features were the ideal of learning for learning's sake

---

[1] Sir Walter Moberly. *Crisis in the University*, p. 17. S.C.M., 1949.
[2] *Ibid.*, p. 21.

and freedom from bias and presuppositions. At the present time, the Liberal idea has been superseded by the Technological and Democratic. The latter is empirical, analytic and selective. In its methods, the new culture 'discriminates between those fields and methods which promise practical results and those which do not. The things with which it has learned that it can deal are those that admit of being measured and weighed and counted and where the results of inquiry can be represented in graphs and statistical tables. . . . It turns its attention away from issues where inquiry is likely to be fruitless because the conditions of testing do not exist. From such aims and methods there results a prevailing mental attitude which is at once activist and optimistic'.[1] Some of the older teachers of the university still cling to the Liberal tradition, so that we have in fact a chaotic university.

He thinks that the university of to-day shirks fundamental issues. Politics, ethics, and religion, which are bound up with deep emotional convictions, are approached from a purely objective or neutral point of view. With due regard to Sir Walter's views, it might be added that this attitude possibly represents a hang-over from the controversies of the mid-nineteenth century when the heated discussions about the subject of religious tests produced in many quarters the conviction that the newer universities ought to approach matters of theology and ethics from a purely factual and objective standpoint. Sir Walter points out that the work of the universities tends to be split up into a number of watertight compartments, with the result that little attempt is made to give the student a working philosophy of life. The neglect of moral and spiritual values suggests to the student that, after all, these are not important. Sir Walter then reviews 'Scientific Humanism', 'Classical Humanism', and a return to the Christian tradition, as suggested remedies which he does not hesitate to describe as spurious. Each has certain merits but also possesses grave defects.

In regard to constructive proposals, Sir Walter admits that 'at best what we have to offer is an interim report'. He suggests that the university's neutrality should be positive and not negative. The university should be a community in which fundamental issues are not ignored, but are stated and thoroughly examined. Just as in a true democracy, differences are resolved through discussions, so the university must become an open forum in which fundamental issues

---

[1] *Ibid.*, p. 45.

of the day are freely discussed. But this is only a beginning. The iron curtain which 'shuts off different groups from all but superficial mental contact with one another' must be removed, and the prime need is to restore communication between the different sections who now live in distinct intellectual worlds. We must discover the basic values for which our present day universities stand and having asserted them, we should be ready to defend them. In Chapter V, Sir Walter enumerates these postulates and shows that there is certainly a Christian ingredient in these basic values. He then emphasizes, 'But in present circumstances and in any near future the university's common basis cannot be specific Christianity, and its Christian members ought not to try to make it so. Yet the university should have a recognizable and conscious orientation'.[1]

The remainder of the book deals with the important problems of specialization, the relation between arts and science, teaching and research, the provision of halls of residence, and the relation of the universities to the State. Space only permits of the mere mention of some of the issues which Sir Walter discusses clearly and logically. He concludes by showing how Christian teachers in the university can take the initiative in the process of self-examination and that a first practical step should be the formation of a Dons' Christian Movement. 'There is a "Student Christian Movement", which does a great deal for students in just these ways. As yet, we have no "Dons' Christian Movement", and it is for urgent consideration whether we do not need to create one, different as some of its techniques might need to be'. The analysis given in his book shows how weighty are the problems which confront the universities to-day, and whether one agrees or does not agree with Sir Walter's diagnosis and conclusions, the suggestions he puts forward are worth much serious thought.

---

[1] *Ibid.*, p. 161.

CHAPTER VIII

ADULT AND TECHNICAL EDUCATION, 1900-50

IT is perhaps true to say that no greater developments have been made in the field of education during the last fifty years than those in connection with adult and technical education. In the first half of the nineteenth century the only agencies for the provision of adult education were the Mechanics' Institutes and the Adult Schools. By the middle of the century the Adult Schools had suffered a temporary eclipse and the Mechanics' Institutes were receiving the bulk of their support from the middle classes for whom, in the first instance, these were not intended. Then a new factor emerged. The universities took a hand in the business of adult education and for some years the University Extension movement, originated by James Stuart of Cambridge, held the field. By the end of the century, University Extension seemed to be losing its original impetus and there was nothing to take its place. Like the Mechanics' Institutes, University Extension classes were being patronized very largely by the middle classes, and provided them with a means of obtaining higher education which for many had previously been impossible. This apparent arrest in the progress of adult education was in fact illusory, for new developments were on the way and were destined to change the whole aspect of adult education. A convenient method of dealing with these agencies is to consider them in chronological order.

From this point of view the first feature that should be noticed was the amazing revival of the Adult Schools. This began when the Society of Friends started to take a vital interest in adult education but the revival quickly spread to other bodies so that a large number of non-Quaker schools were established. They evidently met a long-felt need for after 1874 they developed so rapidly that some form of association to co-ordinate their efforts appeared to be desirable. At first this took the form of local Adult School Unions but as the idea of association grew in strength, the National Council of Adult School Associations was formed in 1899. The Council became the National Adult School Union in 1914.

The next event in order of time was the foundation in 1899 of Ruskin College, Oxford, by three Americans, Mr. and Mrs. Vrooman and Professor Beard. The object of Ruskin College was to provide for working-class students 'a training in subjects which are essential for working-class leadership, and which are not a direct avenue to anything beyond'. In other words, the college was intended to give a liberal and not a vocational training. The motive of the founders was to take 'men who have been merely condemning our institutions', and to teach them 'to transform these institutions, so that in place of talking against the world they will begin methodically and scientifically to possess the world'. Some of the students were dissatisfied with the liberal programme of studies provided and desired to make political ideas, especially the doctrines of Karl Marx, the basis of the curriculum. After a period of internal dissension, this group seceded from Ruskin in 1909 to form the Labour College. This has now been closed but its work is being carried on by the National Council of Labour Colleges. The Ministry of Education does not pay grants to classes conducted under the auspices of the National Council. According to the Adult Education Regulations, grant is only paid to classes in which a non-sectarian and non-political approach to the work is guaranteed. In 1910 Ruskin College was reorganized and its management now is in the hands of the Trade Unions and the working-class societies which support it.

The opening of Ruskin was followed by the establishment of a number of residential colleges for adults, such as, Woodbrooke, 1903; Fircroft, 1909; the Co-operative College, Manchester, 1919; Hillcroft College for Women at Surbiton, 1920; the Catholic Workers' College at Oxford, 1921; and the Avonscroft College for Agricultural Workers at Bromsgrove, Worcestershire, 1925. Wales had no adult residential college until the opening of Coleg Harlech in 1927.

During the period in which the University Extension movement was gaining ground, the Co-operative movement was also developing its educational work but at first it was hampered by the lack of clear ideas about the aims of adult education. It is important, however, because it became one of the parties to what Mr. H. C. Dent has termed the 'Triple Alliance' from which sprang the Workers' Educational Association. The other two parties were University Extension and the Trade Unions. The W.E.A. is the most important agency for adult education that has been born in the last half-century, not only because of its numerical strength, but mainly because it has totally transformed all our ideas about the nature and methods of adult education. Its founder was Dr. Albert Mansbridge and his great contribution to adult education was the bringing together in one association the Co-operative Societies, the Trade Unions, and University Extension.

Albert Mansbridge was born in Gloucestershire in 1876. After a period in the junior ranks of the civil service, he became in 1897 a clerk in the Co-operative Wholesale Society. Mansbridge had attended evening classes, lecture courses organized by the University Extension movement, and classes provided by the Co-operative movement. He had therefore sampled the different types of adult class available at that time and the experience he gained generated a new scheme in his mind. In a number of articles contributed to the *Co-operative News*, he explained his idea of creating an active working partnership between the universities and the people. His fellow co-operators did not take kindly to the scheme but he did not give up hope and as the result of thinking about his plan, he developed a much more far-reaching scheme which was nothing more or less than the 'Triple Alliance' between the three bodies which were most influential in the field of adult education. In 1903 he was given the opportunity of explaining his plan in the *University Extension Journal*. It was approved by a number of working men and later in the same year the Association to Promote the Higher Education of Working Men came into existence with Albert Mansbridge as Honorary Secretary.

The first branch was formed at Reading in October 1904, and this was followed a few months later by the establishment of another at Rochdale, the birthplace of the Co-operative movement. In 1905 the Association changed its title to that of the Workers' Educational Association. There was no doubt about the appeal of the movement. By 1906, 13 branches had been formed. This number grew to 47 in 1907 and to 50 in 1908. The first W.E.A. District was at Manchester. Although the W.E.A. was still in its youth, at a national conference in 1905 it obtained a resolution to request the Board of Education to ascertain 'how far and under what conditions employer and employed in their respective areas, would welcome legislation having for its ultimate object compulsory attendance at Evening Schools'.[1] Sir Robert Morant consented to receive a deputation and the discussion which followed was responsible for the publication of a report by the Consultative Committee in 1909. This was one of the factors which led to the establishment of day continuation schools by the Education Act of 1918.

William Temple (later Bishop of Manchester and afterwards Archbishop of Canterbury) attended this conference and became an enthusiastic supporter of the W.E.A. His interest in the Association was so much appreciated that he was elected its first President. Sir Robert Morant was another who followed the development of the movement with close interest and it was he who was instrumental in persuading New College, Oxford, to make a grant to cover the expenses of an experiment which led to the adoption of the tutorial class system. Mansbridge spoke highly of the support promised by Morant. 'Additional strength was given to the Conference by the presence of Sir Robert Morant, who was then Permanent Secretary to the Board of Education; whilst in that office he was always ready to meet fresh educational demands, and it is literally true to say that, so far as working people were concerned, he never spared himself in his desire to discover their wishes, and to meet them when he had understood them. He spoke in a way that was somewhat unusual for a permanent official, and committed his Department to real and definite aid. . . . Sir Robert said frankly that the Board of Education "is looking for guidance from such an Association as is represented here to-day, to show us the way in which adult education can best be furthered. In particular, we believe it is to small classes and solid, earnest work that we can give increasingly of the golden stream".'[2]

The story of the origin of the tutorial class has often been told. In 1906 the University Extension Committee at Rochdale were sorely perplexed about the progress of their lecture classes. If the approach by the lecturer was too academic, the audience dwindled, but if, on the other hand, the lectures were delivered so as to have a popular appeal, the large numbers in attendance made serious discussion almost impossible. In their dilemma they decided to con-

[1] Albert Mansbridge. *An Adventure in Working-Class Education*, p. 17. Longmans, Green, 1920.
[2] Albert Mansbridge. *University Tutorial Classes*, pp. 24–5. Longmans, Green, 1913.

sult Mansbridge. He asked Rochdale to produce 30 students who would promise to attend the class for two years and do the written work demanded of them. On his part, he guaranteed that he would obtain for them the services of one of the most brilliant scholars and teachers in England. He carried out his promise by securing R. H. Tawney as tutor.

A similar request came from Longton in Staffordshire, where Mr. Tawney also acted as tutor. Rochdale was the first to organize a tutorial class but the first class to assemble was at Longton. The answer to this paradoxical statement is as follows. Rochdale had arranged for the class to be held on Saturdays and Longton on Fridays. Therefore Mr. Tawney met his first class at Longton on the Friday and then went to Rochdale on the following day. The members of these early tutorial classes displayed tremendous enthusiasm. Mr. T. W. Price informs us: 'All shades of political opinion and religious belief were represented, and this gave piquancy to the discussion hour—which was an "hour" in name only, for the discussion went on until the caretaker became restless, and was then continued in the street. At Rochdale Mr. Tawney would frequently arrange to have tea and spend the evening at the home of one of the students, and on these occasions other members of the class would crowd into the house to the limits of the accommodation—and even beyond—and the discussion would often go on until the early hours of the morning.'[1]

The support given by New College to the tutorial class experiment drew forth a similar response from other Oxford colleges and within a short space of time practically every university and university college in England and Wales was sponsoring tutorial classes. In most universities a permanent joint committee of the W.E.A. and the university was set up. In many cases the L.E.A.s were invited to send representatives to the joint committee. Also a central committee known as the Central Joint Advisory Committee for Tutorial Classes was established.

The next step was to obtain assistance from the Board of Education. Already some branches had been receiving aid from local authorities under the clause of the Education Act of 1902 which authorized them to aid education other than elementary. The Board of Education had also given some

[1] T. W. Price. *The Story of the Workers' Educational Association*, 1903-24, p. 14. The Labour Publishing Co. Ltd., 1924.

aid under the Regulations for Technical Schools, Schools of Art, and other Forms of Provision for Further Education in England and Wales, 1918. The Final Report of the Ministry of Reconstruction, 1919, recommended the granting of public money. This was followed in 1924 by the issue of the Regulations for Adult Education which stated the conditions under which the Board of Education recognized adult classes and paid grant on them. These Regulations have been expanded and modified several times since that date. Local authorities also contributed to the work of the W.E.A. and in some cases have taken financial responsibility for classes, e.g. the West Riding of Yorkshire. The relations between the W.E.A., other bodies supplying adult education and the L.E.A.s were discussed in the Report on *Adult Education and the Local Education Authority* (H.M.S.O., 1933).

The W.E.A. has had a remarkable growth. The statistics for the session 1947–8 show that there were nearly 900 W.E.A. branches in the country, federated into 21 districts. The total number of branch members was about 39,000 and over 103,000 men and women were attending the classes. The students represented a fair cross-section of the community. 'The figures describing the occupations of students in classes during 1946–47 show that 21 per cent of students were manual workers, 16 per cent were clerks, draughtsmen, travellers, and foremen, slightly fewer were teachers, civil servants and postal workers, 5 per cent were professional and social workers, 26 per cent were engaged in home duties and nursing'.[1] In 1938–9 the number of students in tutorial classes reached the high-water mark of 12,739. In the middle of the war, as was to be expected, the number had dropped to 6,541 but immediately hostilities ceased, it began to rise again and in the session 1947–48 it had reached the total of 11,893.

W.E.A. classes range from university tutorial classes of three years' duration (there are also a number of advanced tutorial classes) to shorter courses varying from six months to a year. The subjects studied are those which are usually included in the definition of liberal education. Vocational and technical subjects have never formed part of the W.E.A. programme. Economics, history, and literature are the most popular, though in recent years philosophy and psychology have been much in demand. In some areas classes in science, chiefly biology and geology, have been well attended and

[1] *The Future in Adult Education*, pp. 11–12. W.E.A., 1947.

musical appreciation has had a wide appeal. The tutorial class meets 24 times a year, the usual duration of a meeting being two hours. The first hour is normally given over to lecture or exposition but not as formal in character as most university lectures. Students may, and often are, encouraged to ask questions or to raise points about which they would like further information. The second hour is usually devoted to discussion, or if the class has been studying science, to practical work. Book boxes are supplied to classes and students are encouraged to read. Most joint committees have built up libraries which can supply most of the books in regular demand. Written work is done by the students. In the early tutorial classes it was customary for students to write an essay each fortnight but this standard is no longer maintained. Few tutorial class students send in more than three or four essays during a session.

In 1927 the Board of Education selected the Yorkshire area for an inquiry into the work of non-vocational adult classes. The report which was issued in 1928 explained the reason for the choice of this district. 'No review of the progress of this branch of education in England could fail to reveal the important share of Yorkshire and particularly of the West Riding, in promoting and developing on its many sides, popular, academic, social and political, a movement which is not only itself alive but touches life at so many points. Yorkshire in population represents about one-ninth of England and Wales; in the extent of its adult educational enterprise it represents about one-fifth. In other words, out of a number difficult to estimate but probably not exceeding 60,000 students attached to organized bodies, more than 10,000 are to be found in Yorkshire.'[1]

The Report praised the work of the W.E.A. and in comparing it with University Extension, it noted that 'the newer movement represented a revolt as well as a development. The newer demand came from small groups connected for the most part with working class organizations. They were drawn more by their interest in social, economic and political problems than by a desire for general culture. ... From 1905 to 1914, although University Extension was still carried on, adult education in Yorkshire became more and more identified with the spread of the new type of class organized by the Workers' Educational Association; and

---

[1] *Adult Education in Yorkshire.* Board of Education Educational Pamphlet No. 59, p. 3. H.M.S.O., 1928.

when the tutorial class had once been established, there was a strong tendency to regard it as the only kind of class to be fostered. Circumstances, however, proved too strong for this attitude to be maintained. On the one hand the expense of providing for a large number of such classes was more than the Association could bear, and on the other many students interested in the newer form of adult education were not prepared to commit themselves to a three years' course and to do the necessary reading and written work involved. Consequently, many classes were formed which provided courses extending for, at most, one year, and were conducted under local teachers'.[1]

Yorkshire was an example of an area where the L.E.A.s, particularly the West Riding authority, encouraged the movement and supplied financial assistance. The Report considered that since 1918 the W.E.A. had entered upon a third phase of its development in which 'the somewhat narrow aims of the earlier activities of the Workers' Educational Association became widened as more classes were formed. . . . The Workers' Educational Association made itself the agent and organizer of the demand for almost every form of popular culture'.[2] One criticism passed on the classes was that 'many such groups choose subjects of a nature far beyond the capacity of the weaker members. Where the method adopted is purely expository such classes are often successful as pioneer courses, but owing to the fact that the tradition of the tutorial class has dominated the whole field during the last ten or fifteen years, far too many classes have attempted tasks which were unsuitable, when with a simpler objective they might have been extremely useful.'[3]

There was no doubt that the Yorkshire classes had made a definite contribution to educational practice. 'The relations between teachers and taught are not only pleasant and harmonious but are productive of that kind of growth which is part of the meaning of education. It is only necessary to contrast the atmosphere thus created with that of institutions—happily less common now than formerly—in which prestige may mask incompetence and an authoritative manner stifles inquiry—to appreciate the importance of this contribution. It is something at least to have made learning

[1] *Ibid.*, p. 5.
[2] *Ibid.*, p. 5.
[3] *Ibid.*, p. 16.

a pleasure, to have made the common man realize that the heritage of knowledge is his own if he will take it and that one of the chief rewards of learning is the society of those with whom it is shared'.[1]

The Report remarked on two tendencies about which much has been said in these post-war years. The first was that of standards, especially in regard to written work. When the essays of the early days of the movement were compared with those produced at the time of the inquiry, a distinct deterioration was noticed. The Report was quite emphatic about this and it said, 'Probably fewer students find the act of writing a serious difficulty, but on the other hand the essay revealing striking originality of thought couched in language unconsciously inspired by familiarity with the Authorized Version of the Bible is much rarer than it once was. The influence of journalism—not always of the best type—is more apparent. Nor is it at all evident that more time is devoted to reading, although books of the best kinds are more accessible than formerly'.[1] After noting that in some of the more isolated parts of the county many of the best students are found, the Report continues: 'In such places it is still possible to meet the old miner who knows his Butler's Analogy, the labourer who can recite most of Blake's poems, and who can enforce his points with apt quotations from the Bible'.

The second tendency noticed was the change in the character of the people who were attracted to the classes. The Report had previously mentioned that comparatively few ex-pupils of secondary or technical schools found their way to the classes. Nor were they widely patronized by teachers. 'Although there must be many thousands of certificated teachers in the area, only some 200 make use of tutorial classes in pursuit of their further cultural interests'. The composition of the student body was steadily changing. The early tutorial classes in the West Riding had an appeal to a very limited section of the community, namely those connected with the Trade Union organization. One effect of the widening of the curriculum was that the personnel of the classes represented a much broader cross-section of the community. This in turn was having an effect upon the curriculum. The earlier classes had concentrated upon the social sciences. Since the number of women students had

[1] *Ibid.*, p. 17.
[2] *Ibid.*, p. 25.

increased a demand was growing for new subjects, especially literature. 'The clientèle of the tutorial classes is changing, but not very rapidly. As an organization and a method for the pursuit of higher education, the tutorial class is one of the best instruments ever devised.'[1] During the next twenty years the tendencies noted in 1927 accelerated to an extent which has been the cause of grave concern to responsible officers of the W.E.A.

During the second World War many W.E.A. classes were carried on under difficulties. As most of the classes were held in the evening they generally assembled in time to hear the air raid alarm. In those large towns which suffered from aerial bombardment, classes were frequently interrupted while the tutor and students sought safety in the air raid shelters. Frequently discussions continued in the shelters and were punctuated by the noise of exploding bombs and of our anti-aircraft barrage. In smaller towns and rural districts where students frequently travelled considerable distances to their classes, the blackout caused a good deal of inconvenience. In spite of these handicaps the attendance at classes did not suffer unduly. Immediately after the war another difficulty was encountered. The Government introduced 'staggered hours' of work. This interfered with the regularity of attendance, though for grant purposes the Ministry of Education relaxed, for the time being, its grant regulations.

Since the war most of the universities have re-organized their machinery for dealing with adult education in their areas. To obtain fuller co-operation between the different activities in the field of adult education, extra-mural departments have been established with a Director of Extra-mural Studies as the academic head. Many are experimenting with the establishment of residential colleges which will provide courses either of a few days or of longer duration. The work of an extra-mural department is usually organized through a number of committees of which the Tutorial Class and the Extension Committees are the most prominent. Education provided by the universities for the Services is organized through a Services Committee. Universities differ in their practice but as a rule the committees work under the general direction of an Extra-mural Board on which the university, the L.E.A.s, the W.E.A., and other bodies which supply adult education are represented. Full-

[1] *Ibid.*, p. 26.

time tutors have formed an Association of Tutors in Adult Education to look after their interests, and in most cases, they are also represented on the Extra-Mural Board and its committees.

It is now nearly fifty years since the W.E.A. was first started and sufficient time has elapsed to enable a survey of the present situation to be made together with a forecast of future tendencies and developments. This has recently been undertaken by Mr. S. G. Raybould, the Director of the Extra-mural Department in the University of Leeds.[1] Mr. Raybould is quite frank in his appraisement of the present situation, and in regard to the future, his forecast follows the line indicated in the Board of Education Report on Adult Education in Yorkshire. The same tendencies are at work as mentioned in 1927 but since 1939 certain significant changes have occurred which, if they persist, will transform the W.E.A. into an organization quite different from the intentions expressed when it was first founded. Mr. Raybould summarizes the changes as those concerned with the balance in the type of class provided, the kind of student recruited, the subjects which are studied, and the standards of work.

In the early years of the movement the tutorial class (including the preparatory tutorial class) was predominant but in the period following the first World War, one-year and terminal classes began to be more popular. By 1939 tutorial class students represented only one-fifth of the total number and this proportion had decreased to one-eighth in 1947–8. These figures take on an added significance when one realizes that in ten years the total of students had increased by about 40,000 but that the number of tutorial classes was actually less than in 1939.

There has also been a marked change in the type of student who attends the classes. When Dr. Mansbridge founded the Association, he gave as his considered opinion that unless 75 per cent of the students were drawn from the workers, the W.E.A. would fail in its mission. Much depends upon the definition of 'worker' that is adopted. If the use of the term is restricted to manual workers, then one must acknowledge that the fears of Dr. Mansbridge have materialized. In the period between the wars the manual workers constituted one-third of the students and that proportion has now declined to one-fifth. Naturally the proportion of

[1] S. G. Raybould. *The W.E.A., The Next Phase.* W.E.A., 1949.

manual workers varies according to the district and in some areas they are still in the majority but in others they represent less than 10 per cent. On the other hand the recruitment of professional and social workers has increased fourfold and the number of teachers, civil servants, and black-coated workers has doubled since 1939. The problem to which an answer is required is whether the W.E.A. is following the example of the Mechanics' Institutes, which were originally designed for mechanics and which later drew most of their members from the so-called middle classes. In many districts the answer seems to be in the affirmative and it may be asked if this is entirely a retrograde tendency. Many people believe that the restriction of the term 'worker' to one section of the community only is quite indefensible and that any association which draws its members indiscriminately from all who are in receipt of wages or salary will ultimately find this a source of strength rather than of weakness. Nevertheless one cannot deny that a most significant change is taking place in the composition of W.E.A. classes.

The balance of the curriculum in W.E.A. classes has altered considerably. When the movement began, emphasis was upon the social studies, namely, economics, social and industrial history, and political and social science. This was no accident. Although from the start the W.E.A. declared its policy to be non-sectarian and non-political, there was little doubt about which political party provided the majority of its members. It is to the credit of the W.E.A. that it avoided the disaster of becoming an institution for spreading left-wing propaganda and so its policy differed from that adopted by the National Council of Labour Colleges. Thus at the present time one would find that most classes contain representatives of all the main political parties and of many different religious faiths. This state of affairs is a healthy one and is likely to continue in the future when the classes will be composed mainly, though not entirely, of students drawn from the secondary modern schools. The present curricular trends are not entirely dissociated from those changes which have occurred in the composition of the classes and from the point of view of a liberal education are welcome rather than otherwise. Thus one discovers an increasing demand for the study of literature and drama and for classes in psychology, philosophy, and musical appreciation. The liberalizing of the curriculum seems to be no cause for alarm.

The greatest change of all has been with regard to the standards of work. In the early days of the movement, Mr. A. L. Smith, who was Master of Balliol, stated that 25 per cent of the essays sent in by members of tutorial classes were equal to the work of men who had obtained First Class Honours in the Final School of Modern History at Oxford. The Board of Education made it one of the conditions for recognition of a tutorial class that its standard of work should be equivalent to that required for a university honours degree. Apart from the exact meaning that can be attached to the Board's requirement, there was no doubt that both in quantity and quality the written work of the early tutorial classes was eminently satisfactory. It was the common practice for each class to hand in twelve essays in each of the three sessions, that is, one every fortnight. At the present time there are few, if any, classes which can even approximate to this. Most tutors know that apart from certain individuals who are ready to write about anything at any time, the majority of the students require careful coaxing if written work of any value at all is to be obtained. A tutor feels that he has not done so badly if he has been able to obtain four essays in a session.

The quality of the essay work has also suffered. It is true that the writer, in nearly twenty years' experience of tutorial class work, has received essays which have been equal in quality to those he has had from students reading for an honours degree at the university, but these were exceptions and not the rule. The weaker members of the classes had to be tactfully coaxed to write a review of the ground covered in the previous week or a letter to the tutor to state some difficulty that had been encountered and to suggest a tentative solution. Even those students who had taken an active part in class discussions seemed to be overcome with reluctance to express their ideas on paper. There are many causes to account for this. One suspects that the reading of students is neither as wide nor as thorough as it was. One explanation is that in 1908 there were not as many counter-attractions to reading and study as exist at the present day. The B.B.C. was an institution of the future and television was barely conceived even by the most romantic of novelists. The cinema was still in its infancy and the habit of receiving one's opinions ready-made had not then developed to any great extent. The earlier students realized that knowledge and understanding were only to be gained through effort and that progress only came by means of hard thinking. Possibly membership of a tutorial class has become too easy. Students express their willingness to undertake the obligations of membership without serious thought as to their meaning. Tutors may in some cases be to blame when in their eagerness to obtain the requisite numbers for starting a class they are not sufficiently emphatic about the high standards that should be demanded.

The tutors who were responsible for developing the first tutorial classes were mostly outstanding scholars who were not only burning with enthusiasm to talk about their subject but also possessed a large measure of human understanding and sympathy. They entered upon their work in a spirit of missionary zeal that could not fail to communicate itself to their pupils. They laboured unsparingly and thought of their work rather as a vocation than a professional job. One must admit that though there are still many tutors of this type, there are others who have not the slightest spark of the inspiration that animated a Tawney or a Clay and who fail in making the necessary human contacts with their students. Mr. Raybould is on very sound ground when he emphasizes the necessity of selecting the right type of tutor who is able to create in his students the desire to read and to learn. His own wide experience in tutorial class work has shown him the futility of expecting a high standard of work from students who have never been trained in the arts of reading and study. Thus he says, 'Before serious study can really be undertaken with such students, they must be trained in the art of study; in note-taking and note-making, in selective and critical reading, in disciplined discussion, in clear expression in speech and writing. Such training will occupy in most cases the best part of two sessions'.[1]

Mr. Raybould is very concerned with the status of the W.E.A. in the future. It is a voluntary organization which, however, receives considerable support from public funds. Most of our educational ventures started on a voluntary basis and eventually came under the control of the State and the local authorities. Is the W.E.A. to go the way of other voluntary organizations? Will its work of providing classes be taken over by the local authorities and be made part of their scheme for further education? If it still continues to exist, will it cease to be a responsible body and merely confine itself to student organization? Some educa-

[1] S. G. Raybould. *The W.E.A., The Next Phase*, p. 60. W.E.A., 1949.

tion officers have thought that this end is inevitable. Mr. Raybould is in complete disagreement with this view. He believes that it would result in disaster for working-class adult education and he sees in the example of the relations between the universities and the University Grants Commission a means by which the voluntary nature of the W.E.A. may be maintained. He writes, 'Two points are important here for the question we are considering. The first is that, although in the main a democratically elected body, a local education committee is not directly representative, or answerable to adult worker-students in anything like the sense that a W.E.A. Branch Committee, District Council, District Executive Committee, or University Joint Committee is. How much influence, for instance, would students have in the appointment of tutors if all tutors (except those employed by universities, in which case the W.E.A. usually has at least as much voice as the university itself) were employees of the local authorities? The second is that adult education of the kind promoted by the W.E.A.—"education for social purpose"—is just the kind of education which it is most dangerous to put entirely into the control of politicians. If education of this kind is to be really vital, and if the students for whom it is intended are to have confidence in it, it must be carried on in an atmosphere of complete freedom, with nobody, student or tutor, feeling that he had better choose his words carefully lest he offend some local councillor or administrator, who, in pursuance of his official rights, responsibilities or duties, may chance to visit the class'.[1]

There were two interesting developments in adult education in the period between the two wars. The first was an experiment in rural education, the formation of the Cambridgeshire Village Colleges due to the initiative of Mr. H. Morris, the Education Secretary to the County Council. The idea of the village college was to provide at the same time schools for children, and educational, social and cultural centres for adults in the region. The first college to be opened was at Sawston in 1928. Eleven other colleges were projected but their erection was hindered by the economic crisis. It was not until 1937 that the college at Bottisham was opened and this was followed by Linton in 1938 and Impington in 1939. The outbreak of war put an end to this development for the time being and although the building

[1] *Ibid.*, p. 83.

of eight other colleges has been approved, it will be some years before they are ready. The scheme of Mr. Morris was actively encouraged by the Carnegie United Kingdom Trustees. Speaking of the college at Impington, Mr. H. C. Dent writes, 'Twenty-one associations, societies, clubs and groups were meeting at the college: their activities ranged from agriculture to music, from religion to the Red Cross. Fifteen courses and classes, ranging from glove-making to child psychology, were being provided. There were a common-room, a canteen service, a library, a games room and a news-letter. In all the contributory villages further activities were being conducted. And, as in all the colleges, the users were united in the Students' Association, from which was elected the Students' Council, the governing body of the college's internal life'.[1]

The second development was concerned with the new housing estates built after the first World War and its object was to provide a healthy social life amongst the people living on them. Community centres were at first erected through voluntary agency but in 1944 the Ministry of Education in a pamphlet entitled Community Centres stated that the general responsibility for developing them now rested with the Ministry and the local education authorities. The Ministry thought it desirable that all villages with a population over 400 should be provided with a village hall.

In rural districts the Women's Institutes are a most important educational influence. The idea originated in Canada and was implanted here by Mrs. Arthur Watt shortly after the beginning of the first World War. At first their activities were largely practical, being connected with such things as food production, jam making and the bottling of fruit. Very soon they began to develop cultural activities which now range over a very wide field. Each county has its own federation of Women's Institutes, and these are united in the National Federation of Women's Institutes. The latter issues each month its magazine, *Home and Country*, which includes a supplement dealing with the activities of the different county federations. In 1948 the National Federation opened its own college, Denman College, near Abingdon, Berks. At present, 1950, there are 7,281 Institutes containing 438,000 members, and in the two years during which it has been open Denman College has received over

[1] H. C. Dent. *Part-Time Education in Great Britain*, pp. 48–9. Turnstile Press, 1949.

3,000 students for short courses. The very wide range of activities is shown by those carried out in one month in the Lindsey (Lincolnshire) district. They included talks on Lincolnshire Crafts and Industry, France, America, drama, care of the feet, and plants and flowers; there were demonstrations of plastic work, fabric printing, sweet making, salads, smocking, skin curing and dressmaking. Individual institutes organized flower shows, concerts, and competitions. Several of the demonstrations led to a demand for classes to teach the crafts. Most institutes possess a dramatic society and there is a keen competition between institutes in play production.

In the towns the Townswomen's Guilds correspond to the Women's Institutes in the rural areas. The individual guilds are federated in the National Union of Townswomen's Guilds. Members of the guilds show a keen interest in civics, current affairs, social studies, and in choral and dramatic work. Classes providing instruction in homecrafts and various kinds of handwork have been formed and are well attended.

The number of associations at the present day which are connected with some aspect or other of adult education is legion, and space forbids the mention of only those who place education among their principal aims. Two of the oldest are the Y.M.C.A. and the Y.W.C.A. They have always taken a prominent part in adult education and their contriubution to education in the Services will receive mention in the chapter dealing with education in H.M. Forces. Most of the religious denominations have formed voluntary associations which, although mainly religious in character, have also included education in their aims. Examples of these are the Church of England Tutorial Classes, founded by Dr. Mansbridge, the Church of England Men's Society, the Mothers' Union, the Girls' Friendly Society, the Catholic Social Guild, the Brotherhood movement and Men's Fellowships connected with the Free Churches.

The Arts Council of Great Britain had its origin in the war-time organization known as C.E.M.A. (Council for the Encouragement of Music and the Arts). It received the grant of a Royal Charter on August 9th, 1946. From 1940 the Council received a grant from the Board of Education but since 1946 its income has been derived directly from the Treasury and the Chancellor of the Exchequer has been the responsible Minister. As stated in the Charter, the aims of the Arts Council are to develop 'a greater knowledge, understanding and practice of the fine arts . . . and in particular to increase the accessibility of the fine arts to the public . . . to improve the standard of execution of the fine arts and to advise and co-operate with . . . Government departments, local authorities and other bodies on any matters concerned directly or indirectly with those objects'. The Council has eleven regional offices and separate committees for Scotland and Wales. One of its important activities consisted in supplying art exhibitions and this service grew considerably when valuable pictures which had been concealed for safety during the war, became available to the public. Another of its functions has been the establishment of arts clubs in various parts of the country. It also arranges exhibitions in the visual arts, assists symphony concerts in industrial areas, and sponsors a large number of dramatic ventures. Advisory panels for music, art and drama have been established to organize its work in these branches of art.

Another important agency in the field of adult education is the B.B.C. For many years the Corporation has organized systematic broadcasts to schools in a great variety of subjects. In addition to entertainment it has always included in its usual programmes talks and series of lectures for adult listeners. These included symphony concerts, recitals, travel talks and discussion of current affairs, and courses on musical appreciation. In response to demands for a more serious type of programme the B.B.C. introduced the Third Programme, which was designed 'for the alert and receptive listener, who is willing first of all to make an effort in selection and then to meet the performer half-way by giving his whole attention to what is being broadcast.' By this means the B.B.C. has made accessible music and drama which would not appeal to the public as a whole and has been able to broadcast lectures by outstanding authorities in their respective fields. The broadcast lecture has one particular advantage over any other form of adult education. People in remote parts of the country where the formation of ordinary classes would not be practicable are able to listen to the programmes. In some villages listening and discussion groups have been formed and the staff of the B.B.C. has given them valuable help in showing them how a discussion should proceed.

Sir Richard Livingstone in his book, *The Future of Education*, has advocated the establishment of residential colleges for adults on the pattern of those in the Scandinavian countries. He believes that however efficient our primary and secondary schools may be they can only provide the early stages in a liberal education. This would still be true even if the school-leaving age was raised to 16 or 18. The reason is that many of the studies which are essential for adults, literature, history, economics, philosophy and politics, are by their very nature unsuited to schoolboys. Such studies demand a greater experience of life than a schoolboy possesses, so he is unable to fully appreciate them. He may make a beginning with the study of history on the factual side but the real meaning of history will remain hidden from him until he has experienced those aspects of human nature which will illuminate what he has read. Evening classes such as those organized by the W.E.A. or the local education authorities will not supply a solution to the problem. Adults attend these classes after a tiring day and often the environment in which they are held is not such as conduces to study. The ideal conditions, he is convinced, can only be provided by a system of residential colleges planned on the model of the Danish People's High Schools. A necessary supplement to these would be provided by non-residential settlements.

In addition to the voluntary agencies which supply adult education, the local education authorities have been given by the Education Act of 1944 the duty of providing adequate facilities for full-time and part-time education and leisure-time occupation for adults in their areas who are able and willing to profit by them. When the local authorities prepare their schemes for Further Education they are instructed to consult the other agencies concerned, such as the universities and the W.E.A. One of the most serious problems that has to be solved before any system of residential colleges becomes practicable is that of building. It has been suggested that in many parts of the country there are large houses whose owners cannot afford, because of heavy taxation, to maintain them. It would not be an insuperable task to convert them; in fact some of them during the war had been used by the Forces for educational purposes. Another problem is that of the attitude of employers. Would an employer be willing to give an employee six months' leave to attend a college to study literature? The answer usually given is that the Government would have to intervene to protect the interests of the worker and that once the custom had been established of workers spending three or six or even twelve months at a residential college, employers would accept it and make their arrangements accordingly. One can only say that these are hopes for the distant future and that as long as the nation is faced with the necessity of building up its export trade, they are not likely to materialize.

The advances made in the sphere of technical education during the last fifty years are quite as spectacular as those in adult education. In the first half of the nineteenth century, little attention was given to technical education. Britain was the workshop of the world and there was no need to worry. The importance of technical education was first dimly felt at the time of the great Exhibition of 1851. Although in one respect it demonstrated the superiority of British crafstmanship, yet it also revealed potential dangers. Other countries had begun to learn from us and it would not be long before they came into active competition with us. In the year following the Exhibition the Government established the Department of Practical Art and a year later a science division was added. At the same time its title was changed for that of the Science and Art Department of the Board of Trade. In 1856 the Department was put under the supervision of the newly created Education Department of the Committee of Council. The Science and Art Departments of South Kensington started a system of examinations and made grants to institutions, mainly secondary schools, which presented successful candidates. The official mind was seriously disturbed when in 1867 Britain in many classes failed at the Paris Exhibition to gain first place. The consequence was the appointment of the Devonshire Commission which reported in 1875 and which gave a complete account of the technological progress in other countries. The immediate result was the establishment of a number of technical colleges, many of which were developments from the Mechanics' Institutes. Yet another Royal Commission was appointed in 1884 and it was followed by the Technical Instruction Act of 1889. The following year saw the beginning of 'Whisky Money' which was explained in the first chapter of this book.

The subsequent advances in the realm of technical education were so momentous as almost to merit the name of a revolution. The most convenient way of dealing with these changes seems to be that of starting with the evening schools. When they were first instituted the evening schools were intended for older people who had not attended a day school. The instruction was mainly in the three Rs but as elementary education became more widespread, a demand for teaching of a higher type became general. The Code of 1890 authorized instruction in languages, science, art, handicrafts and domestic work. When a separate Code for Evening Continuation schools was issued in 1898, the scope of the evening schools was still further extended. The increase in the range of subjects that could be taken raised an important problem. Students were given the option of choosing the subjects they wished to study. Suppose a certain individual wanted to study engineering. It would not be long before he discovered that he also needed a number of other subjects such as mathematics, mechanics, or machine drawing. This difficulty was overcome by the adoption of the group system. Halifax continuation evening schools were the first to adopt the group system and very soon this policy was approved by the Board of Education. The group system was devised in the interests of those students who intended to carry their studies beyond the range of the evening school. It was organized with regard to the occupations of students or the industries which they hoped to enter. Each grouped course included a number of subjects chosen according to a definite plan. There were five main groups: (1) Industrial, (2) Commercial, (3) Rural, (4) Domestic, (5) General. From the point of view of industry and commerce, the first two groups were considered the most important. Rural courses were not nearly as popular and the General courses, though at first they did not make a strong appeal to students, attracted in later years a large number of students. In all the courses English was a compulsory subject. The subjects included in each of the five grouped courses were chosen on the basis of certain principles. Thus a boy who intended to enter industry should have a knowledge of workshop calculations, be able to read a drawing, to express himself clearly in spoken and written English, and to have some acquaintance with the science of everyday life. Thus the industrial course normally included elementary mathematics, technical drawing, English, and elementary science.

Evening technical schools developed concurrently with the evening continuation schools. At first the range of subjects taught was limited to those which earned grant from the Science and Art Department or which were recognized by the City and Guilds of London Institute, but in 1904 the

Regulations of the Board of Education authorized the payment of grant for instruction in a very wide range of subjects. Although there was an immediate broadening of the curriculum, the full benefits of the revised regulations were not felt until a more adequate supply of qualified teachers of the various subjects was available. The evening technical schools, like the evening continuation schools, adopted the principle of grouped courses of instruction. Eventually courses in evening technical schools were divided into junior, senior and advanced courses. The junior course was usually taken in the evening continuation school and it was not specialized in character. Its object was to provide boys between 14 and 16 years of age with a good foundation for the more specialized studies of the technical school. The senior course was designed as a three years' course to be taken in a technical school. Students who took this course were expected to have received suitable instruction previously, either in a secondary school or in the evening continuation school. The larger technical schools were able to offer an advanced course which was planned to cover two and sometimes three years. The advanced student was allowed greater freedom in the choice of the subjects he wished to study.

At the beginning of this century the recognized view was that the school should be mainly concerned with the theoretical aspect of an industry and that the actual practice should be left to the workshops. Although this view is still widely accepted, it has been considerably modified and in certain industries it has been abandoned. Instruction in the building crafts affords an example of this more recent tendency. Practical training in plumbing, joinery and plastering is now accepted as being an essential part of the course. The same idea has been extended to other crafts. This has given rise to the distinction between Minor and Major courses. There is necessarily some overlapping between the two types but the broad distinction consists in a difference in their aims. The object of a Minor course is to provide instruction for particular occupations within an industry, while the Major course teaches the general principles which belong to an industry as a whole. In many technical schools Minor courses are organized with a view to a subsequent Major course.

At the beginning of the century, as was explained earlier in this chapter, the curriculum of the evening technical schools was largely governed by the examination requirements of the Science and Art Department and the City and Guilds of London Institute. On the whole the certificates of the latter body were designed for craftsmen rather than technicians. It was felt that greater freedom ought to be given to the schools and the Board of Education gave effect to this policy in 1911 when the science examinations in the lower grade were discontinued. The next step was the abolition of all the science examinations except those connected with certain scholarship awards. The lead given by the Board was followed in 1918 by the City and Guilds of London Institute, which only retained the final grade examinations. The Board of Education had in view the establishment of a system of internal examinations conducted by the schools themselves which should issue certificates endorsed by the Board to successful candidates. This proposal met with an unfavourable reception from teachers, local authorities and the industries generally. Their view was that external tests would command greater confidence and would be likely to secure acceptance in all parts of the country. This demand was at first satisfied by examinations conducted by unions of schools and local authorities such as the Union of Lancashire and Cheshire Institutes, the East Midland Educational Union and the Northern Counties Technical Examinations Council. Some of these unions had been in existence for a considerable time; for example, the Union of Lancashire and Cheshire Institutes had been formed as early as 1839. When the Board of Education and the City and Guilds of London Institute relinquished many of their examinations, the regional bodies stepped into the gap and developed a comprehensive system of examinations.

The situation, however, was not completely satisfactory because there were some areas which were not covered by the regional unions. To meet the needs of such districts, the City and Guilds of London Institute restored some of the examinations which had previously been abandoned. There was a widespread demand for a qualification of national standing which would approximate to the standard of a university degree. The Government sensed the direction thought was taking and in 1921 the Board of Education consulted the Institution of Mechanical Engineers in regard to the award of National Certificates and Diplomas in mechanical engineering. The scheme came into operation in the following year and was so well received that further

National Certificates were instituted; chemistry, 1922, electrical engineering, 1923, naval architecture, 1927, building, 1930, textiles and commerce, 1939. Awards are made on two levels; the Ordinary Certificate given on the result of a senior part-time course of three years, and the Higher Certificate awarded for an additional two years of advanced study. Corresponding to the awards for part-time students, full-time students could gain an Ordinary or a Higher National Diploma. The scheme has been extremely successful. It has not only preserved the high standards of work demanded by the great professional institutions but it has also allowed a considerable degree of freedom to the schools. The certificates and diplomas are awarded not merely on results gained by candidates in a specific examination but weight is also attached to each student's record throughout the whole course of instruction.

Technical education in this country owes much to the stimulus and encouragement of Lord Eustace Percy. He was convinced that the position of Britain as one of the leading commercial and industrial nations of the world depended upon the quality of the education given in the technical schools and colleges. When he became President of the Board of Education in 1925 he turned his attention to developing opportunities for technical and technological (higher technical) training and to strengthening the relations between the technological colleges and the universities, the local authorities and the employers of industry. In pursuance of this policy he constituted the Clerk Committee which investigated education for the engineering group of industries and the Goodenough Committee on Education for Salesmanship. These Committees reported in 1929 and 1931 respectively and in reaching their conclusions they received valuable assistance from members of important commercial and industrial enterprises who were represented on the Committees. Lord Eustace Percy was the author of a collection of education essays which were published under the title of *Education at the Crossroads*. The following paragraph from that book, which was written in the midst of the inter-war financial crisis, is fully applicable to the situation of the present day. He said, 'There is to-day in all walks of life less scope for successful careers, and at the same time, within the scope that remains, success requires much deeper knowledge, greater skill, more exact training and stronger character. We are still citizens of a great country, but it is a country in distress. A "boom" philosophy, such as we have inherited from so many years of prosperity will not help us now. Ours is no longer a country to be enjoyed and exploited for its advantages; it is a country to be saved'.[1] Lord Eustace was fully convinced that education, and in particular technological education, would play an essential rôle in the saving process.

The second World War not only brought home to the country the necessity for more highly trained scientists and technicians than those possessed by our enemies but at the same time it threw into relief the lack of co-ordination between the different agencies responsible for the supply of higher technical education. Technology had played a prominent part in winning the war. It was no less important for the peace which was to follow. One of the most urgent problems in this field was that of bringing about greater unity and more useful relations between the bodies responsible for higher technical training and in particular between the universities and the senior technical institutions. To further this aim the Government in 1944 appointed a special committee to consider the problems of technological education. Lord Eustace Percy, because of his long experience in university life, at the Board of Education and in relation to industry, was chosen as Chairman. The Percy Report, issued in 1945, represents the most far-reaching statement of policy regarding technical education that has so far emanated from the Ministry of Education.

The recommendations made in the Report proved that the members of the Percy Committee were fully aware of the issues at stake. Industry in Great Britain suffered from the failure to apply, in the fullest sense, scientific knowledge in its development. This was in part due to deficiencies in technological education. The nation was short of highly trained technological personnel. There was a sufficiency of skilled craftsmen but there was an urgent need for scientists and technologists who not only had expert knowledge but could also apply the results of their researches to industry and who, in addition, possessed ability in organization and administration. In other words, at the lower levels, the nation was adequately served; it was at the highest level that the type of man required was scarce.

The only answer to this problem was to secure a much greater output from the universities and the senior technical

[1] *Education at the Crossroads*, p. 55. Evans Bros. Ltd.

institutions. At the time these two sources of supply were out of touch with each other. Formerly, it had been assumed that one would look to the universities to produce scientists and research workers whilst the technical colleges would train technical assistants and craftsmen. This division of function would become disastrous if maintained and in the future it would be necessary for both institutions to educate students to the stage which would fit them to be senior assistants or even managers of industry. This would involve a far greater degree of co-operation between the universities and the senior technical institutions than had so far obtained. The Percy Report was mainly concerned with the various branches of the engineering industry and it was of the opinion that post-war conditions would require the output of skilled engineers to be at least half as large again as the pre-war number. It was calculated that the minimum ought to be about 3,000 annually, of which about 45 per cent should come from the universities.

In order to bring about this result it was suggested that a limited number of the larger technical colleges should be selected and that the instruction given in them should be equivalent to that of the universities. Special courses should be established for advanced students of technology and one important aspect of the work would be that of research into the problems of local industries. The senior technical colleges which were selected to play a part in the scheme should be granted a large measure of self-government and responsibility. The Government should assist them by means of capital grants in a way similar to the universities and the salaries enjoyed by the staffs should be comparable to those paid in the universities.

The Committee were concerned with the question of recruiting suitable students. The Report quite frankly stated that 'the best material is not being offered . . . in sufficient quantities. In a word, industry, and educational institutions training for industry are not getting their fair share of the national ability'.[1] The advantages that an industrial career offered should be more widely publicized. This would mean a closer co-ordination between the Ministry of Labour, the University Appointments Boards and the Juvenile Employment Bureaux. It was also to be hoped that the expansion of secondary education envisaged by the Education Act of 1944 would have a considerable effect.

[1] Report on *Higher Technological Education*, para. 41. H.M.S.O., 1945.

So far members of the Committee had been in agreement but when they came to the consideration of the award of qualifications by the technological colleges, a divergence of opinion became apparent. It was agreed that the colleges ought to conduct their own examinations and award their own qualifications but it was advisable that some national body should be created in order to guarantee a uniform standard. This need could be met by the institution of a National Council which would work through an academic board. An external examining body would also be necessary and the qualifications given by the major technical colleges should have the prestige of a university degree. Disagreement developed when the actual title of the qualification was considered.

Some members of the Committee thought that it should be a degree, the B.Tech. It was urged that such a course would be of great assistance in attracting students to the colleges. Advanced research might be rewarded by the degree of Tech.D. Others insisted that industrial employers would be more concerned with the kind of training an applicant had undergone than with the exact title of his qualification. They suggested a diploma and not a degree. Opinion was fairly evenly divided on this matter and the decision was left to Lord Eustace Percy. It was again fortunate that he had been appointed Chairman, for not only was he acquainted with the situation in technical education but in addition, as Rector of the Newcastle Division of the University of Durham, he possessed an intimate knowledge of universities. Thus he was an ideal arbitrator and in his *Note to the Report*, he pointed out the difficulties that would arise if the technical colleges were given authority to grant degrees. The matter would not end there. The university colleges, the Royal Colleges of Art and Music and many other institutions for higher education would be justified in making similar claims. Where could one draw the line? He wrote, 'In all civilized countries the power to confer degrees is the distinguishing mark of a university. In this country the power can be exercised only if it is granted by an act of Government, and Government has jealously restricted such grants. Government policy has been based on the principle that a university should be a fully self-governing community of teachers and students, working together in one place, with substantial endowments of its own, mature enough to set its own standards of teaching and strong enough to resist outside pressures, public or private, political or economic'.[1]

His solution was that the selected colleges should be given the title of Royal Colleges of Technology and that they should be authorized to confer at the graduate stage the Associateship of the Royal Colleges of Technology, and at the post-graduate stage the Fellowship. That the idea rejected by the Chairman is not altogether dead is evidenced by recent articles and correspondence in the *Times Educational Supplement* on the subject of a Technical University. The newly elected Socialist Government hastened to implement the Percy Report. As Professor Lester Smith has written, 'Outlining its aims in a short circular, the Ministry demanded "substantial progress" in the course of a few weeks; and accompanying this document was a schedule showing England and Wales sliced into ten regions, in each of which conferences were hastily summoned of representatives, not only of universities, technical colleges and local authorities, but of various bodies associated in any way with further education in its widest connotation. Advisory Councils, representative of the various interests, and Academic Boards were set up; and later, as a coping-stone to this regional mosaic, a National Council was constituted'.[2] He added, ' "This is a time to plan boldly and comprehensively", said the Ministry in a booklet on *Further Education* (H.M.S.O., 1947); there may be some truth in this, but perhaps there is more wisdom in the old French proverb, *Qui trop embrasse mal étreint'*.

---

[1] *Ibid.*, Chairman's Note, para. 4.
[2] W. O. Lester Smith. *Education in Great Britain*, p. 159. O.U.P., 1949.

CHAPTER IX

EDUCATION IN SCOTLAND, 1900–50

SCOTTISH education developed along a path which has been somewhat different from that which was followed in England and the effect has been to produce a system and organization in the former country which still retains certain important characteristics of its own. It is not possible to understand Scottish education of to-day without giving some attention to those historical, geographical, social, and economic factors which have been instrumental in fashioning it.

In England the foundations of a national system of education were not laid until 1902. The first chapter of this book emphasized that English educational institutions came into existence and developed through voluntary effort and only when this was proved to be inadequate the State began to intervene by assisting voluntary effort by means of grants and at a later stage by making good deficiencies in the provision of education. The story in Scotland is quite different. At the beginning of the present century the pattern of Scottish education was that which had been authorized by the Education (Scotland) Act of 1872 which had substituted a State system for one which had existed for many centuries. The chief feature of the history of English education is the creation of a national system, but in Scotland the significant factor was the transference to the State of the organized system of education controlled by the Church. Even before the Reformation, Scottish education was subject to the centralized control of the Church in the primary and university fields, whilst secondary education, at first in the hands of the ecclesiastical authorities, gradually passed into the hands of the municipal councils, either as the sequel to a struggle or as the result of a mutual agreement.

Scotland can boast that the first Education Act in these islands, indeed in Europe, was passed by Parliament nearly five hundred years before any similar measure in England. The reference is to the Act of 1496, which ordered all barons and wealthy freeholders to send their eldest sons or heirs to school from six to nine years of age to acquire 'perfecte

Latine' and then required them to allow their children to spend another three years in the schools of 'Art and Jure'. Non-compliance with the Act was visited by a fine of twenty pounds, though it is doubtful if the penalty was ever enforced.

It was John Knox who was the author of Scotland's national system of education. The *First Book of Discipline*, 1560, which was largely the work of Knox, recommended a comprehensive scheme of education extending from the primary school to the university stage. Although the Kirk was prevented by lack of funds from carrying out this scheme as fully as was intended, nevertheless it remained as a constant ideal for the Scottish people, who regard the Education Acts of 1872, 1908 and 1918 as fulfilling the aspirations of John Knox. Thus Alexander Morgan is justified in saying that 'Most of the progress in Scottish education since Knox's day has consisted in advancing towards his ideals. The great Education Acts of 1872 and 1918 are but modern expressions of some of his ideals, others having still to be fulfilled. These facts, Hume Brown says, "stamp the *First Book of Discipline* as the most important document in Scottish history", and its proposals as a whole cast the mould in which the Scottish character and intellect have been formed for nearly four centuries'.[1]

The striking feature about the proposals of Knox was the insistence that education should be compulsory. The next three hundred years were characterized by attempts to approximate to his ideal and the aim of the Education Acts of 1646 and 1696 was to establish universal primary education. By the nineteenth century the failure of the Church to achieve this task had become apparent. The Great Disruption of 1843 had split the Church so that there was no longer a single authority in charge of education. The failure of the Church to provide schools in a sufficient number caused the appointment of the Argyll Commission of 1868, whose Report, whilst giving well-merited praise to the organization of secondary education, stated that the parish schools, whether in town or country, were totally inadequate to carry out the work for which they had been intended. Already an Act of 1861 had weakened the control of the Church so that when the transference to State control was accomplished in 1872, few obstacles had to be surmounted.

[1] A. Morgan. *Rise and Progress of Scottish Education*, p. 53. Oliver and Boyd, 1927.

The geographical features of Scotland have had a marked effect upon the spread of education. The mountainous nature of the land and the lack of communications in the highlands and the islands presented a formidable obstacle to the establishment of schools in those areas. It is significant that when in the early years of the eighteenth century the S.P.C.K. (Scotland) was founded, its efforts were primarily directed to establishing schools in these regions. The most densely populated area has always been the Lowland Rift Valley and it was here that the majority of the schools were to be found. The only other centres of population were in the coastal areas around the towns of Aberdeen and Dundee. To a lesser extent the Southern Uplands presented similar difficulties. The consequence was that in the sparsely peopled districts the villages developed as self-contained communities and the parish school attained a position of importance that it never achieved in England.

For centuries the Scottish people have been educationally conscious. The proof of this is that during the Middle Ages Scotland was able to maintain three universities whilst her more wealthy neighbour possessed the two universities of Oxford and Cambridge. One should add to the three mediæval universities that of Edinburgh, which was founded at the close of the sixteenth century. All four were in a very real sense 'people's universities'. Their students were drawn from every rank of society and many of them attended classes without further thought of proceeding to a degree. The Scots were always alive to the value of education to a degree that was not to be found in England until recent years. Scottish people of all classes economized in order to send their sons to the burgh schools or to go themselves to the universities. In England it was necessary to prescribe penalties for parents who neglected their duty of sending their children to school to receive adequate instruction in the three Rs. Although during the last fifty or sixty years the attitude of many Scottish parents has changed the old tradition still persists in many places. A few years ago when the writer was being conducted by the gardener round a large estate in Scotland he asked the guide how he spent the gratuities he received. The reply was that the gardener was saving his tips so tht he could enter a university and study for a degree. As Scotland becomes more completely Anglicized such instances become rarer. In the nineteenth century secondary education in Scotland was more widely diffused than in England. Thus in 1868 the Argyll Commission estimated that the proportion of the population receiving secondary education was one in 140. The figure for England at that time was one in 1,300. The sad thing is that Scottish education is inclined to trade with its past capital and in many respects has allowed English education to overtake it. James Grant, the well-known authority for the history of the Scottish burgh schools, wrote, 'In no country did the poorer classes, including the small farmers, crofters, artisans, and labourers, prize a liberal education to the same extent as those classes have done in our own country'.[1]

Another characteristic of Scottish education was the non-existence of a sharp dividing line between primary and secondary schools. Although the typical secondary schools were those supported by the burghs, secondary education was also provided in the parochial schools. The Scottish people possessed a long-standing tradition that the 'lad o' pairts', that is, the intellectually able scholar, no matter from which social class he came, had a right to the best kind of education available for him. One might call this the democratic tradition of Scottish education. Thus the Duke of Argyll, speaking in the House of Lords in 1869 on the subject of the parochial schools, was able to say, 'It is the universal custom all over Scotland that men in very different classes of society should be educated together in the parochial schools. You will have the children of the poorest labourer sitting beside the farmer who employs him, the children of the clergyman of the parish, and even in some cases of the landed gentry, sitting on the same bench and learning from the same master the same branches of instruction'.[2] This still holds good for some of the country districts. The writer, noticing a Rolls Royce waiting outside a village school, inquired who owned it and he was told that it had come to bring the children of the laird to their home.

On the other hand, what one may term the academic tradition has been more firmly rooted in Scotland than in English schools. This is probably due to the natural bias of the Scottish mind. The Englishman is practical by nature and is inclined to mistrust theory and abstract thought. The Scot is more logical and philosophical. He has always possessed a strong belief in the value of a university training

[1] J. Grant. *History of the Burgh Schools of Scotland*, p. 335. W. Collins, 1876.
[2] N. A. Wade. *Post Primary Education in the Primary Schools of Scotland*, p. 29, University of London Press, 1939.

and in university degrees. It is only recently, and that because of war conditions, that non-graduate men teachers in any large number have been employed in Scottish schools. The old-time schoolmaster always cherished the hope that he might leave the profession for preferment in the Church. Scottish universities for centuries have exercised a strong influence upon the national life and education. This tradition has not been an unmixed blessing. Although Scottish schoolmasters have striven to maintain a high standard of 'sound learning' they have been slow to accommodate themselves to new ideas in education. Thus the junior secondary school, which corresponds to the secondary modern school in England, has not so far won general approval in Scotland. It is still regarded as an inferior type of institution.

The Education (Scotland) Act of 1872 under which Scottish education was organized at the commencement of the present century, took full account of these national characteristics. The story of the last fifty years is that of the attempt to bring Scottish and English education into line with each other whilst at the same time retaining those features of Scottish education which are at once characteristic and valuable. One should not compare the Act of 1872 with the English Elementary Education Act of 1870 but rather with the Education Act of 1902. The preamble of the Act specifically stated that its object was 'to amend and extend the provisions of the law of Scotland on the subject of education in such manner that the means of procuring efficient education for their children may be furnished and made available to the whole people of Scotland'. In other words, the Act was concerned with education as a whole and not merely with elementary education. In fact until the end of the nineteenth century, the term 'elementary' was not officially used in Scotland and it was only when the reorganization of Scottish education called for some differentiation between the two stages that it became general.

All state-aided schools were known as public schools and included the parish schools, which provided secondary as well as primary education, and the new schools built under the authority of the Act, which carried on the traditions of the parish schools. The Act explicitly stated that the Government was anxious to maintain the high standards in education which had previously existed. Thus Section 67 declared, 'Due care shall be taken by the Scotch Education Department . . . that the standard of education which now exists in the public schools shall not be lowered, and that, as far as possible, as high a standard shall be maintained in all schools inspected by the said Department.' This encouraged the schools to develop advanced departments in which the instruction given compared favourably with the secondary education provided in the grammar and burgh schools.

The State-aided grammar and burgh schools were known as higher class public schools. In addition the Act recognized higher class schools which were non-public schools maintained by fees, subscriptions and endowments. The higher class public schools were severely handicapped by the Act. They relied for their maintenance upon fees and to a lesser extent upon grants from the 'public good' of the burghs and endowments. As Scottish burgh schools were notoriously poor as regards endowments and the fees charged had always been moderate, they were in an unfavourable position financially. The public 'elementary' schools on the other hand, received support both from the State and from the local rates. The higher class schools, many of which such as Fettes and Loretto corresponded to English public schools, were often more fortunate in the matter of endowments and were able to demand higher fees. As it turned out, the higher class public schools had for some years a desperate struggle to maintain their efficiency.

Scottish education had never been obstructed by religious controversies. Even the Great Disruption of 1843 had been a quarrel about Church organization rather than doctrine. Hence the transference of the schools from Church to State control proceeded quite smoothly. The Act merely stated in the preamble that since religious instruction had always been given in the public schools, the managers should be at liberty to continue such instruction to children whose parents raised no objection to it.

The central authority for administration was the Committee of Council on Education, generally known as the Scotch Education Department. As a committee of the Privy Council, it was presided over by the same President and Vice-President as the English Education Department. Its function was to receive and distribute the Parliamentary grants for education in accordance with a Code of Regulations which had to be approved each year by both Houses of Parliament. It was also given authority to inspect schools. Although the

Act did not expressly define the extent of its powers, the Department was able to extend its authority by the issue of Minutes which when approved by Parliament had the force of law.

For the local administration of education, the country was divided into 984 districts each of which was under the management of a School Board. The desire of the Government to preserve Scottish tradition was exemplified by the fact that the School Board districts roughly corresponded to those of the parishes and burghs. The School Boards were elected triennially and the parish and burgh schools were transferred to them. Other grant-earning schools might also seek transfer. The position at the commencement of the present century was that nearly all State-aided schools with the exception of those belonging to the Episcopalians and the Roman Catholics had been transferred to the School Boards. As in England one of the first duties of the School Boards was to establish schools in those areas in which a deficiency existed. It is important to note that the Scottish School Boards were in charge of all the public schools in their areas regardless of the fact whether they supplied primary or secondary education. The School Boards received the Government grant from the Education Department and distributed it. They had the power of levying a local education rate and of borrowing money for building and equipping schools.

During the transitional period which immediately followed the passage of the Act, the central administration was in the hands of a Board of Education, but when in 1878 the work of transfer had been completed, its duties were taken over by the Scotch Education Department, and Scotland was left free to pursue its own policy without interference from England. Scottish education was fortunate in securing successively the services of two extremely able administrators. The first was Mr. (later Sir) Henry Craik and when in 1885 the Scotch Education Depatment became independent of the English Committee of the Privy Council, he was appointed its first Secretary. In this position he was directly responsible to the Secretary of State for Scotland. Alexander Morgan speaks of his appointment in the following terms: 'At once the effects of his administration were felt in every grade of education. He entered upon a career of reform which he pursued with unflagging zeal during the nineteen years of his Secretaryship. It is not too much to say that during that period he played a dominant part in moulding the educational policy of Scotland'.[1]

The Revised Code of 1862 applied to Scotland as well as to England and although the former country missed the worst features of the system of 'Payment by Results', Scottish schools were examined in the three Rs in the same way as English schools. Craik was determined to abolish the system and he eventually succeeded in doing so in 1890, seven years before a similar step was taken in England. He also tackled the urgent problems of secondary education. The most serious was the unfortunate financial position of the higher class public schools. Many of them had managed to secure additional funds by entering pupils for the examinations of the Science and Art Department. This provided some small assistance but more substantial aid came from the allotment of a proportion of the 'Whisky Money' to Scotland. The amount received by the Burgh and County Councils varied each year but the average sum worked out at about £60,000. About two-thirds of this money was used for education and the remainder for rate relief.

A much more substantial windfall was provided by what was known as the Equivalent Grant. In 1891 Parliament authorized a grant to meet the cost of providing free elementary education in England and Wales. Craik was quick to urge that an equivalent amount should be given to Scotland and his demand was granted by the Education and Local Taxation Account (Scotland) Act, 1892. The sum received by Scotland was £265,000 per annum. £30,000 was assigned to each of the four universities and £60,000 to secondary education. Of the latter amount, a little more than £3,000 was used to cover the cost of inspection of secondary schools and of conducting the Leaving Certificate Examination. The remainder was handed over to Secondary Education Committees which were established in each county and in the five largest towns. The Committees were responsible for distributing the money to the secondary schools. This administrative organization paved the way for the replacement of the parish by the county as the unit of local educational administration, a change which did not take place until 1918. The parallel in England was the authorization of the county and county borough councils as distributors of the 'Whisky Money', which thereby gave them experience in the local administration of education which they were

[1] A. Morgan. *Makers of Scottish Education*, p. 222. Longmans, Green, 1929.

called upon to undertake in 1902. Craik had also been freeing by stages the elementary schools from the payment of fees. In 1891 fees were abolished for all children between the ages of 5 and 14 and this was extended in 1893 to cover the ages from 3 to 15.

Perhaps Craik's crowning achievement was the institution of the Leaving Certificate Examination in 1888. Much tact was required to obtain the support of the schools and universities but Craik wisely avoided making regulations which would threaten the freedom of those schools which entered the scheme. The result was that the number of candidates increased each year and when Craik left the Department in 1904, there were 19,090 pupils who sat for the examination. Many of the schools which were outside the State system entered their pupils and the universities accepted the Certificate under certain conditions as being equivalent to their own awards. The institution of the Certificate was a potent factor in raising the standards of Scottish secondary education. The equivalent in England, the School and Higher School Certificates, were not instituted until 1917. It should be noted that the Leaving Certificate was normally taken a year later than the English School Certificate with the result that the majority of Scottish students enter the universities a year younger than in England. The examination was conducted by the Education Department and not by the universities as in England. Some of the Scottish 'public schools' such as Fettes enter their pupils for the English School and Higher School Certificate examinations.

In 1899 Craik introduced the higher grade school which played an important part in the development of Scottish education. Under modern conditions the teaching of more advanced subjects in the parish schools was becoming increasingly difficult. Craik had encouraged the teaching of science and this called for the use of laboratories which parish schools did not possess. One should also remember that the Act of 1872 had fixed the elementary school-leaving age at 13 and this was not extended to 14 until 1901. The higher grade schools were intended for primary school pupils who were prepared to continue their education for at least three years beyond the statutory school-leaving age. At first they were divided into higher grade science and higher grade commercial schools. The next step was to make these schools available for pupils up to 17 or 18 years of age and to allow them in the final years of their course to specialize in a literary, scientific, technical, or commercial direction. These schools, except in name, were secondary schools and they were allowed to enter their pupils for the Leaving Certificate examination on the same terms as the secondary schools. The institution of the higher grade schools was generally approved by the Scottish people, who had grown accustomed to more advanced education being provided in the parish schools. The weakness of these schools lay in the fact that they overlapped with the secondary schools on the one side, and with the higher departments of the elementary schools on the other. The result was that those schools which offered a five years course eventually became secondary schools and those which retained a three years course took their place in the advanced divisions of the primary schools.

The institution of advanced divisions was the counterpart of the English central and senior school system. The Code of 1903 allowed specialist instruction of an industrial, commercial, rural or domestic character to be given to pupils between the ages of 12 and 14. These courses were known as Supplementary Courses and pupils who completed one of them satisfactorily were awarded a Merit Certificate. The innovation was not at all popular. It was attacked by Professor Laurie, the Educational Institute of Scotland and the press. The main criticisms were that the courses provided an inferior kind of secondary education and that specialization was permitted at too early an age. In 1922 the Supplementary Courses gave place to the system of advanced divisions. Advanced division courses were also included in secondary schools.

In 1904 Sir Henry Craik resigned his Secretaryship and shortly afterwards entered Parliament as member for the Universities of Glasgow and Aberdeen. When the Scottish universities were combined into one constituency in 1918, he still continued as one of the three members allotted until his death in 1927. His work for the schools did not cease and he was a member of the committee which issued what is commonly known as the Craik Report, which established the Minimum National Scales for Scotland, 1919 (cf. the Burnham Committee in England). He was succeeded in the office of Secretary to the Scotch Education Department by Mr. (later Sir) John Struthers, who had worked with him since 1898. Struthers' first concern was with the training of teachers. The Act of 1872 had left the task of teacher training in the hands of the Church. There was now an insufficiency of places in the colleges and many schools had to accept untrained or poorly qualified teachers. As in England at that time, the pupil-teacher system provided the normal means of entry to the profession.

Struthers divided the country into four Provinces each of which was centred upon an appropriate university, St. Andrews, Glasgow, Aberdeen or Edinburgh. In each Province the responsibility for the training of teachers rested with a Provincial Committee of forty members and the Church handed over its colleges to the new committee. The Department issued in 1906 the Regulations for the Training of Teachers. Pupil-teachers were replaced by junior students and all secondary school masters were required to have graduated in honours at a university. Provision was made for the training of specialist teachers of art, handicraft and physical education.

Struthers' reforms in the field of secondary education were drastic. He believed in a much more definite separation between elementary and secondary education and this soon brought him into conflict with Professor Laurie, who was the leader of those who upheld the traditional Scottish view. Struthers saw that in the modern age some of the Scottish traditions would have to be modified. In particular, the claims of the parish school to provide secondary education could no longer be accepted. Sir Henry Craik had gone part of the way when he established the higher grade schools. Struthers wished to go further and this was not possible without fresh legislation. The sequel was the Education (Scotland) Act, 1908 and this measure may be said to have closed one period and to have opened another.

The Education Act of 1908 was based on two main principles which may justly be attributed to Sir John Struthers. The first was the belief in the essential unity of all educational agencies. Thus the Act attempted to survey education as a whole and not merely its component parts. At the same time, Sir John was firmly convinced of the justice of providing equality of opportunity for every child. The value of physical education, which had hitherto been neglected in Scotland, was for the first time adequately recognized. Thus the first important provision of the Act was concerned with school meals. School Boards were given authority to organize schemes for the preparation and supply of meals to children. Normally parents were expected to bear the expense of meals provided for their children but in necessitous cases the school meal service would be free. The Report of the Physical Deterioration Committee had awakened in Scottish parents a considerable concern about the health and well-being of their children. Certain School Boards had already put into operation schemes of medical inspection which applied to all primary and secondary schools in their areas. The Act now made it a duty for all School Boards to arrange for the systematic medical inspection of school children and the Procurator Fiscal was given authority to proceed with the prosecution of those parents whose children were found to be in a filthy or verminous condition or who through parental neglect were suffering from lack of sufficient clothing or food. If the parents could justifiably plead poverty or ill health as an excuse, and if the needs of the child were not supplied by voluntary agencies, the School Boards could make good the deficiencies from public funds. It also became an obligation of a parent to ensure that any physically or mentally defective child belonging to him received efficient education until the age of sixteen.

Geographical conditions in the northern part of Scotland had for years proved a serious obstacle in securing regular attendance at school. The Act empowered School Boards to provide means of conveyance and to defray the travelling expenses of teachers and pupils. In regions where the conditions of travelling to and from school were exceedingly difficult, as in some of the islands, the cost of boarding pupils could be met from public funds. The onus of providing efficient education for their children was placed upon parents. The School Boards were also given power to award bursaries to enable children who could profit from secondary education to attend a secondary school or an institute for higher education. Continuation classes for pupils over the age of fourteen were to be established and the subjects of the curriculum were to include the study of the English language and literature and instruction in the crafts and industries of the neighbourhood. In Gaelic-speaking districts, instruction in that language would also be provided. In all such classes instruction in the laws of health should be given and adequate opportunities for suitable physical training should be provided.

For the first time a scheme for the superannuation of teachers was established and this was to apply to secondary as well as to primary school teachers. Previously, only primary school teachers had been eligible for pensions under the scheme of the Elementary School Teachers' Superannuation Act of 1898. A necessary simplification in the administration of the different Government grants for education was achieved. With the exception of grants paid to universities and the Art and Science grant, all other sums paid by the Government were consolidated into one fund known as the Education (Scotland) Fund and the Act laid down the principles which the Education Department should follow in distributing the grant. After certain services which were given priority had been satisfied, the distribution of the balance of the Fund was placed in the hands of the Burgh and County Committees on Secondary Education. This was a further step towards the replacement of the School Boards by the burghs and the counties as the local authorities for education.

A serious weakness in the Act of 1908 was that it placed additional burdens upon the School Boards without at the same time overhauling the whole of the machinery for the local administration of education. Although by amalgamation the original 984 School Boards had been reduced to 947, there were still many small authorities which were unable to shoulder the financial responsibility which the Act of 1908 placed upon them. This was particularly noticeable in the field of post-primary education. A much larger unit than the parish was needed and this could only be supplied by the counties and the larger burghs. The Government had originally wished to establish the councils of the counties and the five largest burghs as local education authorities but the time was not yet ripe for this step and the strong opposition aroused led to the abandonment of this policy. The Scottish people had long been accustomed to *ad hoc* authorities for education and they showed no desire to change.

The Government was forced to accede to the popular wish and the next Education Act in 1918, which abolished the School Boards set up, *ad hoc* authorities for the local administration of education in each of the 33 counties and the burghs of Edinburgh, Glasgow, Aberdeen, Dundee, and Leith. The new authorities were elected triennially by a system of proportional representation. Leith was later amalgamated with Edinburgh. All the powers and duties of the School Boards were transferred to and vested in the new authorities. The central authority was not changed but it was given the new title of the Scottish Education Department.

The Act placed upon the local authorities the duty of preparing and submitting to the Department schemes for the constitution of School Management Committees for each school or group of schools within their districts. The School Management Committee was composed of representatives of the local authority, teachers, parents and other persons living in the district who were appointed by bodies connected with education. The work of the committees was confined to the supervision and management of the schools and did not include finance and control of expenditure, the appointment, remuneration and dismissal of teachers, all of which powers remained in the hands of the local authority.

In one sense the Act of 1918 may be regarded as an extension of the policy initiated by the Act of 1908. Thus its guiding principle was that no child who could benefit from the education given in an intermediate or secondary school should be debarred from entry by reason of poverty. Local authorities were therefore given the power to pay fees and travelling expenses, or the cost of residence in hostels or to grant bursaries and pay maintenance allowances to enable suitably qualified young people to enter a training college or university.[1]

Hitherto Scottish secondary schools had not been well equipped as regards libraries. The Act sought to remedy this deficiency by giving power to local authorities to supply books, not only for children attending school and for young persons engaged in a course of further education, but also for adults. This policy resulted in a considerable development of the library services and the demand for books from all sections of the community steadily increased. As in England, many of the clauses of the Scottish Act were permissive and not mandatory. This applied to those sections of the Act which conferred the power of establishing nursery and continuation schools. During the slump which followed the conclusion of the war, these projects suffered the same fate as the corresponding institutions in England. The Act also placed restrictions upon the employment of children

[1] The policy of the Scotch Education Department in the period 1905–7 was that of assimilating the programme of the higher grade schools with that of the intermediate departments of secondary schools. Schools which offered a three years course presented their pupils for the Intermediate Certificate Examination. They corresponded to the selective central schools in England. The Intermediate Certificate gained so high a prestige that a considerable number of parents allowed their children to remain at school for more than three years. Statistics, however, showed that a large number of pupils failed to complete the three years course.

under the age of 13. It should be noted that the corresponding English Act adopted the age of 12.

One of the most important parts of the Act was that which made it an obligation of the local authority to adopt a scale of salaries for teachers in accordance with conditions prescribed by the Education Department after consultation with the teaching profession and the local education authorities. Dr. John Strong, at that time Rector of the Royal High School, Edinburgh, and later Professor of Education in the University of Leeds, was largely instrumental in securing the new salary scales. Certain important administrative changes were also effected. An Advisory Council was instituted to assist the Department, which was obliged to take into consideration any representation submitted by the Council. In this respect it was more akin to the Central Advisory Councils for England and Wales established in 1944 than to the Consultative Committee of the Board of Education. Every local education authority was also directed to constitute a Local Advisory Council to which were allocated functions in regard to local education similar to those exercised by the Central Council.

The original intention was to raise the school-leaving age to 15 on a date to be announced by the Education Department but the Geddes Axe prevented this clause from coming into operation. Perhaps one of the most important administrative provisions of the Act was that concerned with the transfer of voluntary schools by sale or lease to the local authority. Once terms had been agreed, the local authority was bound to accept the transfer. This was an amendment of the Act of 1872, which had not made it compulsory for School Boards to accept a transfer. Any school transferred under the new regulations became a public school and teachers who were appointed to serve in it had to satisfy the Department in regard to their professional qualifications and to be approved as to their religious belief and character by the representatives of the denomination in whose interests the school was conducted. A time limit of two years was fixed beyond which no school could be accepted for transfer and no grant could be paid to any voluntary school which had not been transferred. Roman Catholic and Episcopalian schools availed themselves of these conditions with the result that most voluntary schools have been transferred to the local authorities. Thus there is no Dual System in Scotland.

Struthers began to work out his schemes for the re-organization of Scottish education as soon as the Act became operative. The first step was the issue of a Circular which advised every local authority to appoint a Director of Education. This was followed by a simplification of the grant system. A uniform rate of grant per pupil was to be paid each year irrespective of the type of school he attended, primary, intermediate or secondary. At the same time it was announced that the Merit and the Intermediate Certificates, which were bound up with the old system of allocating grants, would be abolished in 1924. Sir John Struthers felt that the time was now ripe for a complete overhaul of post-primary education and his last act before his retirement was the issue of the famous Circular 44 in December, 1921. Education was in future to be regarded from an 'end on' point of view, primary followed by post-primary education. The pupil who entered school at the age of five would pass from the infant department to the junior and senior divisions of the primary school at the ages of seven and nine respectively. At 12 years of age he would sit for the qualifying examination. If he showed ability to benefit from a full course of secondary education, he would pass to the secondary school. Such pupils would be comparatively few in number. The majority would be found in the non-secondary and would carry on their education in an Advanced Division until they left school at the age of 14 or 15. The two groups, secondary and non-secondary, were to be quite distinct, although opportunities would be given for the transfer of individuals from one type of school to another in cases where at the time of the qualifying examination it was discovered that a wrong selection had been made.

As soon as the proposals of the Circular had been studied, a storm of criticism rose from widely different sections of the community. Members of all three political parties, Conservative, Liberal and Socialist, condemned them on the ground that they fostered class distinction and delivered a vital blow at the Scottish democratic tradition. The teaching profession through its representative organization, the Educational Institute of Scotland, was almost unanimous in its opposition. In 1922 the Educational Institute presented its own proposals for re-organization which were based on the conception of a national system of education embracing all stages from the primary school to the university with the recognition of the principle of a full course of secondary education for all children. The Advisory Council considered the proposals of the Circular and in 1923 issued their own report which recommended three stages of education beyond the nursery school, namely, primary (5 to 12 years), intermediate (12 to 15 years), and secondary (15 to 18 years). It is important to note that this organization was based on age groups and the fact that many pupils under the existing circumstances would not stay at school longer than 15 years of age justified the retention of the term 'intermediate'. The Report of the Advisory Council was on the whole acceptable and criticism was confined to certain details.

To the astonishment and dismay of many people, the Education Department turned down the recommendations of its Advisory Council. The primary school Code and the secondary school Regulations of 1923 embodied, with certain modifications, the proposals of Circular 44. Supplementary courses were replaced by advanced divisions which were now to be conducted under the primary school Code on the plea that it was cheaper to do so. The Merit and the Intermediate Certificates were discontinued and their place was taken by the Day School Certificate (Lower) and the Day School Certificate (Higher). The former was issued by the local education authorities to those pupils who had successfully completed two years in an advanced division. The Department issued the higher award to those who left school after the successful completion of a three years' course. It was assumed that pupils from the advanced divisions would proceed to a day or evening continuation school but those clauses of the Act of 1918 which authorized these institutions were never put into operation.

Struthers was responsible for a very important change in the arrangements for the training of teachers. In 1920 a National Committee for the Training of Teachers was constituted and the four Provincial Committees, who were now relieved of financial responsibility, were charged with the supervision of the four training centres at St. Andrews, Glasgow, Aberdeen, and Edinburgh. Episcopalian and Roman Catholic training colleges were also transferred to the National Committee. It was proposed that after 1924 all men entrants to the profession with the exception of specialist instructors in physical training, handicrafts, music, art, and domestic science should be graduates. At first this policy brought about an immediate increase in the proportion of graduate teachers, both men and women. We shall see, however, that since the second World War this tendency is no longer operative.

The *ad hoc* education authorities were abolished by the Local Government (Scotland) Act in 1929 and their powers were transferred to the councils of the counties and the four largest towns of Edinburgh, Glasgow, Dundee and Aberdeen. As in England, the new education authorities were required to appoint education committees.

The year 1936 saw yet another Education Act which roughly followed the pattern of the corresponding English Act. The school-leaving age, with certain exemptions, was to be raised to 15 on September 1st, 1939. All post-primary education was to be included under the generic term 'secondary', but as in England, the commencement of the second World War rendered the Act inoperative.

For some time before the outbreak of hostilities the Scottish authorities had prepared schemes for the evacuation of school children from the danger areas. As soon as war was declared the plans were put into operation. The country had been divided into evacuation areas in which the average density of the population was about 14,000 to the square mile; reception areas with an average density of about 100 per square mile, and neutral areas in which it was considered that the normal educational services might continue without interruption. The evacuation areas were Edinburgh, Rosyth, Glasgow, Clydebank, and Dundee. At a later stage the list was increased by the addition of Inverkeithing, North and South Queensferry, Greenock, Port Glasgow and Dumbarton. Suitable reception areas corresponding to these were allotted. The progress of the evacuation was similar to that south of the border. At the commencement of hostilities, 175,812 persons were evacuated. About one-third consisted of unaccompanied children and the remainder of mothers and accompanied children, teachers and voluntary helpers. The number of evacuees fell considerably short of the total which had been expected, and some who had not previously registered took part in the evacuation. As in England, when large scale air raids did not materialize, the drift back assumed alarming proportions. When Glasgow and the Clydeside areas suffered from severe bombing attacks in the spring of 1941, a second evacuation began. At the end of 1940 only about 20,000 children remained in the evacuation areas but this figure had risen to 83,000 in July, 1941, and after that date it began to fall.

Only about a quarter of the children whose homes were in the danger areas remained evacuated. Nearly 3,000 children were sent overseas.

The process of evacuating the children was characterized by muddle and chaos due to lack of administrative foresight. Many mothers and young children were forced to travel from 7 a.m. to 9 p.m. without any arrangements having been made for their meals. The following account is typical of those who had to undertake a long journey. 'The journey from Glasgow was the most depressing, deplorable, and disgusting journey I have ever had the misfortune to make. The train took $12\frac{1}{2}$ hours to reach Aberdeen. Half-hours and hours were spent in railway sidings until the line was clear. The journey was a positive nightmare, increased by the darkness of the train (lit by blue lights) and the wretched rainstorm which greeted our arrival at our station. The evacuees were famished when they arrived, having had no food for a matter of 12 hours. . . . The babies-in-arms kept howling for milk which was unobtainable at any station. Mothers began to grow hysterical, two in particular crying like children. Many children became trainsick. There was a lack of water on the train. . . . On arrival at midnight the evacuees, teachers and helpers were so exhausted and depressed that the term 'refugees' applied to them by some of the houscholders seemed more appropriate than offensive'.[1]

A special investigation of a selected evacuation area, that of Clydebank, showed some interesting features. There was a considerable number of Roman Catholic families in the district and it was noticed that there was a marked tendency on the part of Catholic mothers to accompany their children. This suggested a greater cohesion in the Catholic than the Protestant family. Hence it was not surprising to find that the drift back of Catholic children was more rapid and that 90 per cent had returned home by Christmas, 1939. Although Clydebank was a vulnerable area and eventually suffered from air bombardment, even at the height of the raids the number of children who remained in the town exceeded the number who had been evacuated.

As in England, many parents visited their children too frequently with the result that the children were unsettled and emotionally upset and wanted to return home. Weekly

[1] *Evacuation in Scotland*, Edited by W. Boyd, pp. 55–6. University of London Press, 1944.

visits by parents caused the most damage but those children who were not visited at all seemed to be almost equally upset. There were, as in England, complaints made by the evacuees about their hosts and by the latter about the children they received but the account given in the Press was somewhat exaggerated. There were certainly areas where dirty or verminous children seemed to be fairly numerous and there were other districts in which the attitude of the householders was lacking in friendliness and sympathy. One of the greatest difficulties was the failure of some children to adjust themselves to their new surroundings. 'Town dwellers did not take to the country. They missed their neighbours, their ordinary occupations and their amusements, and they found the country boring. . . . Time sometimes rectified matters, but the majority did not give time any chance of work'.[1] One widespread problem was due to food differences. 'Town-bred children, used to "fish suppers", chip potatoes and tinned foods, objected to good plain cooking. It is possible, of course, that the cooking was not always "good"; but despite this it seems indubitable that apart from mere unfamiliarity the palates of a large number of the children were vitiated. One case is recorded of children who had never eaten a boiled egg before'.[2] On the whole, evacuation in Scotland was just as much a failure as in England, and the demand for the re-organization of Scottish education was widespread.

This was effected by the Education (Scotland) Act, 1945. In the following year a consolidating Act was passed which collected together all the previous enactments about education in Scotland which still remained in force. The Scottish Act of 1945 was based on the same general principles as the English Act of 1944 but there were important differences in details. As we have already seen, Struthers had organized Scottish education from an 'end on' point of view or in progressive stages. Hence there was no necessity to change this arrangement. The Act of 1872 had only recognized one type of school, the public school, within the State system. There was no Dual System to complicate the administrative pattern. The preamble of the English Act stated that the new legislation was designed to reform, i.e. to reshape the law about education. The Scottish Act aimed at amending the law so as to bring education into line with the general

[1] *Ibid.*, p. 71.
[2] *Ibid.*

policy of the Government in regard to education in Britain. At the same time the distinctive features of the Scottish system were retained.

Some of the differences between the two Acts are due to the logical Scottish mind which demands a precise and accurate definition of the terms employed. For example, the Scottish Act attempted to define primary and secondary education in accurate terms. ' "Primary education" means progressive elementary education in such subjects as may be prescribed in the code, regard being had to the age, ability, and aptitude of the pupils concerned, and such education shall be given in primary schools or departments. Primary education includes training by appropriate methods in schools and classes (hereinafter referred to as "nursery schools" and "nursery classes") for pupils between the age of two years and such later age as may be permitted by the code.'

' "Secondary education" means progressive courses of instruction of such length and in such subjects as may be approved in terms of the code as appropriate to the age, ability, and aptitude of the pupils who have been promoted from primary schools and departments and to the period for which they may be expected to remain at school. Such courses shall be given in secondary schools or departments.' (Part I, section 1).

The Scottish Act required every education authority to prepare and submit for the approval of the Secretary of State a promotion scheme. This should show the method adopted in the authority's area for promoting pupils from primary to secondary education and the means employed for ascertaining the kind of courses from which each pupil would be likely to benefit. In England, the arrangements for transfer from one type of school to another are the concern of the local education authority. Clause 11 of the Act allows tuition fees to be charged in maintained primary as well as secondary schools. Fees may be charged at the discretion of the authority in a limited number of primary and secondary schools, provided that 'the power to charge fees may be exercised without prejudice to the adequate provision of free primary and secondary education'. There are a few schools where tuition fees are payable in the primary but not in the secondary departments. In schools where education is free, the authority must provide books, stationery, mathematical instruments and other necessary articles free of charge.

Most education authorities already possessed a Director of Education as chief executive officer. This was now made compulsory and each authority was required to set out a scheme detailing the functions and duties of this officer. It should be noted that in Scotland the local education authority is the council of a county or of one of the four large burghs. The authority may, and must if required, by the Secretary of State, constitute an education committe and draw up a scheme to show what functions have been delegated to the committee. The restrictions imposed in 1872 about the times at which religious instruction may be given, have now been removed.

A very important feature of the Act is that which is concerned with teachers' salaries and superannuation. Each teacher is required to pay 5 per cent of his salary towards superannuation and the education authority, governors or managers have also to contribute an equivalent amount. The minimum national salary scales for teachers were abolished and all education authorities were required to pay salaries in accordance with scales to be set up by the Secretary of State. The National Joint Council which had been constituted before the war to investigate the problem of salaries had been obliged to postpone its decisions because of the commencement of hostilities. During the war, the Department gave teachers a war bonus to assist them in meeting the rising cost of living. In 1943 the Advisory Council recommended the abolition of the minimum national scales and the substitution of standard national scales. The National Joint Council was reconstituted. It now consisted of 24 representatives, half from the authorities and half from the Educational Institute of Scotland. Six assessors were also appointed. The Council met in December, 1944, with Lord Teviot as an impartial chairman. After a long series of negotiations, agreement was obtained and the Teviot Scales (in some respects more generous than the Burnham Scales) were adopted.

The Secretary of State for Scotland issued draft regulations for teachers' salaries on November 29th, 1950. In many respects these differ from the recent Burnham recommendation in England. 'These regulations emphasize once again the fact that, in spite of the agreement on general principles underlined in the principal Education Acts for England and Scotland (those of 1944 and 1945 respectively), there are notable differences in the organization of the two educational systems, and that these organizational differences reflect fundamentally different national histories, traditions and philosophies'.[1] The Educational Institute of Scotland had demanded a flat rate increase for Scottish teachers but this policy was rejected. It should be remembered that until recently all Scottish men teachers were graduates and that the policy of the Scottish Education Department seems to favour a return to this position. The only exceptions to the rule about graduation were the teachers qualified under Chapter VI, that is teachers of art, music and physical education. Hence the new recommendations, unlike the English, provide for additional increments for graduates with first—or second—class honours. One must remember, however, that the honours course at a Scottish university is four years and is followed by a year at the training college. The Scottish recommendations do not include a 'pool' for posts of special responsibility and a Scottish teacher is longer in reaching his maximum than his counterpart in England. The decrease in the number of women graduates had been very pronounced and to counteract this tendency the new scales offer a strong inducement to women to graduate, especially in the case of teachers of science. Similar incentives are offered to teachers of domestic science and physical training, of whom there is a considerable shortage.

The problem of the independent schools was met by the appointment of one of the officers of the Secretary of State to be Registrar of Educational Endowments, and arrangements were made for setting up an Independent Schools Tribunal and for hearing complaints and appeals. Provision was made for further education up to the age of 18 but it should be noted that the equivalent of the English County College is in Scotland known as a Junior College. On the whole it may be said that the central authority exercises a closer supervision and control of the local authorities than is the case in England.

The Advisory Council on Education has issued three important reports which are of value to English as well as to Scottish teachers—the Reports on Primary Education, 1946, Technical Education, 1946, and Secondary Education, 1947. The first of these reports deals with the utilization of present school buildings which are not well suited to modern ideas about education. Most of these schools were erected

[1] *Times Educational Supplement,* December 8th, 1950.

in the days of the School Boards and they are lacking in the provision of playgrounds and facilities for physical education. Unfortunately it will be many years before they can be replaced so that the immediate problem is how to make the best use of them. The report suggested that the number of pupils on roll should be reduced to give more space for practical work and that the interior decorations of the buildings should be as attractive and bright as possible. Where circumstances admit, the schools should be reconstructed to allow of the provision of assembly halls, dining-halls, and gymnasia.

The report considered that the academic traditions of Scottish education had strongly influenced the curriculum of the primary schools with the result that too much attention had been given to the three Rs and to book learning and that learning through practical activities had been neglected. Useful advice about the curriculum and methods of teaching were included and it was suggested that there was an urgent need to re-think the primary school curriculum. On the other hand, the Council believed that it is important to retain all those aspects of Scottish tradition which still have value. It was considered that it would be a grave error to copy the English system in detail. For some years there had been a growing nationalist feeling amongst the Scottish people which has recently found expression in the demand for a greater control of their own affairs. It is not based upon any antagonism towards England but it emphasizes the fact that the Scottish people are in many ways a distinct nation with a history, a character, and a tradition peculiar to themselves. Hence the importance of keeping this feeling alive. It can be fostered in school through a study of the Scottish traditions and language, through closer attention being given to the literature of Scotland, both prose and poetry, the learning of traditional Scottish songs and dances and by bringing into the school the industries and crafts practised in the locality. This would not involve the teaching of Gaelic in districts where that language is not in common use but all children should be taught something of Gaelic life, legends and traditions.

The setting of compulsory homework was deprecated. Circular 122 accepted the findings of the Council on the whole but it gave a warning that great care should be exercised in teaching the Gaelic language and customs in Lowland schools. Over-zealous teachers inspired by pride in the history of Scotland might be tempted to introduce the study of Gaelic in districts where it could serve no practical value, or, in their archæological interest, might carry the instruction in Gaelic life and traditions to a stage at which it would be out of touch with the pupils' present-day interests. The Circular was unwilling to advocate the complete abolition of homework but it suggested that teachers should be careful not to overburden children with home lessons and that some of these might take the form of simple projects which would make use of the child's activity and perhaps lead to observation out-of-doors.

The Report on Secondary Education in Scotland was much concerned with the future organization of secondary schools. It was quite emphatic that the title 'junior secondary school' should be abolished, since the name suggested a position of inferiority. Neither the tri-partite organization of secondary education nor the multilateral school in the form in which the term is usually understood in England was favoured. The assumption of the Norwood Report that children at 12 years of age can be neatly sorted out into three categories to which the three types of school, grammar, technical and modern, correspond was summarily rejected. It was asserted that the tri-partite organization could never bring about that parity of esteem that is desired and the modern school would always suffer from the taint of inferiority. The alternative, the multilateral school, would be too large a unit and therefore could not achieve that organic unity which is essential to the life of the school community. Instead of a school containing about 2,000 pupils, it would be more practicable to limit the secondary school to a maximum number on roll of 800 or 900. Even this would be a compromise, for the maximum allowed for an ordinary secondary school should be about 600 pupils. The compromise was justified, however, in the case of the 'omnibus' type of secondary school which could not be effectively organized unless the number of pupils was about 800. The special advantages of this type of school, it was thought, outweighed the drawback of having rather larger numbers.

Kirkaldy High School, at that time under Dr. F. M. Earle, was an omnibus school of the type the Report wished to see established.[1] The system adopted in this school was some-

---

[1] The organization introduced by Dr. F. M. Earle is described in detail in his book, *Reconstruction in the Secondary School*, University of London Press, 1944.

what intricate but it may be briefly described as follows. The school provided secondary education for all children in the area. Every child who entered the school was studied most carefully. The results he obtained in the selection tests, the records of intelligence tests he worked and the diagnosis of his special aptitudes and interests as set down in his primary school record were all assessed. On the basis of this, an individual programme was made for him. If at any time it was found that part of the programme was unsuitable, modifications could be made. Thus no pupil was able to claim that he was a member of the grammar, technical or modern stream. In practice he would be receiving instruction in all three streams. In some subjects he would be a member of what might be called the grammar school stream; he would also study other subjects which would normally be emphasized in a technical or modern school. The writer visited the school shortly after Dr. Earle had retired and he asked the acting-headmaster whether the organization was successful in eliminating all class distinctions. He was told that two distinctions still remained. The majority of the pupils left school at about 15; the remainder stayed to study for the Leaving Certificate Examination.

The Report on Secondary Education advocated an examination policy which should be compared with that recommended by the Secondary Schools Examination Council in 1947. It suggested that the Senior Leaving Certificate should be abolished and that two new examinations should take its place. At the end of the fourth year of the secondary school course, pupils should sit for a School Certificate examination. Those who left at 15 without obtaining a School Certificate should be given a record containing particulars of their work during the school course. The School Certificate examination should be an internal test carried out by the school staff and standardized according to a process recommended in the Report. Like the English General Certificate of Education, the Scottish School Certificate should not be awarded on a group basis but should indicate the subjects included in the school course

At present Dr. Earle is a Senior Research Fellow of the University of Leeds Institute of Education. Dr. Earle has been investigating the attitudes and interests which may be regarded as characteristic of students in training colleges and university departments, to determine what appear to be the 'normal' groupings of such attitudes and interests and to consider what significance, if any, attaches to the more extreme variations from the 'norms' thus established. He will be shortly publishing a monograph giving an account of his research.

and those in which the pupil had secured a pass. A similar type of examination for the Higher School Certificate, which should be an external test conducted by the Scottish Education Department, would mark the completion of various types of sixth form course.

The Education Department in Circular 145, January, 1949, agreed with the general principles of the Report but modified it with regard to certain details. The group system of the Senior Leaving Certificate was discontinued after 1949, but every candidate is obliged to follow a programme of studies approved by the Department. Thus although at pass in arithmetic is no longer necessary, every candidate should have studied this subject during his school course. The number of subjects offered by a candidate is decided by the school authorities, but the Certificate is awarded on a subject and not a group basis. As in England, the universities have their own entrance requirements and these will naturally influence the choice of candidates who wish to proceed to the university. The new examination is intended to mark the successful completion of a five years' secondary school course, but a loophole is still left for those pupils in the fourth year who wish to offer at the lower grade as many subjects as the school considers they are capable of attempting. This proviso is in force from 1951 and is intended to meet the needs of pupils who leave school at the end of the fourth year. As the old Leaving Certificate marked the completion of a five years course, the age at which the examination is taken has not changed. The examination is now known as the Scottish Leaving Certificate Examination.

The Educational Institute of Scotland has been mentioned several times in this chapter. In England the teaching profession has been divided amongst numerous professional organizations such as the National Union of Teachers, the National Association of Schoolmasters, the Assistant Masters and Assistant Mistresses' Associations. Until recently all Scottish teachers were members of one professional association, the Educational Institute of Scotland. This was founded in 1847 and has always exercised a beneficial influence upon the development of Scottish education. It has not only been concerned with the material welfare of teachers, e.g. salaries, superannuation and tenure of office, but it has consistently stood for the tradition of sound learning and the encouragement of educational experiment and research. In recent years, many teachers believed that the Institute was not paying sufficient attention to the special problems of the secondary school. The Scottish Secondary Teachers' Association was formed in 1944 within the parent body but in the following year it broke away from the Institute. The new association comprises about a quarter of the Scottish secondary school teachers.

Until recently, adult education of the pattern provided by the W.E.A. and University Extension had not flourished to the same extent as in England. There are several reasons to account for this late development. Originally adult classes received no aid from public funds and were not eligible for local authority grant unless they were organized by the School Boards (after 1918 by the local education authorities). The universities have always been more accessible to the people than in England. From quite early times the ambition of the intelligent Scot was to spend some time at the university and he was prepared to deny himself all luxuries to satisfy his desire. In later years the bequest of Andrew Carnegie assisted poor students in the payment of their university fees.[1] During the last two decades, especially in industrial areas, the W.E.A. has made considerable progress. In 1937, Newbattle Abbey, Dalkeith, was opened as a residential college for adults and was recognized by the Scottish Education Department.

The Youth Movement has received strong encouragement from the Scottish authorities. In 1943 the Scottish Youth Advisory Committee was asked to make an inquiry into the needs of youth and to discover how far they were satisfied by existing voluntary agencies. The report of 1945, entitled *The Needs of Youth in These Times*, was a valuable and comprehensive survey which dealt competently with the social, psychological, cultural, and religious aspects of the problem. A second report followed which dealt more explicitly with the organization and control of the youth service. In 1947 the Secretary of State appointed the Scottish Committee for the Training of Community Centre Workers and Youth Leaders. This replaced the Scottish Youth Leadership

---

[1] In 1901 Mr. Andrew Carnegie left the sum of £2,000,000 to the Scottish universities. Some of the money was used for new buildings, the extension of research and the foundation of additional chairs. The capital brings in an annual income of over £120,000 and half of this amount, according to the terms of the will, is used to assist poor students in the payment of their fees. Alexander Morgan estimated that about seventy per cent of Scottish university students received help from the Carnegie Trustees.

Training Association and has since formed a voluntary body known as the Scottish Leadership Training Association. The first training course of the new association was held in 1948 and lasted for sixty weeks. Besides youth organizations provided by voluntary bodies, the education authorities have opened youth clubs and centres to cater for the needs of boys and girls above statutory school age.

Like the schools, the Scottish universities possess many characteristics peculiar to themselves. All the Scottish universities are ancient foundations; three of them originating in the Middle Ages, and the fourth at the close of the sixteenth century. The mediæval universities were founded considerably later than Oxford and Cambridge. In the thirteenth and fourteenth centuries, Scottish students attended both the English universities and the University of Paris. In fact almost every European university possessed its contingent of Scottish students. The constant border warfare between England and Scotland made residence at Oxford or Cambridge impossible for Scots and those who wished to travel to the Continent had to run the risk of interception by English ships. The result was a demand for the establishment of universities in Scotland. At this time the theory had crystallized that Papal sanction was necessary for the foundation of a university. Thus unlike Oxford and Cambridge which originated without any definite Papal or Royal authority, the mediæval Scottish universities owed their foundations to Papal Bulls.

The oldest university is that of St. Andrews, which was authorized in 1411 by a Papal Bull obtained by Bishop Wardlaw of St. Andrews from Benedict XIII. It is interesting to note that King James I, who warmly approved the foundation, was a captive in England, and Benedict XIII, who had recently removed from Avignon to Aragon, was recognized as Pope by less than half of Europe. Like other Scottish, and indeed, most European universities in their early days, St. Andrews had practically no permanent buildings. The professors taught in hired rooms and received no salary. By the middle of the sixteenth century, St. Andrews possessed three colleges; St. Salvator (the College of the Holy Saviour), founded in 1450 by Bishop Kennedy, who succeeded Wardlaw; St. Leonard's, founded in 1512 by Archbishop Alexander Stewart; and St. Mary's, founded in 1538 by Archbishop James Beaton. During the Reformation period the fortunes of St. Andrews were on the wane but by the beginning of the seventeenth century the university had recovered much of its prestige. This was largely a consequence of the reputations of three well-known scholars; John Major, Provost of St. Salvator, the last of the scholastics; George Buchanan, the humanist and Principal of St. Leonard's, and Andrew Melville, the Principal of St. Mary's.

In the early part of the eighteenth century, numbers declined rapidly and to offset this the two colleges of St. Salvator and St. Leonard were in 1747 amalgamated into the one institution known as the United College. Conditions within the university grew worse and when the Royal Commission on Scottish universities was appointed in 1826, it was found that not a single graduation had occurred between 1804 and 1826. The Commission found a similar state of affairs at Glasgow and Edinburgh; Aberdeen was an exception. It had become customary for students to enter universities and attend classes without any intention of graduating. The recommendations of the Commission did not take effect until the University Act of 1859. This Act brought the constitutions of all the Scottish universities into line and effected a number of administrative and academic reforms. In 1876 the Andrew Bell Trustees used their surplus funds to endow two chairs in the History, Theory and Practice of Education. One was at St. Andrews and the other at Edinburgh. Thus the first professorships in education in Britain were established at the Scottish universities.

Further reforms were effected by the Scottish Universities Act of 1889. University College, Dundee, had been founded in 1881 and the executive commission set up under the Act recommended that Dundee should be incorporated in the University of St. Andrews. After lengthy and not altogether friendly negotiations this was accomplished in 1897. Dundee possessed departments of medicine, law, and engineering and it brought to the University of St. Andrews advantages somewhat similar to those which accrued to Durham when Armstrong College, Newcastle, became a member of the federal University of Durham. Strictly speaking, Dundee was not a federal but an incorporated college of the University of St. Andrews.

Glasgow was the second university in order of foundation. William Turnbull, Bishop of Glasgow, persuaded James II to petition Pope Nicholas V for a Bull to authorize its establishment. Glasgow received a Royal Charter in 1433. The university was poorly endowed and for many years teaching had to be carried on in the Cathedral and other church buildings. During the sixteenth century Glasgow existed in what has been described as a state of 'suspended animation' and it was not until the famous scholar Andrew Melville was appointed Principal in 1574 that its fortunes began to revive.

Scotland's third university was that of Aberdeen. In 1494, James IV at the instigation of Bishop Elphinstone secured a Bull from Alexander VI. Elphinstone had previously been Rector of Glasgow and his experience showed him the difficulties that beset a university which possesses insufficient endowments. He took steps to avoid a like disaster and as a result, in its early days, Aberdeen had a more flourishing career than the two older universities.

Andrew Melville, who had infused new life into the University of Glasgow, now turned his reforming zeal upon Aberdeen in 1575 and St. Andrews in 1579. The original college of Aberdeen was King's College but in 1593 George Earl Marischal, because of his disappointment at the progress made by the older college, obtained a Royal Charter to establish Marischal College. In 1641 the two colleges were united to form one university under the name of King Charles's University but within a few years the rival colleges once more became independent institutions until they were again united in 1860.

The University of Edinburgh was a product of the Reformation. Edinburgh, although it was the administrative capital of Scotland, was not a bishop's see and this explains why its university was not established earlier. The Royal Charter was granted to the Town Council of Edinburgh in 1582 for the foundation of a 'Tounis College' with power to grant degrees. The college began its work in the following year when its first Principal or Regent, Robert Rollock, was appointed by the Town Council. For several centuries the university was almost entirely under the jurisdiction of the municipal authorities and in this respect its career resembled that of University College, Nottingham. The Principal and the teaching staff were appointed by the Town Council, who also issued regulations governing the courses of study and setting forth the conditions under which degrees could be granted. A dispute between the university and the Town Council about the content of the course for medical graduation led to the appointment of the Royal Commission of 1826 and the subsequent University

Act of 1858 which affected all the Scottish universities. The Act, together with the later University Act of 1889, was the work of John Inglis, who was Chancellor of Edinburgh from 1868 to 1891. These two Acts with subsequent modifications are still the basis of the organization and government of the Scottish universities.

Many Englishmen have wondered why the M.A. and not the B.A. is the initial degree of the Scottish universities. The answer is that the B.A. was originally the first award but for some years prior to the Commission of 1826 it had fallen into abeyance. An attempt to revive it met with no success and the Act of 1858 established the M.A. as the initial degree. The reforms inaugurated by the Act of 1858 were carried a stage further in 1889. The University Court, which appointed the professors, except those nominated by the Crown, and which was in charge of the revenues and the internal administration of the university, was considerably enlarged. Its functions were defined and brought into line with the Senate, which controlled academic matters. A new administrative body known as the Scottish Universities Committee of the Privy Council was created and all fresh ordinances had to be submitted for its approval. The Students' Representative Council, which was the outcome of a student movement, received official recognition. New courses of study were approved and a pension scheme for professors was adopted. Women were given the right of graduation in 1892.

In the three pre-Reformation universities, the Principal is appointed by the Crown and he usually holds the office of Vice-Chancellor. Prior to the Act of 1858 he had to be an ordained minister of the Church of Scotland. Edinburgh, because of its origin and development, differs from the other universities. When the Act of 1858 removed the university from the control of the Town Council, the latter were allowed to retain certain powers. Thus the appointment of the Principal is in the hands of seven curators, three elected by the town and four by the university. The Curators of Patronage also appoint a considerable number of the professors. In the other universities, professors are appointed either by the Crown or the University Court. This body, which is a large one in English provincial universities, consists of only fourteen members in a Scottish university. It controls the whole of the administration and the business side of the university and is presided over by the Rector, who is elected triennially by the undergraduates. It roughly carries out the functions exercised by the Council of an English provincial university. In the latter, although in theory the University Court is the supreme governing body, in practice it usually confirms the decisions of the Council. As in England the titular head of the university is the Chancellor. All ordinances proposed by the University Court must be confirmed by him and he also confers the degrees of the university. Each university has in addition a General Council consisting of the Chancellor, the members of the Court, the staff and all registered graduates. It is mainly an advisory body and corresponds to the Convocation of an English provincial university.

In the early nineteenth century it was common for students to enter the university direct from the parochial schools. It was thought unwise to make any break with past tradition and thus neither the Act of 1858 nor that of 1889 suggested the institution of a university entrance test. When secondary education was re-organized by Sir Henry Craik, a change of policy became desirable and a preliminary examination for university entrance was instituted in 1892. This examination was completely recast in 1927 and the conditions under which the Senior Leaving Certificate could be accepted were formulated.

In 1922 another University Act introduced some important modifications. Previously the superannuation of professors had been quite inadequate and there had been no pension scheme for the majority of the staff. This Act brought all members of the staff under the Federated Superannuation Scheme which is now common to nearly all of the teachers in the universities and university colleges of Britain. The Act also gave power to each University Court to fix the age limit at which professors and other members of staff should retire. Like the English, the Scottish universities now participate in the grants made by the University Grants Commission. They are also facing similar problems in the post-war period to those discussed in connection with the English universities.

The incorporation of University College, Dundee, in the University of St. Andrews has not proved altogether a happy arrangement. The former institution believed that its incorporation in St. Andrews constituted a restriction to its development and it has made a claim to independent status. The Secretary of State for Scotland agreed to the request of the University Court that the problems raised should be the subject of an impartial inquiry. This was conducted by Lord Cooper, President of the Court of Session, and two assessors. The report was issued in 1949 and it recommended the full absorption of Dundee into the university and that the two institutions should be integrated into a single whole. This result could be achieved if the colleges which seemed to be the centres of discord were dissolved. The University Court was prepared to accept as a compromise many of Lord Cooper's recommendations but it rejected the proposal to dissolve the colleges and it pointed out that if St. Salvator's College, the oldest college in Scotland, were abolished, a great deal of opposition would be encountered. It seems unlikely that Lord Cooper's report will be wholly acceptable to the parties of the dispute, but his emphasis on the need for integration, however difficult it may be to realize, is a step in the right direction. The existence of two independent universities, separated by a bare twelve miles, would seem to be a great mistake and it is to be hoped that both institutions will be able to devise means by which they can, without sacrificing their distinctive characteristics, contribute to the good of the whole. The only solution seems to be the appointment of a Royal Commission with power to investigate the whole situation and by the time this book has appeared in print, this may probably have been done.[1]

---

[1] The appointment of a Royal Commission under the Chairmanship of Marshal of the Royal Air Force, Lord Tedder, was approved in May, 1951.

CHAPTER X

EDUCATION IN H.M. FORCES, 1900-50

EDUCATION in the Army as in civil life had its beginning in voluntary effort. In the latter part of the eighteenth century there are instances of individual officers who secured the services of a non-commissioned officer as a schoolmaster to teach the men reading, writing and arithmetic. William Cobbett as a sergeant-major taught in a school of this kind and whilst he was teaching he both wrote and tried out his well-known English Grammar. Sir John Moore in training the newly formed Rifle Brigade at Shorncliffe made instruction in the three Rs a regular part of the programme. The Commander-in-Chief, Frederick, Duke of York, suggested the appointment of a sergeant-schoolmaster in every regiment and this was carried out by the general orders of 1811 and 1812. The sergeant-schoolmaster's duties included not only teaching young soldiers but also the children of soldiers. Two features should be noted; education in the Army was concerned with both children and adults, and it was at first organized on a purely regimental basis. The schoolmaster was a member of the regiment and wore its uniform. Much of the education given in the early part of the century must have been singularly ineffective. An Army chaplain once complained, 'If you get a man of character, the chances are that his intellectual attainments are defective. If you get a scholar, he either turns out to be a drunkard, or wanted in the paymaster's office, or in the adjutant's orderly room, and the school is left to shift for itself. Besides, not one of them, not the best of them, understands the art of teaching'.[1]

In 1840 Thomas Macaulay as Secretary-at-War signed a Royal Warrant for the appointment of Army Schoolmistresses. There was, however, no central control or supervision of Army education. This defect was remedied by the Rev. R. C. Gleig who was appointed Inspector-General of Army Schools in 1846. It is recorded that his discovery of the shocking conditions prevalent in the Duke of York's

---

[1] *The Story of Army Education, Centenary Souvenir*, 1946, p. 8.

School decided his policy. The result was the issue of a Royal Warrant dated July 2nd, 1846, which established the Corps of Army Schoolmasters. The reasons for its institution were given in the preamble: 'Whereas . . . we have deemed it expedient to introduce in our Army a class of man better calculated to perform the duties of Schoolmaster, Our Will and Pleasure is that such persons shall be appointed schoolmaster-sergeants and shall take rank next after the sergeant-major. . . . An inspector of regimental schools shall be appointed by our Secretary at War'. Another Royal Warrant later in the same year established a normal school for training schoolmasters and a model school for boys.

It is not relevant to enter into the detailed history of Army education during the nineteenth century but one development, however, should be mentioned. This is the introduction of the system of Army Certificates of Education. In 1860 three classes of certificates were instituted. A fourth class certificate was introduced in 1871 but its standard was so elementary as to be almost valueless. It was discontinued after 1877.

The modern period in Army education was the result of the Cardwell reforms of 1870 which by introducing the short-service system produced a completely new outlook. Every year, thousands of soldiers in early middle-age would be returned to civilian life and therefore it was a matter of the greatest importance that their education whilst in the Army should not only aim at making them more efficient soldiers but should also take into account the problems they would encounter when they had left the Army. Thus a Select Committee of the House of Commons in 1895 recommended that soldiers should be encouraged to attend technical and commercial schools. This policy was carried a stage further by a War Office Committee in 1906 which proposed that some degree of vocational training should be available for the soldier during his period of service.

The educational situation in the Army at the close of the last century was by no means satisfactory although statistics suggested that considerable progress had been made. The returns showed that more than 4,000 men had gained a first class and about 45,000 a second class certificate, but these figures concealed the real weakness of the system. Many high ranking officers were either apathetic or believed that Army education was of little value. Lord Wolseley reported in 1898, 'The time will soon come when we shall be able to dispense altogether with Army schoolmasters and schoolmistresses'. Such a forecast was entirely out of touch with reality. The Corps of Army Schoolmasters found their work hindered on every side by numberless petty regulations which stifled initiative and encouraged formalism. At one time the authorities prescribed the exact number of words and sentences which would be accepted as a minimum in the essay examination for the second class certificate of education. Small wonder, indeed, that this narrow outlook caused difficulty in obtaining the right type of man for the Corps.

It is to the credit of the War Office that the higher authorities began to entertain some doubts about the progress of education in the Service and in 1906 the Board of Education was requested to conduct a searching inquiry into Army education. The Board's inspectors who had been seconded for this purpose made their report in the following year and many of their suggestions were put into operation. The methods of training Army schoolmasters were brought into line with those employed in civilian training colleges and in 1909 the Board of Education took the significant step of recognizing trained Army schoolmasters as certificated teachers. Men could now enter the Corps with the assurance that when they left the Service they could obtain appointments in civilian schools together with adequate recognition on the salary scale for their previous experience.

The outbreak of the first World War brought about the dispersal of the Corps of Army Schoolmasters and although a few individuals were retained for the instruction of enlisted boys and for duties in Army schools, the Corps never fully assembled again. The military situation in the autumn of 1914 was much too critical to allow the War Office to pay attention to the education of the soldier. Every effort had to be exerted to supply reinforcements for the hard-pressed British Expeditionary Force and for training the personnel of the New Army which Lord Kitchener was forming. It was at this juncture that civilian aid came to the rescue. The Y.M.C.A. had for many years carried out religious, educational and welfare work amongst young soldiers. The Y.M.C.A. tent with its familiar red triangle was to be found at summer training camps of the Territorials and during manœuvres of Regular troops. Soldiers could use it as a quiet room for reading and for writing letters to those at home, and after parade hours, concerts, debates, lectures, and religious services were held in it. Early in 1915, a committee with Dr. Temple (later Archbishop of Canterbury) as chairman and Dr. Basil Yeaxlee as secretary, was formed to develop educational work in the Forces.

The Y.M.C.A. got down to work very quickly and arranged lectures and classes in the training camps in Britain and for the troops on all the main battle-fronts: e.g. France, Salonika, Mesopotamia, and British East Africa. In France this work was carried out on the lines of communications, where troops were visited by university lecturers and other teachers who provided instruction in a large variety of subjects. Because of the exigencies of the campaign, most of the work was restricted to single lectures, though at G.H.Q. and the base camps certain short courses were possible. The military authorities and in particular Sir Douglas Haig were intensely interested in the experiment and this led to a further development.

The Y.M.C.A. in co-operation with the universities formed in April 1918 the Y.M.C.A. Universities Committee. This body included representatives of numerous organizations which were interested in adult education in the Forces; e.g. the Y.M.C.A. and Y.W.C.A., the senior members of university staffs, the local education authorities, the N.U.T. and the W.E.A. The Y.M.C.A. undertook to bear the whole expense of the work carried out by the Universities Committee and spent more than £250,000 on the project. University lecturers were sent to undertake educational work on the lines of communication in France and later, distinguished scholars and lecturers visited the other battle areas. At base camps it was found possible to arrange for longer courses and to provide opportunities for a certain amount of continuous study. One feature was the universal demand for instruction in modern languages. Thus at Etaples, in the early months of 1918, more than a thousand men were learning French.

In addition to the facilities provided under civilian auspices, educational efforts from within the Army arose itself. At first these were entirely due to the zeal and initiative of individual officers. The earliest organized experiment was made at Brockton Camp, Cannell Chase, where young soldiers, that is recruits between the ages of 18 and 18 years 8 months, were undergoing their training. Members of the battalion who either had received a secondary education or who possessed some teaching experience consented to give the instruction. Classes of approximately fifty men were formed and graded according to the previous education and attainments of the personnel. Ten hours per fortnight were allotted for educational purposes and the instruction included the English group of subjects (English literature, history, geography and composition), science and mathematics, ethics and hygiene. About the same time a similar scheme was started in the Southern Army, later the 23rd Army Corps. The latter scheme emphasized the aspect of training in citizenship and defined its aim as 'the development of the soldier not only as an efficient fighting man, but also as a citizen'.

When the great German offensive of 1918 had been contained, the War Office began to look ahead to the post-war period and decided that a comprehensive educational scheme would be necessary for the stage of demobilization and resettlement. Army Order X, September 24th, 1918, marked the commencement of the official scheme of Army education. At the time nobody expected a sudden collapse of German resistance but it was realized that a great deal would have to be accomplished in a very short space of time. The official scheme was under the control of a newly formed branch of the War Office (S.D. 8) which had been established at the end of August. Events moved much more rapidly than had been expected, with the consequence that every step taken by the War Office was always a few weeks behind time. Lord Gorell was brought from France to take charge of the new branch with the title of Deputy Director of Staff Duties (Education). The scheme was still in the process of formation when news of the Armistice burst upon the world. At once appeals for help came in from training camps and units in the field. When fighting suddenly ceased, thousands of men were idle waiting until orders for demobilization reached them. All the wartime enthusiasm quickly evaporated and unless something was done, and that quickly, there would be a marked decline in morale.

Once the authorities realized this fact they acted with alacrity and in an incredibly short space of time an educational scheme of gigantic proportions was launched. Army Order X was extended by the issue of Army Order XVIII, December 20th, 1918, which not only applied to Great Britain and France, but also to Italy, Salonika, and Egypt. The new Army Order recast the establishment by providing an education officer at brigade level and instructors on the scale of four officers and 12 N.C.O.s per 1,000 men. Education officers were authorized for hospital areas and special provision was made for the instruction of backward men in the three Rs. The collapse of the Empires of Germany, Austria and Russia led to political changes which puzzled even well-educated men. In order to stimulate discussion on these changes, regimental officers were issued with 'outline lectures' which anticipated the A.B.C.A. pamphlets of the second World War. Two things were immediately necessary; a supply of suitable textbooks and an adequate number of trained instructors. The first need was met by the printing and distribution of books on a grand scale. By April 1919, nearly three-quarters of a million textbooks had been issued. The supply of teachers was maintained by the opening of two schools of education, one at Oxford and the other at Cambridge. The latter was eventually transferred to Newmarket. It was estimated that nearly 3,000,000 men would be brought under the influence of the educational scheme.

Army Order VII dated May 13th, 1919, made provision for the systematic education of men in the home armies and in the armies of occupation. A pamphlet issued with the Order emphasized that education would henceforth be an essential element in the training of the soldier and related the Army scheme to the further education envisaged by the Education Act of 1918. Courses were established for the education of illiterates whilst those above this level were given facilities to attend classes in a wide variety of subjects.[1] A special Army Education Certificate was issued to those who successfully completed courses in the advanced stages of group A and at least, but not more than, three of the optional subjects in groups B to F. This certificate was accepted by the universities and by a large number of the

---

[1] The scheme set out by Army Order VII consisted of the following groups:
    A. (1) English, (2) Arithmetic or elementary mathematics, (3) Civics, history and geography.
    B. Languages and history.
    C. Political economy (Economics and industrial history).
    D. Pure science (Chemistry, physics and botany).
    E. Mathematics, including higher and practical mathematics.
    F. Engineering course.
    G. Commercial subjects.
    H. Agricultural science.
    I. Music, including choral singing.
    J. Drawing, art and design.
    K. Hygiene and first aid.
    L. "Handyman training" (Shoemaking, tailoring, cookery, etc.).
    M. Practical trades.

professional associations as equivalent to their own entrance requirements.

Probably the most complete educational organization was that of the Army of the Rhine. The army was given four officers and eight N.C.O.s to each battalion, double the number allotted to the other armies. Education in general subjects (group A) was the responsibility of the unit. Technical training could not be carried out at unit level and therefore a special organization had to be created to deal with this problem. A G.H.Q. Army General and Commercial College for 300 students was established in January 1919, and a few months later an Army Science College for 220 students and an Army Technical College for 200 students were added. When the soldier returned to his unit after completing the course at one of these establishments, he was able to continue his studies by means of the G.H.Q. Correspondence School. At corps and divisional levels, schools which provided general, commercial and technical training were authorized. The divisional schools included an agricultural wing to meet the popular demand for this subject. Civilian instructors were used in these establishments to augment Army resources. The premises of German universities and technical colleges were requisitioned for this work. By the summer of 1919 about 75,000 soldiers were pursuing regular courses of study in these colleges.

Less spectacular but perhaps of even greater importance was the extension of the educational scheme to military hospitals in Great Britain. The larger military hospitals were insufficient to cope with the 250,000 patients who required medical and surgical treatment and a large number of auxiliary hospitals and convalescent homes had been established. More specialized treatment could be given in the larger and better equipped hospitals and this entailed the continual movement of patients from the larger to the auxiliary hospitals and convalescent homes. Thus the author after spending a short time in a military hospital was moved to an auxiliary hospital in London and eventually to a convalescent home on the south coast. The continual movement of patients from one institution to another made it difficult to form an adequate educational organization. The problem was solved by the appointment of education officers to the larger hospitals and then working outwards to the auxiliary establishments. Patients who possessed the necessary educational qualifications were also used as instructors. Another obstacle was the attitude of some of the patients. Many of them were incapacitated from following their normal occupations and an important aspect of the training was fitting them to take up new types of employment when they received their discharge. At first some patients regarded these educational activities as attempts to deprive them of their pensions but by degrees their hostility was overcome through the understanding and sympathetic treatment they received.

The inspiration behind all this organization came from Lord Gorell and no praise can be too high for the devoted service he rendered to the cause of Army education during the period of the first World War. The Ministry of Reconstruction summarized what had been accomplished in the following paragraph: 'It is clear, however, that any attempt at judgment of the work must be made in the light of the resources available and the conditions under which it had to be conducted. Viewed as a whole, it was a triumph of improvisation, and the surprising thing is that these widespread activities were found possible at all in the face of the difficulties which must inevitably accompany any attempt at education among the soldiers of armies taking part in a great war, when all such attempts must be subject to the overwhelming claims of military necessity. Indeed, when sufficient time has elapsed to enable the events of the war to be seen in their true perspective, the rise and development of the educational movement among the armed forces will stand out as one of the most striking and unpredictable. As the President of the Board of Education, speaking at the Cambridge School for Army Education Instructors, said: "Nothing in the shape of adult education has ever been attempted on the same scale in the whole history of the world".'[1]

The most significant aspect of education in the Army during these years was the outstanding contribution of civilian educationists. Mr. Fisher paid them this tribute: 'To them, and to the Army Authorities in France, under whom they worked, belongs the credit of introducing and developing the largest scheme of adult education which has ever at any one time been launched from this country; and it is satisfactory to know that the pioneer work which was begun by the Y.M.C.A. in the Army Areas as far back as

[1] *Ministry of Reconstruction Adult Education Committee. Final Report*, p. 349. H.M.S.O., 1919.

1916 is now, upon a larger scale and in easier circumstances (though the circumstances are still by no means easy), being continued by an able staff of teachers working under the Army Education Scheme'.[1] Although the amount of civilian assistance decreased rapidly in the period between the wars, it never entirely disappeared and as late as 1938 the author was lecturing to N.C.O.s in Northern Command. Civilian resources remained as a potential which was there to be realized when hostilities once more broke out.

Certain features of special interest were to be found in the educational activities of the Royal Air Force. The R.A.F. Education Scheme began to take shape in August 1918, and it was preceded by an attempt to secure a complete census of the educational requirements of R.A.F. personnel who were serving in France. Because of the large numbers involved, no similar attempt had been made by the Army. The returns are instructive since at this time no systematic educational work had been carried out in the R.A.F. and therefore officers and men had no previous experience which influenced them in their choice of subjects. The Royal Air Force contained a much larger proportion of skilled and semi-skilled men than the Army and therefore it is not surprising to learn that requests for various kinds of technical and practical training preponderated.

The special circumstances under which the R.A.F. worked produced a development along lines somewhat different from those in the Army. The R.A.F. had few centres in which large numbers of men and women were congregated. Units were much smaller and more widely scattered. They were frequently situated in places where few local educational facilities were available. Hence the education scheme needed to be decentralized. The general organization of the scheme was in the hands of the Directorate of Training at the Air Ministry. Arrangements were made for regular fortnightly conferences between area education officers and the Deputy Director of Education at the Air Ministry. Whenever possible, educational staff officers from France attended. The conferences proved invaluable as a means of pooling information and experience and for securing unity in educational policy.

The R.A.F. scheme was organized in the belief that it would be permanent. Hence it followed principles which

---

[1] *Army Education, the Journal of the Army Educational Corps*, vol. XVII, No. 4, p. 141.

would be suitable for normal conditions and which were then modified to meet the special requirements of the war and demobilization periods. The Army scheme had been improvised under war conditions and one of the urgent problems which had to be solved after the Armistice was that of deciding to what extent education should remain as a permanent feature of military training. The necessity for decentralization in the R.A.F. threw greater responsibility upon the commanding officers and education officers of units and consequently they were given wider discretionary powers. The establishment provided for a maximum of four officers and twelve N.C.O.s for each thousand men, and as in the Army the services of volunteers in the Service and of civilian tutors were utilized. In addition education in the R.A.F. was helped by the fact that a considerable number of educated women had joined the W.A.A.F. (now the W.R.A.F.), and could be used as teachers. These special features of the R.A.F. made for greater elasticity. The central control which resulted in carefully planned courses was not nearly so prominent as in the Army, with the consequence that education officers had to rely more on their own initiative and were able to organize courses with a view to the needs of individuals rather than of large groups. The R.A.F. also gained much benefit from a close liaison with the War Office and the Board of Education. Airmen could present themselves as candidates for the Army Education Certificate and attend courses provided by the War Office. Assistance was given by inspectors of the Board of Education and schemes for co-operating with local education authorities were put into operation.

Education in the Royal Navy can be traced as far back as the end of the seventeenth century. In certain of the larger ships, education officers were to be found whose duty it was to instruct young officers in writing, arithmetic and navigation and to teach the youths of the ship. The Newcastle Commission investigated the educational facilities provided by the Admiralty and their criticisms embodied in the Report of 1861 brought about many improvements. When war broke out in 1914, the educational work of the Royal Navy was considerably extended and even more than was the case with the R.A.F. the emphasis was on scientific and technical instruction. General education was by no means neglected. Individual officers at the home ports arranged lectures and debates, organized classes in modern languages and other subjects, and provided facilities for instruction in various handicrafts. On the larger ships young seamen received regular instruction from naval schoolmasters who were appointed by the Admiralty.

When the Regular Army was being reconstituted in the summer of 1919, the future status of Army education became a prominent subject of discussion. There still remained a large number of senior officers who were not convinced of its value and for the time being its fate was in the balance. Were the experiences of the last two years to be ignored or would some provision be made for the continuance of education in the peace-time Army which would embody what had been learned during the stress of war and demobilization? The answer came from Mr. Winston Churchill, who was Secretary of State for War. In a reply to a question asked in the House of Commons on August 5th, 1919, he said, 'It has been decided that education is henceforward to be regarded as an integral part of Army training'. This reply at once raised the problem whether it would be sufficient to return to the pre-war system of education or whether a new type of organization would be necessary. The first alternative was impracticable. Many members of the Corps of Army Schoolmasters were serving under the Government of India. Others were dispersed amongst Army and Corps Headquarters or were still being employed in Army schools teaching the children of soldiers. The War Office decided upon a complete re-organization. The Corps of Army Schoolmasters was dissolved early in 1920 and in May of that year a scheme for the constitution of an Army Educational Corps was presented to Parliament. The Corps of Army Schoolmistresses still continued to exist but the conditions of its members were improved by the adoption of the Burnham Scales.

While arrangements were going forward for the creation of the new Corps the War Office issued the manual, *Educational Training: Part I, General Principles*. This was an enlightened document dealing with the principles and practice of adult education. 'The manual illustrated the position of the Corps that was to be formed by stating "it is not to be regarded in any other light than as a combatant corps of the army". This followed necessarily on the decision to regard education as an integral part of military training. "Its duties are exclusively educational," the paragraph continued, "but its members are distributed through units and accompany units to which they are attached, wherever and upon whatever duty the units may be dispatched".[1] The Royal Warrant of June 15th, 1920, transferred members of the Corps of Army Schoolmasters in their respective ranks to the Army Educational Corps. The establishment of the new Corps totalled 1,023 (428 officers and 595 warrant officers and sergeant instructors). Advertisements in the Press invited applications from officers and those who were already serving as instructors, ex-officers and N.C.O.s who had served as instructors during the war, officers and other ranks on the active list who were serving in other branches of the Regular Army, and university graduates and others with special qualifications in education. A selection board under the chairmanship of Lord Gorell was set up to interview candidates and in November 1920, the *London Gazette* published the first list of those who had been commissioned in the Corps.

Since 1811 the Army Schools had worked under the Adjutant-General's department but now a change was made and the A.E.C. was placed under the Director of Staff Duties. As soon as educational training became restricted to members of the Regular Army, the responsibility for it was transferred to the Directorate of Military Training. This change may not at first appear significant but it really indicated that a new attitude towards Army education was developing. The military aim of producing an efficient soldier now became foremost and education was valued as a means of rendering the man more fit to receive his military instruction. This should be borne in mind; otherwise the educational developments of the second World War will not be seen in their right perspective. As previously mentioned, A.E.C. officers were regarded as combatant and until 1930 they were required to pass the tactical tests undergone by infantry officers of the same rank. Even in wartime the A.E.C. officer fired his annual musketry course and if events demanded it he was available for fighting. In other words, he was primarily a soldier and secondarily an educationist though there were times when the rôles seemed to be reversed.

In spite of this, however, for some years the problem of re-settling the soldier after the expiration of his service remained an important one for the A.E.C. This problem was almost non-existent in the technical branches of the

[1] *The Story of Army Education, Centenary Souvenir*, 1946, p. 16.

Army such as the Royal Engineers or the Royal Army Service Corps. It was an urgent one in non-technical units like an infantry battalion where with the exception of a few men employed in the regimental tailor's or cobbler's shops, there were no facilities for teaching a trade. Opportunities were now made for men to receive instruction in various kinds of manual work, e.g. woodwork, gardening, sheet metal work, and the elements of electrical engineering. This was given in the unit, but in large garrisons the instruction could be provided at brigade level.

The unit scheme of vocational training was extended by the establishment of special vocational training centres situated at Hounslow and Catterick. These had been instituted for men in Eastern and Northern Commands, respectively, in 1919 but in 1923 men in other commands became eligible for the courses. Suitable W.O.s, N.C.O.s and men who held a second class certificate of education were selected and posted to these centres for the last six months of their military life. Such establishments were organized to accommodate about two hundred men each. In the Catterick centre the emphasis was on agriculture. About 120 acres of arable land and 500 acres of grassland were available for those who desired instruction in the methods of farming and there were sections dealing with pig and poultry keeping.

The system of Army Certificates of Education was revived and a Special Certificate was added to the original three. The 3rd class certificate became a test which was given to recruits at an early stage in their training; the 2nd class was designed for trained soldiers and was made a necessary qualification for proficiency pay, and the 1st class certificate (about School Certificate level) became a requirement for promotion to warrant rank. The Special Certificate was a qualification for commissioned rank. The candidate was required to pass in English, mathematics, a foreign language (classical or modern), map-reading and two optional subjects taken from a list provided. The two lower examinations were organized locally and most of the instruction for them was given by unit instructors. The two higher examinations were controlled by the War Office and preparation for them was a responsibility of the A.E.C.

Since the promotion and pay of both officers and men depended upon success in examinations, this system lent itself to cramming. Lord Wavell saw the danger and remained a vigorous opponent of the system, working to bring about the abolition or reduction of compulsory examinations. He said, 'As an instance of the results to which this examination system may lead I remember an officer in my Division at Aldershot, shortly before the War, who had made several unsuccessful attempts to pass for promotion to the rank of Major. He had won the D.S.O. and M.C. in the 1914–18 war, and had subsequently been given a brevet majority for good work in peace as a Regimental Officer. I asked the War Office to excuse him from further examination, saying that he was one of the very best Company Commanders in my Division, and thoroughly efficient; but that he lacked book learning and got confused in these written examinations. The War Office was hard-hearted and insisted that he should have another attempt. The poor officer gave up his hunting all one winter to study with a crammer, and failed again. The War Office then agreed to promote him, which they might just as well have done at once. He justified my opinion of his efficiency by commanding a Battalion and then a Brigade with considerable success in the late war'.[1]

In spite of the lack of encouragement received from many commanding officers and the depressing effect of War Office regulations which seemed designed to strangle the newly-formed Corps with red tape, the A.E.C. struggled manfully and achieved an astonishing degree of success. Its work in various parts of the Empire cannot be recorded in this volume but it shouldered heavy responsibilities in Britain. Personnel of the Corps were allotted to units to act as the expert educational advisers of commanding officers. In addition to carrying out the more advanced instruction they were made responsible for the supervision and training of the unit instructors. The latter attended a course at the Army School of Education, Shorncliffe, for which again the A.E.C. held the responsibility. Officers of the A.E.C. also carried out specialist instruction at Sandhurst and Woolwich, and others were allotted for the general education of Army apprentice tradesmen at the Military College of Science and at the Army Boys' Technical Schools. The special and technical education at these establishments was the responsibility of the technical corps concerned. The A.E.C. was also responsible for the two boys' schools, the Duke of York's and the Queen Victoria School, Dunblane.[2]

[1] *Army Education*, vol. XXII, No. 1, p. 8.
[2] There had originally been a third boys' school, the Royal Hibernian Military School, Dublin, which had been incorporated under a Royal Charter

In 1922 the Geddes Committee imposed sweeping cuts on the Services which resulted in the establishment of the A.E.C. being reduced to one half. This policy seriously interfered with the promotion and pay of officers and other ranks and thus discouraged the right type of man from joining the Corps. It is said that between 1921 and 1937 no officer was gazetted to the Corps. Although in 1931 the retiring age of officers was extended from 55 to 60 years of age with a consequent benefit to their pensions, this step was offset by a further reduction of the establishment of officers to 100. In 1928 the department of Army Schoolmistresses became the Corps of Queen's Army Schoolmistresses under the patronage of Queen Mary. Members of the Corps, much to the disgust of many of them, remained civilians and were largely recruited from the teachers' training colleges. For practical purposes, on service abroad, they ranked as warrant officers.

It was unfortunate that in the period between the two wars Army education was to a large extent isolated from the main current of development in civilian education and it is to the great credit of the A.E.C. that in spite of the obstacles, intentionally or unintentionally placed in its way, the officers and other ranks of the Corps preserved the Army Education Scheme from stagnation. In 1931 yet another responsibility was thrust upon the Corps. Until this date, the personnel for carrying out work in connection with codes and ciphers had been provided by the Royal Corps of Signals. The introduction of radio transmission had made the task of maintaining secrecy more difficult and in order to lighten the burden of the R.C.S. the responsibility for codes and ciphers was transferred to the A.E.C. All ranks were trained in code and cipher work and at the outbreak of war most of the personnel were dispersed to undertake these duties.

The Munich crisis was followed by the National Service Act of 1938 which introduced a modified form of conscription. The Y.M.C.A., the W.E.A. and the universities immediately demanded that steps should be taken to provide for the education of the young men who had been called up for service with the militia. The War Office issued a scheme for the establishment of Advisory Regional Committees

in 1769. When the Irish Free State came into existence in 1922, the school was transferred to the Duke of York's and was finally dissolved in 1924. The colours of the school were deposited in Windsor Castle.

based on the extra-mural departments of the universities. Hostilities commenced, however, before the scheme could be put into operation. All the plans were abandoned and it was officially declared that educational training in the Army was suspended.

Once again civilian educational bodies sprang into the breach in response to requests from men in the Forces. The Y.M.C.A., the W.E.A. and the universities offered their assistance and there was an insistent demand in the Press and by the various educational associations that something at a national level should be done to co-ordinate these different activities. The result was the formation in January 1940 of the Central Advisory Council for Adult Education in H.M. Forces which co-ordinated the activities of 23 regional committees based on the areas served by universities and university colleges. Sir Walter Moberly was appointed chairman and Dr. A. D. (now Lord) Lindsay, Master of Balliol, as vice-chairman. The Council was fortunate in once more securing the services of Dr. Basil Yeaxlee as secretary. The regional committees organized the civilian educational resources in their areas and placed them at the disposal of the three Services. As in the war of 1914–18, the Y.M.C.A. took a leading part in the creation of this organization.

The Central Advisory Council made repeated demands that the Army should co-operate with civilian organizations by reviving its own educational activities. The War Office was impressed by the unanimity of public opinion and realized also that steps would have to be taken in order to maintain the morale of the troops. In March 1940, a small committee with Lieut.-General Sir Robert Haining as chairman was appointed to consider a scheme for adult education in the Army during the war period. The Haining Committee believed that it was essential to provide means of mental stimulus to keep men's minds interested and alert but it was emphasized that war conditions would make it extremely difficult to arrange for systematic and continuous instruction. In order to carry out the recommendations of the Committee a Directorate of Army Education was instituted. Mr. F. W. D. Bendall was released from his duties at the Board of Education to become the first Director and he was assisted by Brigadier C. G. Maude, the Chief Inspector of the A.E.C.

Officers and other ranks of the A.E.C. were re-assembled

and since the task which confronted them was so great, it became necessary to expand the membership of the Corps. The Army School of Education was re-opened at Brockenhurst and later moved to Wakefield and special efforts were made to train both new entrants to the A.E.C. and unit instructors. Within three years the Corps had grown to about three times its original size. The new Army education scheme was put into operation by A.C.I. 1138 of 1940. The recently trained members of the A.E.C. were posted to units or formations, where they quickly discovered numerous difficulties that had to be surmounted. Apart from problems arising from the necessity of getting the scheme working as soon as possible, officers and other ranks of the Corps discovered that in most cases they would have to convert commanding officers to a belief in the value of education before much headway could be made. This was not always a simple matter. There were, of course, a few commanding officers who eagerly welcomed the education scheme. There were others who regarded education as a sheer waste of time and a serious obstacle to effective military training. The majority were either apathetic or somewhat suspicious and it was therefore necessary to win them over and to secure their cooperation.

Although many members of the A.E.C. were actually engaged in instruction the task which had to be accomplished was far too great for the comparatively small numbers of the Corps. Much of their time was taken up by organizing duties in commands or divisions and in units they carried out the rôle of expert educational advisers to the commanding officer. Hence the War Office decided that each unit should have its own education officer. On the whole, commanding officers selected their education officers wisely though there were some instances where a junior officer who had not shown a great deal of initiative in the work he had been doing was given the job. Some soldiers had been preparing for professional examinations and their studies had been rudely interrupted by the outbreak of war. It was not always possible to cater for them through either the existing civilian or military organizations. To meet their needs, Army Correspondence Courses were started in December 1940. Originally there were available courses in 46 different subjects but as the demand for this type of instruction increased, more subjects were added. The cost of providing the courses was fairly heavy. Hence it was desirable that they should be restricted to genuine students. Each student who enrolled was asked to pay a fee of ten shillings for the course. In less than a year about 8,000 correspondence course students had been enrolled.

The Auxiliary Territorial Service (A.T.S.) presented a special problem. Many women attended mixed classes taught by civilian lecturers belonging to the regional committees, by the A.E.C. or by regimental instructors. It was soon discovered, however, that women differed considerably from men in their interests and were asking for instruction in such subjects as needlework and dress-making, cookery, home nursing and domestic science. Many of the recruits to the A.T.S. were young and immature and felt keenly the separation from their homes. It was therefore thought advisable to attach A.T.S. officers and N.C.O.s to women's units to carry out duties parallel to those performed by the personnel of the A.E.C.

So far the educational work carried out in the Army had been mainly on a voluntary basis. In spite of the efforts of the regional committees, the local education authorities and the technical institutes and the Army's own instructors, it was estimated by the summer of 1941 that roughly 80 per cent of the Army was untouched by any specific educational influence. The military authorities were growing increasingly anxious about the morale of the Forces. The Germans had clear ideas about the objects for which they were fighting but the Adjutant-General, Sir Ronald Adam, realized that it was not so in the British Forces. Large numbers of men and women in the Army had completely lost touch with the major issues of the day at home and abroad. The ideal was to produce soldiers similar to those who had served in Cromwell's New Model Army; who both knew the ideals for which they were fighting and loved them. It was this situation which brought about the establishment of the Army Bureau of Current Affairs of which Mr. W. E. Williams, who had a long experience in the field of adult education, was chosen as Director.

In August 1941 the War Office issued the pamphlet *Current Affairs in the Army* which explained how A.B.C.A. should be carried out in units. Attendance at an A.B.C.A. course for at least one hour a week was made compulsory for everybody. The actual running of the course would be in the hands of the regimental officers and it was to be organized at the platoon level. The platoon or its equivalent in other branches of the Service would provide a class of approximately 30–35 men which would be of a suitable size for the kind of work contemplated. A.B.C.A. involved an innovation which produced considerable disquiet in the minds of some senior officers. It was decided that the main part of the session which should follow a brief talk by the platoon commander would be an open discussion in the course of which any man would be free to express his own opinions. Some of the older officers thought that free discussion might encourage the crank and the extremist to air their views. Moreover, the discussion leader might quite easily discover that some of his men knew more about the subject than he did himself and this might result in the lowering of his prestige as an officer.

In practice these fears proved to be groundless. The common sense of the soldier prevailed and it soon became apparent that the individual who spoke merely because he wished to put over a particular kind of propaganda would receive short shrift. Most A.B.C.A. discussions were conducted in an orderly way and in a friendly spirit by men, who, if they were often lacking in factual knowledge, were anxious to make use of the information they possessed. For the assistance of the discussion leader, the Army Bureau of Current Affairs issued a weekly bulletin to all regimental officers. There were two types of bulletin issued alternately. The first, *Current Affairs*, aimed at providing a background which would give the officer the vital information to enable him to assess and understand the significance of current events. The other, *War*, was designed to provide a commentary on the progress of the Allied forces in the different theatres of war and which, as it often contained information semi-secret in character, was distributed to officers only. The former bulletin was issued to civilian lecturers working under the regional committees.

The scheme was launched by the first issue of *Current Affairs*, September 27th, 1941. The first issue was prefaced by useful hints to regimental officers, e.g. "This new job of keeping your men abreast of current affairs may at first seem out of your line of country. You are used to teaching your men tactics, weapon-training and so on, and you've probably worked out a useful technique. You know what snags are likely to develop, where the tricky questions arise. You may feel diffident about tackling a subject which seems so very different from your usual line. But if you deal with it with the experience you have gained from instructing your men in other branches of their training, you will soon find it no more difficult to teach current affairs than to teach those other subjects in the Army time-table about which you knew nothing or next to nothing a few months ago'.[1] Later issues of the bulletins contained useful advice about the technique of the discussions, the use of questions, the blackboard, maps, pictures and other kinds of visual aid. The Army Bureau of Current Affairs issued map summaries, photographs, and information films. In all important training centres, information rooms were set aside, furnished with chairs and tables and stocked with reference books, visual aids of all kinds and pamphlets dealing with current affairs. One important feature of the information room was the wall newspaper and regimental officers displayed much ingenuity in developing new and striking ways of bringing home to their men the salient facts about the war and the world situation. The bulletins and other publications of the Army Bureau of Current Affairs were also distributed to the Royal Navy and the Royal Air Force.

The reader will probably have realized that these new developments came, not as the result of a plan which had been carefully thought out beforehand, but they were improvisations forced upon the authorities by the actual situation. It was inevitable that in the early stages the different activities would be to a large extent unrelated. Once the first stages had been successfully carried through it became possible to provide for a more systematic approach. This took place in the summer of 1942 when plans were made for a 'winter scheme' to be in force from November to February.

During these months, three hours a week from training or working periods were given to education. The winter scheme was an attempt to deal with the three aspects of the soldier's education, i.e. as a soldier, a citizen and as an individual. The first of these periods was placed at the disposal of the commanding officer, who could use it for such purposes as instruction in map reading or in such technical subjects as would be of use to the soldier or in talks about the history of the British Army and the regiment which would assist the development of morale. As an individual the soldier had certain interests and hobbies which should be catered for as far as possible. Many units formed classes in handi-

[1] *Current Affairs*, Number 1, p. 1. September 27th, 1941.

crafts, arts, music and dramatics. On A.A. and searchlight sites where the personnel was fairly permanent instruction over a long period could be given and men were able to develop their hobbies both during and after working hours. Toy-making was very popular. The author still possesses an exquisite model of a British destroyer presented to him by men of an A.A. battery to whom he lectured.

The education of the man as a citizen presented peculiar difficulties. In the first place, the number of existing instructors was too small to cope with the task. The universities were able to give assistance in this matter. Most of them provided short intensive courses for the training of regimental instructors. During this period the author was in charge of courses at Leeds where over 400 N.C.O.s and men were briefed for their work. The second difficulty was that no suitable up-to-date textbook on this subject existed. It was therefore necessary to issue a series of pamphlets entitled *British Way and Purpose*. The pamphlets were written by experts and were so successful that they were extended to cover the winter schemes of 1943–4 and 1944–5, and finally a consolidated edition was issued in book form by the Directorate of Army Education at the close of 1944.

Space forbids all but the mention of the important work carried on in hospitals, in military prisons and detention barracks, and amongst Polish soldiers in training in this country. Facilities for study and for classes were also provided by the libraries and the local education authorities. Although in 1944 hostilities were by no means at an end, it was realized that if the hasty improvisation which followed the Armistice of 1918 was to be avoided, plans would have to be prepared for the demobilization period. These were carefully considered and in March 1945 the *Organization Handbook* for the release period was issued followed by others on the curriculum, methods of instruction, equipment and materials, correspondence courses and libraries. The Government took in hand the publication of adequate numbers of selected textbooks and an inter-Services Committee in Educational Broadcasting was set up in consultation with the B.B.C. V.E.-Day, May 8th 1945, came sooner than was expected but the educational organization for the release period was in being. The author well remembers that date, a day of pouring rain which he spent in conference with Major-General Cyril Lloyd and Mr. W. R. Grist, the Secretary of the University of Leeds Regional

Committee, working out schemes for the demobilization period.

It would be difficult to give excessive praise to the leadership provided by successive Directors of Army Education. In 1942, Mr. Bendall returned to his post at the Board of Education and was succeeded by Mr. J. B. Bickersteth, who had been in charge of education in the 1st Canadian Army since September 1940. His successor at the end of 1943 was Mr. P. R. (later Sir Philip) Morris, who at that time was Director of Education for the county of Kent. Sir Philip Morris was given the new title of Director-General of Army Education which was to emphasize that the appointment had been made with a view to the special problems of the demobilization period. It was his task to organize the new education scheme. The first step consisted in re-organizing and co-ordinating the two directorates of Army Education and A.B.C.A. One of the essentials of the planning was to ensure that when the time arrived to put the scheme into operation, an adequate number of regimental instructors would be available. Once again the universities co-operated through their regional committees. The Army authorities also took the matter in hand. For some time, Coleg Harlech (requisitioned by the War Office) had been used as a centre for training A.B.C.A. instructors. Now a new school of education was opened at Cuerdon Hall near Preston, May 1944, to provide training for regimental instructors.

Under the able direction of Sir Philip Morris, the main features of the scheme for the release period had been completed by the end of 1944. The Army Council appointed Brigadier (later Major-General) Cyril Lloyd to fill the vacant post of Director of Army Education and to work in collaboration with Sir Philip Morris. At the time of his appointment, General Lloyd was Deputy Adjutant-General to 21st Army Group and the fact that Field-Marshal Montgomery released him from his duties was a sure sign that the authorities were alive to the importance of Army education.

The work accomplished by Sir Philip Morris and General Lloyd enabled the scheme to commence by July 1st 1945 in Home Commands, the Middle East and the Central Mediterranean Force. Within a month it was also in operation in the British Army of the Rhine. The military authorities had forecast that at least more than a year would be needed to bring the war with Japan to a close and it was anticipated that demobilization would take place in stages. The sudden collapse of Japan, August 15th, 1945, drastically altered the plans for demobilization and as a consequence the release scheme had to be speeded up. There was at first a good deal of confusion because of the enormous numbers of men and women whose requirements had to be met and also on account of the difficulty of evolving continuous courses of instruction when through releases and postings the personnel was constantly changing in units. At some centres the scheme was a great success. In some units it failed conspicuously. Everything depended upon the sympathy and enthusiasm of commanding officers.

The details of the scheme were set forth in the *Organization Handbook*. It was organized on a unit basis (an A.T.S. group was counted as a unit) and six hours a week were allocated from training or working time for education. Commanding officers who wished to do so could allocate additional periods. The syllabus of instruction in each subject was divided into three grades, elementary, intermediate and more advanced. Where suitable instruction could not be provided by units, classes could be organized at brigade level. More advanced study could be pursued at the Formation Colleges. These were distributed as follows: one college in each Home Command and one in each of the British Liberation Army, Central Mediterranean Force and Middle East Force. Arrangements were also made for lecturers selected by the C.A.C. to visit the armies in Europe, North Africa and the Far East.

Some men and women were anxious to obtain a qualification which would enable them to enter a training college, a university or one of the professions. For this purpose the Forces Preliminary Examination was instituted. The standard demanded is roughly equivalent to that of School Certificate and the examination can be taken in two parts. Part I consists of English, mathematics or Latin or an approved subject taken from Part II, and General Knowledge, which includes Current Affairs and Citizenship. Candidates are required to select two subjects for Part II from the following list: natural science or household science or Latin (if not already taken in Part I), French or German, history or geography, social sciences, additional mathematics or geometrical and mechanical drawing.

As soon as hostilities ceased, the pamphlet, *War*, was discontinued and at the end of 1945 the Army Bureau of Current Affairs was replaced by a civilian bureau under the control of the Carnegie Trustees. When the release scheme was fully working, Sir Philip Morris retired to take up the appointment of Vice-Chancellor of the University of Bristol and his duties were continued by General Lloyd. By the summer of 1946 it became clear that the release period was nearing its end and the educational scheme would have to be replaced by one designed for the peace-time Army. This took place early in 1947. In planning for the post-war scheme of education the authorities had to consider a number of problems. The new scheme must be free from the restrictions which nearly killed pre-war education in the Army. It would have to incorporate the lessons that war experiences had taught and it would be necessary to bring the scheme into line with the plans for further education envisaged by the Education Act of 1944. The unsettled state of international affairs required that some form of conscription should be continued. Hence the scheme would have to provide for the education of National Servicemen as well as of regular soldiers.

The most convenient procedure will be to deal with the case of the national serviceman first. Intakes are usually received at intervals of a fortnight and as soon as possible, each new arrival is interviewed by the Personnel Selection Officer (P.S.O.) who estimates the educational standard of the recruit and gains as much information as he can about the individual's ambitions both whilst in the Service and after his Army life has ended. These particulars are of considerable assistance in deciding to which arm of the Service the recruit should be posted when his initial six weeks of basic training have been satisfactorily completed. During this period the recruit has much to learn about his military duties so that his education is restricted to two periods a week in current affairs and citizenship.

As soon as the recruit has 'passed out' and has been posted to his training unit, the educational standard allocated to him by the P.S.O. becomes operative. Those who possess a School Certificate or some higher qualification are known as 'exempted soldiers' and can attend courses of instruction which are planned to meet their special requirements. These are usually conducted by university lecturers appointed by the extra-mural departments and who work in close liaison with the R.A.E.C.[1] Most of this work is carried out in small

---

[1] The distinction of the title Royal Army Educational Corps was conferred, December 10th, 1946, to recognize the valuable services the Corps had provided during the war.

tutorial groups. Thus at Catterick, the Services Committee of the University of Leeds Extra-mural Department maintains a staff of full-time lecturers to deal with the requirements of exempted soldiers. The remainder of the National Servicemen are required to attend the courses in General Education which include the following subjects: English, mathematics, history and geography, general science, citizenship and current affairs. All these subjects are graded into three stages according to the capacity of the pupils. 'Thus in English and Mathematics men will acquire the skills of language and number; in history, geography and science they will learn of the heritage of the past and the opportunities of the present; in citizenship and current affairs they will face the challenge of the community and study the art of living together. It is important to emphasize that these subjects will not be taught in isolation; lines of approach will be carefully interwoven to produce a pattern which might well be described as a design for living. History and geography will include the study of the locality in which the men are stationed, and, at the appropriate time, countries to which they are going; science, except for advanced classes, will concern itself with science in the home and in society; citizenship and current affairs will, again, be closely inter-related with the history and geography so inextricably mixed in the pattern of national and international affairs.'[1]

The syllabuses are given in detail in the *Handbook of General Education*, 1948. In its introduction, the Handbook indicates the spirit in which the peace-time education of the soldier should be approached. It says, 'It will be realized, therefore, that Army education should be regarded as one facet of the national system. When the Education Act, 1944, is fully implemented, the education of youth will form a continuous process extending from school through county college to National Service. National Service especially will mark the transition from the shelter and influence of the home to the responsibilities and obligations of the community. This is the natural time for the development of a flexible and inquiring mind, essential both for efficiency as a soldier and alertness as a citizen. This period of National Service also provides an opportunity to foster in the individual the spiritual qualities and humane influences which are a heritage from

[1] Supplement to No. 46, *Education in the Services*, pp. 4–5. Bureau of Current Affairs, Carnegie House, 1948.

the past, without which there can be but little hope for the future'.[1]

The Regulars and National Servicemen give three hours a week to General Education. When the latter have finished their service, the regulars alone remain and those of them who are not actively engaged in training others, devote four hours a week to education. When a regular soldier has completed three years' service or has reached the standard of Part I of the Forces Preliminary Examination, his compulsory education ceases but he will be encouraged to continue his studies on a voluntary basis. Similar regulations apply to women's units, now renamed the Women's Royal Auxiliary Corps (W.R.A.C.). Officers and N.C.O.s of the W.R.A.C. now bear the titles of rank hitherto given to men only. Thus a Junior Commander of the A.T.S. is now a Captain in the W.R.A.C. The correspondence courses of the war period are still available for men and women and all ranks are encouraged to make use of civilian educational facilities.

Two Army Colleges at home and two overseas are retained and where there are large concentrations of troops, Army Education Centres at home and abroad have been established. The unit education officer is retained on a part-time basis but regimental instructors are gradually being replaced by personnel of the R.A.E.C. In each unit, the commanding officer is still responsible for the education of his men. One problem that had to be faced in the change-over from war to peace was that of staffing. In order to train the instructors required, two Army Schools of Education were set up, one for N.C.O.s at Buchanan Castle, close to Loch Lomond, and the other for officers at Eltham Palace, Kent. In September 1948 the two schools were amalgamated and moved first to Bodmin, Cornwall, and then to Beaconsfield.

A recent development in Army education is the re-introduction of the three classes of Army Certificates of Education. A.C.I. 349, April 20th, 1949, announced that the starting date would be October 1st of that year for the examinations for the second- and third-class certificates and March 1st, 1950, for the first-class. Unless this scheme is wisely administered, it may prove to be a retrograde step. Future promotion is to depend on the possession of the appropriate certificate. No doubt a good deal of extraneous interest may be created by this means but it also presses

[1] *Army Education Scheme, Handbook of General Education (Provisional)*, p. 3, 1948.

hardly upon a number of highly efficient N.C.O.s who make very capable instructors in such subjects as drill and weapon training. In the author's own unit there are several extremely competent instructors in military subjects who are seriously perturbed about their prospects of promotion if they fail to pass the first-class certificate.

The syllabus for the lower certificates comprises English (oral and written), elementary mathematics and a general paper which includes history, geography, general science, current affairs and citizenship. The second-class certificate also requires a pass in map reading. The first-class certificate is divided into two parts. In Part I the candidate is required to pass in English, mathematics and current affairs. In Part II candidates are given a choice of history, geography, general science and citizenship. Subjects such as additional mathematics, physics, chemistry, engineering drawing, map reading or modern languages may be offered for special requirements. In addition candidates may also offer themselves for the Forces Preliminary examination.

One of the most troublesome problems that has to be faced is that of illiteracy. This is not so prominent in the Royal Navy and the Royal Air Force, which only accept recruits who have reached a certain standard in educational attainments. In the Army the problem of illiteracy existed from the beginning of the last war. Sir Ronald Adam drew attention to it in 1941 and in 1943 it was stated in the House of Commons that slightly under $1\frac{1}{4}$ per cent of recruits were illiterate. The War Office was greatly concerned, for illiteracy is a grave handicap to the production of an efficient soldier. Basic Education Centres were authorized in 1943 and special reading books (*English Parade*) were prepared for the instruction of illiterate soldiers in reading.

The problem has become even more serious since the advent of National Servicemen. It has been stated that the number of illiterates is about 10 per cent of the intake with semi-illiterates double that number. These figures are probably exaggerated but it still remains a fact that a large number of men who enter the Army at 18 years have retained little or nothing of what they have learned at school. Such men are not all dull and backward; many have normal or nearly normal intelligent quotients. They are often difficult to discover, as a soldier who is illiterate naturally does not want to advertise the fact. He often asks a comrade to read company orders for him and excuses his own inability by saying, 'Sorry, but I have left my spectacles in the barrack-room'.

Several investigations have been conducted to discover the causes of illiteracy. Sometimes it can be accounted for by the circumstances of early childhood, e.g. children of gipsies and bargees who have missed much of their schooling. Sometimes the large classes of the junior school are to blame. Pupils pass from them to the secondary modern school without acquiring a firm hold of the essential skills of reading and writing and are not able to gain much help in their new surroundings because of the lack of suitable books for children of that age, In other cases, the prevalence of illiteracy and semi-illiteracy constitutes a very serious criticism of our educational system. Pupils have left school without there being awakened any desire to continue their studies. The incentive to keep up their work has been absent. In some schools this may be due to the formal nature of the work, which has been divorced from the circumstances of everyday life, and in others to a lack of understanding of modern 'activity' methods and a tendency to allow the three Rs to take care of themselves. Frequently an illiterate becomes engaged and his desire to write to his beloved provides a motive to acquire the arts of reading and writing.

The Army Council decided that the war-time Basic Education Centres should be continued under the name of Preliminary Education Centres. When an illiterate is discovered, he is given a six-weeks' full-time course under specially selected instructors and when this has been completed he continues with Preliminary Education in his own unit. Much has been done to remedy defects of early education but it must be admitted that unless the illiterate discovers some motive to consolidate what he has learnt he quickly relapses. Modern warfare is very technical and the presence of even a small proportion of illiterates means that the efficiency of the Army will be considerably impaired.[1]

[1] The following item from a recent issue of the *Yorkshire Post* provides an interesting comment on the educational attainments of some boys between 16 and 18 years of age.
'A would-be recruit to the Black Watch (the Royal Highland Regiment) has written to Leeds Recruiting office in the following terms: "I am writing about putykulers of the Black Wotch. I am 17 yers of hage and I ma very kene of joieing that Redjimened I am a diveever—Yor Frend."—The Army can work wonders with recruits of low educational standard, provided the intelligence is not lacking. But nearly 50 per cent of boys in Leeds and district who offer themselves for general duties cannot pass the simple educational test given them'

It is now time to leave the subject of education in the Army to consider what has been carried out in the other Services.

Reference has already been made to the long tradition of education in the Royal Navy. Before 1946, the Education Branch was divided into two categories—Instructor Officers and Schoolmasters. The Royal Marines had also a separate Schoolmaster Branch. Schoolmasters who were qualified teachers were classed as Warrant Officers and it was their duty to provide for the education of the Lower Deck. All young seamen under 18 are required to spend a certain proportion of their time in school each week. Promotion for all ratings depends upon passing certain educational tests which range from a test in reading, writing and arithmetic for Able Seamen to an examination of School Certificate standard for Warrant Rank. Instructor Officers were concerned with the education of Midshipmen in navigation, astronomy, ship-stability, and meteorology. The development of the Fleet Air Arm made the scientific knowledge of weather forecasting extremely important and as the majority of Instructor Officers are science graduates, this duty is assigned to them. In aircraft carriers there are Instructor Officers employed full-time on meteorological duties.

In 1946 certain changes were made which involved the abolition of Warrant Schoolmasters. At the present time the whole branch is staffed by Instructor Officers and the establishment, which in pre-war days was about 400, has been doubled. Most Instructor Officers possess a first- or second-class honours degree in science or technology but there are also a few graduates in arts. The Instructor Officer may be assigned to a variety of jobs. His duties may include the organization of debates, discussions, all forms of educational or vocational training, and at sea he is in charge of the Strategical Plot, i.e. he is the intelligence officer of the ship. He may be allocated to a shore station for Basic Education (the equivalent to General Education in the Army), or if his qualifications are suitable, he may be engaged on scientific research.

Unlike the Army, in which General Education is provided for men throughout their period of service, the Royal Navy concentrates upon Basic Education while the sailor is training, which is mostly at shore stations (ports or 'concrete' ships). When afloat there is so much to be done aboard ship that there is little time for any studies except those which have a direct bearing upon the sailor's work. Hence the Navy is concerned to give every sailor a sound educational training before he is sent aboard ship. When at sea, conditions are not ideal for education from a landsman's point of view. Space is very restricted and although on board large ships it may be possible to set aside a space as a classroom, library, information room and handicrafts room combined, on smaller craft this is impracticable and the education officer is forced to improvise. Larger ships such as battleships and aircraft carriers are allotted two education officers whilst smaller ships such as cruisers and destroyer flotillas carry one. The education officer is always free to call upon the part-time services of other members of the ship's company and in the very small craft education has to be carried out by one of the ship's officers who is detailed for the purpose.

Like the Royal Navy, education in the Royal Air Force has a definite technical bias. Under modern conditions, the R.A.F. contains a large proportion of craftsmen, technicians and skilled tradesmen. Its officers include a large number who have been specially trained for flying duties or who have a specialist knowledge of various branches of engineering—mechanical, electrical, radio or aeronautical. Hence the educational training provided has to be divided between the technical and the education officers. During the war, the airmen received instruction from R.A.F. education officers and N.C.O.s but the services of civilian lecturers provided by the C.A.C. and the facilities offered by local education authorities were utilized to the full. Until October 1946, the education service of the R.A.F. was recruited from civilian teachers who were given the status of officers and permitted to wear uniform. Since then an Education Branch of the R.A.F. consisting of officers serving on permanent or short service commissions has been formed.

The war-time education scheme of the R.A.F. was similar to that of the Army although, because of the exigencies of the service, more emphasis was placed upon discussion groups than upon longer courses of instruction. During the release period, the R.A.F. adopted a compulsory scheme known as E.V.T. (Educational and Vocational Training). The National Service entrants created a difficult problem for the R.A.F. Most of the trades require a long period of training and the time available (at present two years) is all too short. Unless a recruit has had previous experience of a trade, it is essential to allocate him to one which does not require a very long period of training.

The recruit undergoes a preliminary training course of about eight weeks at a Recruit Centre. His education is limited to two periods a week, mainly in current affairs and citizenship. The course which follows this depends upon whether he is selected for aircrew or for work as a mechanic or tradesman. In all cases he will receive instruction in current affairs and citizenship for one period a week. If he is selected to be a member of an aircrew, his educational course will largely consist of mathematics, physics and aerodynamics. Those who are to become technical tradesmen will be posted to a school of technical training or in the case of radio mechanics to a radio school. Apart from their purely technical training, they will receive instruction in English, mathematics, mechanics, machine drawing and the theoretical principles of the sciences with which they are concerned. The time given to these studies depends upon the standards which are required in them but it varies from two to six hours a week.

When an airman has completed his training, he is examined by a Central Trade Test Board. According to the standard he reaches, he is classified as aircraftman 1st or 2nd class (A.C.1. or A.C.2). If he shows exceptional knowledge or skill, he may be placed in the highest category of leading aircraftman (L.A.C.). After this he is posted to a station and if he wishes he can make use of the facilities provided by the General Education Scheme. The object of this scheme is to develop through education a high standard of morale and at the same time to meet the requirements of airmen and airwomen in their capacity as citizens and as individuals. This work is undertaken by the education officers of the station, who are assisted by part-time teachers provided by the R.A.F., the university extra-mural boards and the local education authorities. The General Education Scheme also prepares all ranks for returning to their civilian occupations when their service has been completed and gives them information and guidance about possible careers for them to choose. As in the Army, correspondence courses are available for students who require specialist qualifications. A recent development has been the introduction of courses and examinations for officers and other ranks who are seeking promotion.

The R.A.F. is very proud of its training scheme for boy

apprentices. These are chosen by means of a competitive examination and successful candidates are given a three-year course in a highly skilled technical trade. This course is designed to give a boy a first-class technical training. At least a third of the time is spent in the study of mathematics, physics, mechanics, theory of flight, theory of structures, mechanical drawing and the theory of the internal combustion engine. Those who are entering the electrical or radio trades receive instruction appropriate to their needs. In addition, they are taught such general subjects as English, history, geography and current affairs. They also receive suitable training in physical exercises and games. The training is carried out in the R.A.F. training schools, the best known of which is the School of Technical Training at Halton, Bucks.

The R.A.F. also requires the services of a large number of clerical staff who are trained through the administrative apprentice training scheme. Boys of a mechanical turn of mind who have not reached the high standard required for entrance to the School of Technical Training, can be prepared for entering less highly skilled trades. There are also specialist training establishments for officers in such subjects as aircraft engineering, armaments, signals and radio.

In the above brief account of education in the Services, the work of the civilian lecturers under the C.A.C. and the regional committees has frequently been mentioned. Although the C.A.C. came to an end on December, 31st 1948, it was realized that the Services would still need civilian assistance. The universities were invited to take over, through the Service Committees of their extra-mural departments, the work previously carried out by the regional committees. So far, not all institutions of university rank have established Service Committees. University lecturers have been appointed to teach students of School Certificate standard and over whilst the W.E.A. and the local education authorities provide staff to assist with the education of non-exempted men. Some of this work, especially with the Royal Navy and the Royal Air Force, consists of single lectures or short courses, but wherever possible the emphasis has been placed upon continuous courses of instruction. In some cases the instruction takes place in university buildings whilst in others courses in residential or centralized schools are organized by the universities.

The volume of civilian aid to adult education in H.M.

Forces has reached considerable dimensions and is still increasing. For example, in Great Britain and Northern Ireland, during the year 1949–50, the universities and associated bodies were responsible for organizing 3,783 single lectures, 942 short courses, 168 residential courses, 267 courses for exempted soldiers and airmen and 372 classes. The recruiting of lecturers for units overseas has been continued. In place of the C.A.C., a Central Committee for Adult Education in H.M. Forces has been established for the purpose of co-ordinating the work carried out by the separate universities and for maintaining close liaison with the education staffs of the three Services.

SUGGESTIONS FOR FURTHER READING

General Histories of Education in Great Britain

ADAMSON, J. W., *A Short History of Education*, C.U.P., 1919.
English Education, 1789–1902, C.U.P., 1930.
Both these have long been standard works. They provide an excellent survey of the development of education before the opening of the present century and carry the story down to the Education Act of 1902.

ARCHER, R. L., *Secondary Education in the Nineteenth Century*, C.U.P., 1921.
In addition to the account of secondary education up to the end of the First World War, this book contains much useful material about the development of the universities and pays special attention to the growth of secondary education in Wales.

BARNARD, H. C., *A Short History of English Education, 1760–1944*, University of London Press, 1947.
A useful work which summarises the events of the last fifty years and refers to the principal writers on education during the period with which it is concerned. The book contains a full bibliography and a chronological chart.

BIRCHENOUGH, C., *History of Elementary Education in England and Wales from 1800 to the Present Day*, U.T.P., 1938.
This is the most detailed history of Elementary Education that has been produced. It includes the period between the great wars and ends with the Spens Report.

CURTIS, S. J., *History of Education in Great Britain*, U.T.P., 2nd edition, 1950.
The reader who wishes to familiarise himself with the development of British education from the earliest times to 1950 will find this a useful companion to the present work. The scope of the book necessitates a less detailed treatment of the last fifty years. It contains a date chart and an extensive bibliography.

GRAVES, J., *Policy and Progress in Secondary Education*, Thomas Nelson & Sons, 1943.
Provides much factual material. In reading the earlier chapters one should bear in mind the author's bias which tends to make him under-estimate the really solid achievements of Sir Robert Morant.

LESTER SMITH, W. O., *Education in Great Britain*, Home University Library, No. 210, O.U.P., 1949.
A brilliant summary of the development of British education. *To Whom Do Schools Belong?* Blackwell, 1943. A very able study in the development of the English educational system. It is most valuable for the light it sheds upon the events which led to the Education Act of 1944.

LOWNDES, G. A. N., *The Silent Social Revolution*, O.U.P., reprinted, 1948.
Deals with the development of English elementary, secondary and technical education from 1895 to the end of the period immediately preceding the Second World War. As its title indicates, special attention is paid to the 'civilizing' influence of English schools and such topics as the career of Morant, the work of the School Medical Service and the development of secondary and technical schools are admirably presented.

The reader should not neglect such valuable sources of information as the annual Reports of the Board of Education and the Ministry of Education, and the Scottish Education Department. The Report of the Ministry of Education for 1950, *Education, 1900–1950*, Cmd. 8244, H.M.S.O., 1951, reviews the events of the last fifty years under appropriate headings.

Additional reading in connection with particular chapters.

c. I. The student is recommended to study the Reports of the Cross and Bryce Commissions. *The Minutes of Evidence* throw much light upon educational ideas during the last decade of the nineteenth century. It is not an exaggeration to say that in many respects the Education Act of 1944 represents the fulfilment of suggestions latent in the report of the Bryce Commission. The Bryce Commissioners selected certain districts for special study, e.g., the north of England, south-west England, Bedfordshire, etc., and in reading these the student will obtain a clear picture of the state of secondary education in 1895.

c. II. The Board of Education Act, 1899 and the Education Act, 1902 should be carefully studied. Sir G. W. Kekewich, *The Education Department and After*, Constable, 1920, is a very readable book, but the account of the Duke of Devonshire and Sir John Gorst should be interpreted in the light of the relations between them and Sir George. In assessing the personality and character of Morant, the reader should consult Lowndes, G. A. N., *The Silent Social Revolution*, O.U.P., reprint, 1948, Allen, B. M., *Sir Robert Morant, a great Public Servant*, Macmillan, 1934, Michael Sadleir, *Michael Ernest Sadleir*, Constable, 1949, and Leese, J., *Personalities and Power in Education*, Arnold, Leeds, 1950. Dr. Allen is an admirer of Morant and plays the part of an apologist and Mr. Sadleir is advowedly partisan.

c. III. The facts about the Sadler-Morant controversy as far as they have been released may be studied in *Papers relating to the Resignation of the Director of Special Inquiries and Reports*, H.M.S.O., 1903.

Sadler's work as an educationist may be studied in the first three volumes of *Special Reports on Educational Subjects*, H.M.S.O., 1896-8, his reports on secondary and higher education prepared for various local education authorities and his books of which *Continuation Schools in England and Elsewhere*, Manchester University Press, 1907, is an excellent example.

The effects of Morant's administration of education are summarized by Mr. Lowndes (op. cit.), by Dr. Young in his admirable historical introduction to the Spens Report and by Dr. Leese (op. cit.). The student should also consult *The Code for Public Elementary Schools*, 1904, *Suggestions for the use of Teachers and Others concerned in the work of Elementary Schools*, 1905 (the latter should be compared with the later editions of 1926 and 1937), and the *Regulations for Secondary Schools*, 1904. The *Reports of the Chief Medical Officer to the Board of Education* contain detailed information about the health of school children and the progress made through medical inspection and treatment. The Reports of 1908 and 1909 should be compared with later ones.

For the Holmes Circular see Hayward, F. H., *Educational Administration and Criticism*, Ralph Holland, 1912. (Part I. *The Holmes Circular.*) See also Appendix I, *The Text of the Holmes Circular*. Holmes, E., *What Is and What Might Be*, Constable, 1911, gives a good picture of the inadequacies of Edwardian schools, the prevailing ideas about education and the new outlook which was beginning to develop.

c. IV. For the work of the McMillan sisters see McMillan, Margaret, *The Nursery School*, J. M. Dent, revised edition 1930 and Mansbridge, A., *Margaret McMillan, Prophet and Pioneer*, J. M. Dent, 1932. The text of the Education Act of 1918 should be studied and Mr. H. A. L. Fisher's *An Unfinished Autobiography*, O.U.P., 1940.

The following official publications are indispensible for the study of the period between the two wars:—

The Education of the Adolescent, 1926, *The Primary School*, 1931, *Infant and Nursery Schools*, 1933, *Spens Report*, 1938, *The School Certificate Examination*, 1931, *Humanism in the Continuation School*, 1921. The *Report on Education by the Bradford I.L.P. Committee*, Thornton and Pearson, 1931, gives in detail the views of the Labour Party on education. Mr. H. C. Dent's *Secondary Education for All*, Routledge and Kegan Paul, 1949, is a valuable summary of the growth of the new ideas about post-primary education.

c. V. Dent, H. C., *Education in Transition*, Kegan Paul, Trench, Trubner, 1944, is the best book about the progress of evacuation and the growth of the demand for educational re-construction. In the latter connection, *Educational Reconstruction* (White Paper), 1943 and a good commentary on the Education Act of 1944, e.g. Dent, H. C., *The Education Act of 1944*, University of London Press, revised edition, 1947, should be studied. A full account of the Emergency Scheme for the Training of Teachers is given in *Challenge and Response*, Ministry of Education Pamphlet, No. 17, H.M.S.O., 1950.

SUGGESTIONS FOR FURTHER READING 307

The following official reports are essential for further study:—
>Report on Curricula of Secondary Schools and Examinations (Norwood Report), 1943.
>Public Schools and the National System (Fleming Report), 1944.
>Training of Teachers and Youth Leaders (McNair Report), 1944.
>Ministry of Education Pamphlets:—
>>The Nation's Schools, 1945.
>>A Guide to the Educational System of England and Wales, 1945.
>>Youth's Opportunity, 1945.
>>The New Secondary Education, 1947.
>>Further Education, 1947.
>>School and Life, 1947.
>>Our Changing Schools (Professor Armfelt), 1950.
>Report of the National Advisory Council, Training and Supply of Teachers, 1951.
>Report of the Secondary Schools Examinations Council, 1947.

c. VI. The Fleming Report has already been mentioned. Important books on the Public Schools are:—
>Hughes, D., *The Public Schools and the Future*, C.U.P., 1942.
>Partridge, E. H., *Freedom in Education*, Faber & Faber, 1943.
>Spencer Leeson, *The Public Schools Question*, Longmans, Green, 1948.
>Wolfenden, J. F., *The Public Schools To-day*, University of London Press, 1949.
>Sanderson's work at Oundle is described in:—
>*Sanderson of Oundle*, Chatto & Windus, 1924.
>>This is an account of Sanderson's achievements compiled by members of his staff.
>Wells, H. G., *The Story of a Great Schoolmaster—Sanderson of Oundle*, Chatto & Windus, 1924.

c. VII. The following official publications are important:—
>*Royal Commission on London University*, 1913.
>„ „ „ *Oxford and Cambridge Universities*, 1922.
>„ „ „ *the University of Durham*, 1935.

University Development, 1935-47—Report of the U.G.C., 1948.

University Awards—Report of the Working Party on University Awards, 1948.

Important works on universities in the modern period are:—

Childs, W. M., *Making an University*, J. M. Dent, 1933.
The story of the University of Reading.

Flexner, A., *Universities, American, English, German*, O.U.P., 1930.

Fiddes, E., *Chapters in the History of Owens College and of Manchester University*, Manchester University Press, 1937.

Humberstone, T. L., *University Reform in London*, Allen & Unwin, 1926.

Moberley, Sir Walter, *The Crisis in the University*, S.C.M. Press, 1949.

Nuffield College Survey, *The Problem Facing British Universities*, O.U.P., 1948.

Truscott, Bruce, *Redbrick University*, Faber, 1943.

Whiting, C. E., *The University of Durham, 1832-1932*, Sheldon Press, 1923.

c. VIII. The most complete account of the development of technical education in England in the pre-war period is Abbot, A., *Education for Industry and Commerce in England*, O.U.P., 1933. The following official publications on adult and technical education are important:—

The Development of Adult Education in Rural Areas, 1922.
Adult Education in Yorkshire, 1927.
Pioneer Work and other developments in Adult Education, 1929.
Suggestions in regard to Teaching in Junior Technical Schools, 1937.
Report on Higher Technological Education (Percy Report), 1943.

The following books on Adult and Technical Education are recommended:—

Dent, H. C., *Part-Time Education in Great Britain*, Turnstile Press, 1949.

Livingstone, Sir Richard, *The Future in Education*, C.U.P., 1942.
Mansbridge, A., *An Adventure in Working Class Education*, Longmans, Green, 1920.
   This is an account of the formation and early years of the W.E.A.
    University Tutorial Classes, Longmans, Green, 1913.
Peers, R., *Adult Education in Practice*, Macmillan, 1934.
Percy, Lord Eustace, *Education at the Crossroads*, Evans Bros. Ltd. (no date).
Price, T. W., *The Story of the Workers' Educational Association, 1903–24*, Labour Publishing Co. Ltd., 1924.
Raybould, S. G., *W.E.A., The Next Phase*, W.E.A., 1949.
Richardson, W. A., *The Technical College*, O.U.P., 1939.
Scott, R., *The Story of the Women's Institutes*, Village Press, Idbury, Oxon, 1925.
Yeaxlee, Basil A., *Spiritual Values in Adult Education*, 2 vols., O.U.P., 1925.

c. IX   There is at present no complete history of Scottish education which covers the whole period up to 1950. The best book is Morgan, A., *Rise and Progress of Scottish Education*, Oliver and Boyd, 1927, which includes the Education (Scotland) Act of 1918. Post-primary education up to the commencement of the Second World War is covered by Wade, N. A., *Post Primary Education in the Primary Schools of Scotland (1872–1936)*, University of London Press, 1939.

Later developments in Scottish education are covered in Belford, A. J., *Centenary Handbook of the Educational Institute of Scotland*, Edinburgh, 1946. Rusk, R. R., deals with teacher training in the *Training of Teachers in Scotland*, Educational Institute of Scotland, 1928, but more recent changes are recorded in the annual reports of the Scottish Education Department.

Morgan, A., *Makers of Scottish Education*, Longmans, Green, 1929, contains a very readable account of the work of Craik, Struthers and Lord Haldane. The story of evacuation in Scotland is given in *Evacuation in Scotland*, edited by W. Boyd, University of London Press, 1944. *Reconstruction in the Secondary School* by Dr. F. M. Earle, University of London Press, 1944, furnishes details of a Scottish 'omnibus' school (Kirkaldy) as it was when he was headmaster.

The following publications of the Scottish Education Department are important:—

Reports of the Advisory Council on Education in Scotland:—

> *Training for Citizenship*, 1945.
> *Training for Teachers*, 1946.
> *Primary Education*, 1946.
> *Technical Education*, 1946.
> *Secondary Education*, 1947.

Reports of the Scottish Youth Advisory Committee:—

> *The Needs of Youth in These Times*, 1945.
> *The Recruitment and Training of Youth Leaders and Organisers*, 1946.

c. X. So far little has been written on adult education in H.M. Forces. Hawkins, T. H. and Brimble, L. J. F., *Adult Education. The Record of the British Army*, Macmillan, 1947, is the most complete account of Army education.

Lloyd, C., *British Services Education*, Longmans, Green, 1950, contains chapters on education in the Royal Navy and the Royal Air Force. Details and syllabuses of the scheme of General Education in the Army are given in the *General Education Handbook*, War Office, 1948.

APPENDIX

Since the above was written, the General Election, October, 1951, resulted in the return of a Conservative administration with Mr. Churchill as Prime Minister. Miss Florence Horsbrugh was appointed Minister of Education.

During the course of 1951 the economic situation of the country had considerably worsened and the new Government viewed with grave apprehension the increasing dollar-gap and the all round rise in the cost of living. The overwhelming necessity for speeding up rearmament added to the burden and it was felt that something drastic would have to be done. The problem facing the Government was one of introducing economies without inflicting serious damage to the essential fabric of the social services. Miss Horsbrugh intimated that all local education authorities should consider means of curtailing their expenditure on education by five per cent on the previous year's estimates. Circular 242 suggested five main headings under which savings might be effected: administration, capital expenditure from revenue, transport of school children, further education and the grants made for recreation and social or physical training. The problem was complicated by the rapidity with which costs had risen so that to effect the desired economy, in most cases, more than five per cent on last year's estimates would have to be saved.

Local education authorities carefully surveyed their estimates. Some were fortunate enough to be able to announce that they could carry out the request but others found it next to impossible to effect the full amount of the saving. Economies were made as regards administrative staff and programmes of school building. A determined attempt was made to reduce the cost per school place. Some minor savings could be effected in the school transport services but the main economies were found to be in the field of adult education and in the grants made for recreational purposes. Some authorities have decided to increase the fees for students attending evening classes and to reduce the amount spent on equipment in technical schools and colleges. A certain amount of saving could also be made in the grants to school camps, young farmers' clubs and the youth service.

A good deal of irritation was created through rumours spread by ill advised and irresponsible persons that the Government intended to shorten the length of the child's school life either by raising the age for compulsory schooling to six or by reducing the school leaving age. A short reflection would have shown that it was unlikely that Mr. Butler, now Chancellor of the Exchequer, would agree, unless it was absolutely necessary, to measures which would cut out some of the fundamental features of the Act for which he was responsible. These wild rumours were dispelled by his broadcast statement: "I am determined to make the Act which I introduced go on and do the great job for which it was intended." Miss Horsbrugh, in a recent speech, deprecated the action of those local authorities who through panic were contemplating too drastic or indiscriminate cuts. She pledged herself to do her utmost to safeguard education in these most difficult circumstances. One of the most serious problems was the shortage of essential materials such as steel, but she suggested that it might be solved by utilizing new methods in building.

The Government's policy on grants to universities has yet to be announced. If the situation deteriorates further, it may be necessary to economize on nursery schools by introducing legislation authorizing the payment of fees. The whole of the divisional executive system may be re-considered with a view to saving time and money. (See p. 129.) Whether additional economies of the nature of those outlined in this paragraph will become necessary is something that cannot be foreseen at present. *The Times* Educational Supplement, 1st February, 1952, adopted a reasonable point of view quite free from panic when it commented: "Education has got off lightly for stern and practical reasons; the argument that education pays is beginning to tell. There will be more money for its essentials if savings are made on the frills which still remain."

INDEX OF NAMES

ABERDARE, Lord, 196
Abbot, A., 308
Acland, A., 29, 30, 49
Adam, Sir R., 287
Adams, Sir J., 99
Adamson, Professor J. W., 9, 303
Allen, Dr. B. M., 33, 65, 305
Anson, Sir W., 36, 46, 47, 49
Archer, Professor R. L., 303
Argyll, Duke of, 239
Armfelt, Professor R., 98, 104-5, 307
Armstrong, Professor, 21
Arnold, Matthew, 50
Arnold, Dr. Thomas, 161, 167

BADEN-POWELL, Lord, 154
Balfour, A. J., 35, 36, 38, 39
Barnard, Professor H. C., 303
Beale, Miss D., 172, 173
Bendall, F. W. D., 285
Bickersteth, J. B., 291
Birchenough, C., 303
Bigge, Sir Selby, 66
Birrell, A., 40, 188
Bowen, E., 162
Boyd, W., 310
Buchanan, G., 265
Burnham, Lord, 86
Buss, Miss F. M., 172, 173
Butler, R. A., 26, 120-3, 135, 137, 138, 165, 166
Butler, Dr. S., 161

CARNEGIE, Andrew, 194, 263
Chamberlain, Joseph, 36, 194
Childs, W. M., 308
Churchill, W. S., 119, 123, 280
Clough, Miss A. J., 172
Clifford, Dr., 38, 40, 65
Cobbett, W., 102, 270
Cockerton, T. B., 35
Colet, Dean, 167n.
Cook, Caldwell, 167
Cooper, Lord, 269
Craik, Sir Henry, 242-5, 246, 268
Curtis, S. J., 52, 75, 81, 121, 137, 303
Curzon, Lord, 183

DAVIES, Miss Emily, 172
Dent, H. C., 88, 107, 110, 114, 115, 124, 143, 209, 223, 306, 308
Devonshire, Duke of, 24, 25, 26, 27-8, 29
Dewey, Professor, 99

EARLE, Dr. F. M., 260-1, 310
Ede, Chuter, 55, 125, 133
Edgeworth, R. L., 164
Elphinstone, Bp., 266

FEARON, Mr. 137
Fiddes, E., 308
Firth, Mark, 194
Fisher, H. A. L., 26, 77-81, 84-5, 168, 277, 306
Fitch, Sir J., 17, 137
Flexner, A., 190, 308
Forster, W. E., 8, 23
Froebel, 68, 98

GAINFORD, Lord, 72
Garnett, Dr., 35
Geddes, Sir E., 81, 86
Gleig, R. C., 270
Gore, Bishop, 183
Gorell, Lord, 274, 277
Gorst, Sir John, 24, 26, 28, 29, 33, 34, 35, 69
Graham, Sir James, 20, 78
Graves, J., 49, 90, 304

HADOW, Sir Henry, 90
Haining, Sir Robert, 285
Haldane, Lord, 39, 156, 188-9
Hawkins, T. H., and Brimble, L. J. F., 310
Hayward, Dr. F. H., 306
Hoare, Sir S., 64
Holmes, Edmond, 64-5, 306
Holmes, Sir M., 46, 66
Hoole, Charles, 164
Hughes, D., 307
Humberstone, T. L., 308

INGLIS, John, 267

JAMES, Professor William, 99
James, Thomas, 161
Jones, Viriamu, 196

KAY-SHUTTLEWORTH, Sir James, 7, 53
Kekewich, Sir George, 24, 28, 30, 32, 33, 34, 35, 36, 64, 305
Kerr, Dr., 69
Knox, John, 237

LAURIE, Professor, 245, 246
Laxton, Sir W., 174
Law, Richard, 123

Leese, J., 53, 305
Leeson, Canon Spencer, 166, 307
Lindsay, Lord, 285
Livingstone, Sir R., 225-6, 309
Lloyd, Cyril, 290, 291, 293, 310
Lloyd George, D., 39, 40, 65, 77
Londonderry, Lord, 36
Lowe, Sir R., 42, 81
Loundes, G. A. M., 18, 32, 33, 76, 304, 305

MACAULAY, Thos., 270
MacDonald, Ramsey, 96
Major, John, 265
Mansbridge, Dr. A., 210, 211, 218, 224, 306, 309
Mason, J., 193
Maude, C. G., 285
McDougall, W., 100
McKenna, 40, 58, 188
McMillan, Rachel and Margaret, 60-61, 69-70, 71, 99, 306
McNair, Sir A., 151
Melville, A., 265, 266
Moberley, Sir W., 205-7, 285, 308
Montessori, Madam, 99
Moore, Sir John, 270
May, Sir George, 96
Morant, Sir Robert, 27, 32-6, 37, 38, 39, 40, 45-67, 83, 84, 88, 93, 188, 211
Morgan, Alex, 237, 309
Morris, H., 222
Morris, Sir P., 149, 291, 293

NEWMAN, Sir Geo., 60
Norwood, Sir C., 143

OWENS, John, 192

PARTRIDGE, E. H., 307
Peers, R., 309
Percy, Lord Eustace, 26, 89, 231-2, 234-5, 309
Pestalozzi, 98
Phillips, Sir Thos., 174
Price, T. W., 212, 309

RAMSBOTHAM, Mr., 119-20
Raybould, S. G., 218-222, 309
Richardson, W. A., 309

Rollock, Robt., 266
Rosebery, Lord, 24, 187
Rouse, Dr., 69, 167
Runciman, W., 40, 65
Rusk, R. R., 309

SADLER, Sir M. E., 16, 24, 28, 30-2, 46-9, 50, 55-8, 305
Sadleir, M., 33, 305
Sanderson, F. W., 162, 167, 174-80, 307
Sandon, Lord 24, 134
Scott, R., 309
Smith, A. L., 220
Smith, Professor Frank, 98
Smith, Professor Lester, 46, 119, 120, 235, 304
Spens, Sir Will, 107
Strong, Dr. John, 250
Struthers, Sir J., 245-6, 251-2
Stuart, Jas., 208

TAWNEY, Dr. R. H., 88-9, 212
Tedder, Lord, 269 n.
Temple, Archbishop William, 119, 211, 273
Thring, E., 162, 165, 166, 177
Tomlinson, G., 123, 150
Trent, Lord, 197
Trenchyan, Sir Chas., 26, 89, 95
Truscott, Bruce, 308
Turnbull, Bp., 265

WARDLOW, Bp., 264
Wade, N. A., 309
Watt, Mrs. A., 223
Wavell, Lord, 282-3
Webb, S., 36, 39
Wells, H. G., 175, 179, 307
Whitehead, Professor A. N., 111
Whiting, C. E., 308
Wilkinson, Miss Ellen, 123, 149
Williams, W. E., 287
Wolfenden, J. F., 307
Wolsely, Lord, 271
Wyatt, Joan, 174
Wykeham, William of, 167 n.

YEAXLEY, Dr. B., 273, 285, 309
Young, Dr. R. F., 51-2, 101, 109, 305

INDEX OF SUBJECTS

ACTS of Parliament quoted or referred to:
England and Wales—
  Board of Education (1899), 25–7, 166
  Education (1870), 8; (1876), 24, 134; (1902), 36–44; (1918), 78–81; (1936), 106, 131; (1944), 121–40, 226; (1946, 1948), 139
  — Administrative Provisions (1907), 59–63
  — Local Authorities Default (1904), 39
  — Provision of Meals (1906), 59; (1914), 75–6
  Endowed Schools (1869), 8
  Local Taxation (Customs and Excise), (1890), 12
  Public Schools (1868), 8
  Technical Instruction (1889), 12, 227
  Voluntary Schools (1897), 24–5
Scotland—
  Education (1496), 236; (1646, 1696), 237; (1872), 240–2; (1908), 246–8; (1918), 248–50; (1936), 253; (1945), 255–7
Adult Education, 9, 208–227; (Scotland) 263
— Residential Colleges, 209, 225–6
— Schools and Colleges, 208, 209
Advanced Divisions, 245, 251
Advisory Councils, Ministry of Education, 122–3; (Scotland) 250, 251–2, 258
Age, school leaving, 63, 78, 95, 135–6, 244, 251, 253
Agreed syllabus, 132–3
Air Training Corps, 156
Army Bureau of Current Affairs, 287–9
— Certificates of Education, 271–2, 282, 295–6
— Colleges and schools, 270, 273, 276, 281, 295
— Education in the, 270–8, 280–96, 296–7
— Illiteracy in the, 296–7
— Schoolmasters, Corps of, 271, 272, 280
— Schoolmistresses, Corps of, 280, 284
Arts Council of Great Britain, 224–5

Association of Headmistresses, 173

B.B.C., 225
Bibliography, 303–310
Board of Education ,25–7, 29, 36, 41, 42, 45, 50, 51 ,54, 60, 65, 69, 73, 74, 75, 77, 92–3, 114, 119, 121, 183, 187, 213, 230, 272, (Scotland) 242
Boy Scouts, 74, 154
Burnham Scales, 86, 142
Bursars, 54

CAMBRIDGESHIRE village colleges, 222–3
Challenge of Youth, 155
Charity Commission, 8, 10–11
Circular 44 (Scotland), 251–2
Cockerton Judgment, 35
Code for Public Elementary Schools (1904), 52–3
Commissions, Royal:
England—
  Bryce, 9–18, 23, 24, 51
  Clarendon, 11
  Cross, 9, 10
  Newcastle, 136–7
  Taunton, 10, 16, 17, 42, 51, 138, 165
Scotland—
  Argyle, 237
Committee of Privy Council on Education, 7, 10
Common Entrance Examination, 170
Community centres, 223
Consultative Committee, 26, 122 (*see* Reports other than Royal Commissions)
County Colleges, 135

DEVELOPMENT Plans, 130
Divisional Executives and Excepted districts, 125–30
Dual System, 37–8, 93, 95, 131–2

EDUCATIONAL Institute of Scotland, 245, 251, 262–3
Education (Scotland) Fund, 248
Elementary Education, definition of, 50
Emergency Training Colleges, 140–1
Employment of School Children, 78–9
Equivalent Grant, 243

INDEX

Evacuation (England), 113–18; (Scotland), 253–5
Evening Play Centres, 75
Evening Classes, 227–8
— Institutes, 228–9
Examinations, school, 81–84, 111, 148–9 149–51 (Scotland), 261–2;
Extension, University, 208

First Book of Discipline, 237
Free places, 61–3, 76

GAMES (*see* Physical Training)
Geddes Axe, 86, 87, 250
Girls' Schools, 172–3
Governing Bodies Association, 165, 173
Grants, Government, 42, 79
Great Disruption, 237, 241
Great Exhibition, 227
Green Book, 120

HALF-TIMERS, 20–1, 78
Halls of residence, university, 203, 204–5
Headmasters' Conference, 26, 164–5, 173
Heuristic method, 21
Higher School Certificate, 83

IMPERIAL College of Science and Technology, 187, 188, 189
Inspectors, 45–6, 93, 149
Institute of Christian Education, 134

LABOUR Colleges, 209
Labour Party and education, 58, 88–9, 95, 135, 138
Liverpool Secondary Education in, 56–8
Local Education Authorities, 15, 27, 77–8 (Part II and Part III), 37, 43–4, 72, 77, 93–5, 111–12, 123–5; (Scotland), 248–9
Local Government (Scotland) Act, 253

MANAGERS and governors, school, 11, 37–8, 42, 131–2
Manchester Grammar School, 17–18
Mechanics' Institute, 9, 208
Medical Service, school, 21, 59–61
Merit Certificate, 245
Ministry of Education, 121–3

NATIONAL Certificates and diplomas, 230–1
— Fitness Council, 155
— Society, 23–4
— Union of Teachers, 29, 64–5, 67

National Certificates and diplomas cont.
— Youth Advisory Council, 157
— — Committee, 156–7

OFFICERS' Training Corps, 156
Owens College, (*See* University of Manchester)

PASSIVE resisters, 38–9
Payment by results (Revised Code), 21, 29, 243
Physical Education, 21–2, 59
— Deterioration Committee, 59, 247
Prefects, 167 n.
Pre-Service training, 156
Pupil Teachers, 53–4

REGISTER, teachers', 15, 63–4
Religious instruction, 38, 131–4
Reports (other than Royal Commissions):
England—
 Fleming (1944), 163–174
 Hadow Reports—
  Education of the Adolescent (1926), 90–3
  Infant and Nursery Schools (1933), 103–4
  Primary School (1931), 97–103
 McNair, (1944) 151–4
 Norwood (1941), 143–9, 171
 Percy (1945), 201, 232–5
 School Returns (1870), 137
 Secondary Schools Examination Council (1917), 84; (1947), 149–51
 Spens (1938), 107–112
Scotland—
 Primary Education (1946), 258–60
 Secondary Education (1947), 260–2
 Technical Education (1946), 258
 Youth (1945), 263; (1946), 263
Reserved teachers, 106, 131
Royal Air Force, education in, 278–9, 296, 299–301
— Army Educational Corps, 281–3, 293–4
— Navy, education in, 279–80, 298–9
— Society of Teachers, 63–4
Ruskin College, 209

SCHOOL Attendance Committees, 11
— bank, 74–5
— Boards, (England and Wales), 8, 11–12, 21; (Scotland), 242, 246–8
— buildings, 103–5, 140

INDEX

School Attendance Committees cont.
— Certificate Examination, 82–3, 111, 148
— Leaving Certificate, 244, 261–2
— types of:
  Aided, 131
  Boarding, 134, 162, 167, 169, 173
  Burgh, 241
  Central, 70–71
  Controlled, 131
  Day Continuation, 80–1, 247
  Direct Grant, 169
  Elementary, 7–8, 10, 37, 50, 52–3 (*see also* Primary)
  Grammar, 8, 17–20, 42, 50–2, 61–3, 73, 76, 90, 107–8, 110–111, 150
  Higher-elementary, 49
  Higher-grade, 10, 34–5, 51; (Scotland), 244–5
  Independent, 136–8, 258
  Infant, 68, 98–9, 103–4
  Junior Technical, 55, 71–2
  Modern, 91–2, 107–8, 145
  Multilateral, 145–6, 167–8, 260
  Non-provided, 37–8
  Nursery, 69–70, 79, 103–4, 135
  Omnibus, 260
  Organized Science 10, 11, 19–20
  Preparatory, 170–71
  Primary, 88–9, 90, 97–8, 100–103, 256
  Private, 136–7, 139
  Provided, 37
  Public, 158–180
  Secondary (*see* Grammar or Modern)
  Senior, 79–80
  Special, 59
  Special-agreement, 131
  Technical High, 108, 110
  Trade, 110
  Voluntary, 21, 23–4, 37–8, 96, 131
Science and Art Department, 9, 10, 11, 20, 227
Scottish Education Department, 241, 242, 248
Secondary Education, definition of, 16–17, 50
— — for all, 88–9, 134
Settlements, educational, 226
Special places, 96
State scholarships, 148–9, 204

Suggestions for Teachers, 53, 305
Superannuation, 86–7, 247, 257
Supplementary Courses, 245
TEACHERS' Registration Council, 63–4
Technical Education, 227–35
Teviot scales, 257–8
Townswomen's guilds, 224
Training of teachers, 43, 54, 151–4

UNIVERSITIES, 8, 181–207, 264–9
— (Particular Universities)
  Aberdeen, 266
  Birmingham, 193–4
  Bristol, 197, 200
  Durham, 194–6
  Edinburgh, 266–7
  Glasgow, 265–6
  Leeds, 192–3, 194
  Liverpool, 193, 194, 200
  London, 186–91, 200–201
  Manchester, 192–3, 194
  Nottingham, 197–8
  Oxford and Cambridge, 181–5
  Reading, 197
  St. Andrews, 264–5, 268–9
  Sheffield, 194
  Victoria, 192–3, 194
  Wales, 196–7
— Royal Commissions on:
  Durham, 195–6
  London (Haldane), 188–190
  Oxford and Cambridge, 182–5
University Colleges, 198
— Extra Mural Boards, 217–18
— Grants Committee, 198–9, 202, 203–5, 268
— Institutes of Education, 151–3

WALES:
  University of, 196–7
  Welsh Department, 40
  Welsh Secondary Education, 174
War Savings, 74–5
War-time Education, 72–6, 113–18
"Whisky Money", 12, 198, 243
"White Paper", 120, 125
Women's Institutes, 223, 224
Workers' Educational Association, 209–222, 284–5; (Scotland), 263

Y.M.C.A. and Y.W.C.A., 224, 272–3, 277–8, 284–5
Youth Service, 154–7; (Scotland), 263–4